PAJ Books
Bonnie Marranca and Gautam Dasgupta,
Series Editors

Art + Performance
1. Deborah Jowitt, ed., *Meredith Monk*
2. Moira Roth, ed., *Rachel Rosenthal*

Art + Performance

Rachel Rosenthal

Edited by Moira Roth

The Johns Hopkins University Press   Baltimore + London

© 1997 The Johns Hopkins University Press
All rights reserved. Published 1997
Printed in the United States of America on acid-free
paper

06 05 04 03 02 01 00 99 98 97   5 4 3 2 1

The Johns Hopkins University Press
2715 North Charles Street
Baltimore, Maryland 21218-4319
The Johns Hopkins Press Ltd., London

Library of Congress Cataloging-in-Publication Data

Rachel Rosenthal / edited by Moira Roth.
    p.   cm.—(PAJ books.   Art and performance mono-
graphs ; 2)
    Includes bibliographical references.
    ISBN 0-8018-5628-0 (hc : alk. paper).—ISBN 0-8018-5629-9
(pbk. : alk paper)
    1. Rosenthal, Rachel, 1926–   —Themes, motives.   2. Per-
formance art—United States.   3. Feminism and theater—
United States.   I. Roth, Moira.   II. Series.
NX512.R68R3   1997
700′.92—dc21   97-9332   CIP

A catalog record for this book is available from the British
Library.

Permission credits may be found on page 225.

Contents

III Writings and Scripts by Rachel Rosenthal

Photograph gallery follows page 116.

Acknowledgments

Many people have helped me on the creation of this book. First and foremost, I owe an enormous debt of gratitude to Rachel Rosenthal, for her time and hospitality, and to both her and her assistant, Tad Coughenour, for their meticulous and patient responses to my many requests for material and information. I am most grateful to Bonnie Marranca for inviting me to be part of this series, and I also want to thank the Johns Hopkins University Press staff, especially Kimberly F. Johnson. Maria denBoer did a splendid job of the initial copyediting and continued to be a wonderful mainstay in the later stages of the book. Whitney Chadwick has been, as always, invaluable in her critical reading of my text. Equally, invaluable as always, Annika Marie contributed long hours helping me at many points in the research and process of putting the book together. David Sweet worked diligently on, among other tasks, the copyright permissions. At an early stage in the manuscript, Elise Griffin and Lorraine Lupo did a tremendous amount of research and compilation of information, and together we worked on the first drafts of the bibliography and chronology. In a later stage, I was helped by Kim Haglund, Heather Heise, and Katherine Mills. Finally, I want to thank the intrepid Cheryl Leonard, who spent so many hours on painstaking proofreading and general organization.

Moira Roth

Introduction:

Journeying with Rachel Rosenthal,

January 17, 1995–June 1, 1996

Los Angeles, Rosenthal at Home, January 17, 1995. Rachel Rosenthal and I watch the CNN reports on Kobe, struck twenty-four hours earlier by the worst earthquake in Japan in over fifty years. On the screen are image after image of fires, and people lying on stretchers, and bodies being dug out of collapsed buildings, with narrations concerning the mounting number of deaths and injuries. The reporter intones, "The Japanese are experiencing helplessness in the face of nature's terrible force despite Japan's being the most advanced country technologically in the world." Rosenthal, watching with deep compassion, comments ironically, "People think they can control nature. How wrong they are."

Rosenthal's building, which she owns, is a comfortable and active one. Here she reads, writes, conducts daily business, organizes workshops, holds rehearsals with her newly formed company, plays with her two dogs, and feeds her cats. The phone rings constantly. Her space consists of two rooms, together with a kitchen and a bathroom. They are crowded with huge ferns, her early large sculptures made up of tightly coiled clay tendons, old family photographs, a large cloth-stuffed gorilla, collections of stones, an early Betye Saar assemblage, and an array of artwork on the walls—Rosenthal's series of landscape photographs and pieces by other artists—together with an assortment of furniture, a tatami-mat platform shrine, and crowded bookcases. Shelf upon shelf of books on theater, animals, shamanism, art, collections of fairy stories from all over the world, volumes by Derrida, Lévi-Strauss, and Foucault, Ilya Prigogine and William Irwin Thompson, *The Education of Koko* by Francine Patterson and Eugene Linden, *The Case for Animal Rights* by Tom Regan, and a few shabby and tattered brown paperbacks in French, including Simone de Beauvoir's *Le Deux-ième Sexe* and André Malraux's *La Condition Humaine*. On the ground floor of the building is Rosenthal's business office, run by a full-time assistant, and a large studio. Outside are the sounds of Los Angeles, an insistent, discordant city in which Rosenthal, now sixty-eight years old, has lived since 1955.

Over the past few months I have spent much time in this space, traveling down from Berkeley, where I live, to study Rosenthal's large and orderly archives, skimming through albums of cuttings and photographs, reading scripts, and looking at videos of performances—and ceaselessly talking with Rosenthal herself. It is here that I am trying to construct a bare-bones account of her unruly, sprawling biography, and to gather and select texts and photographs for this slim volume. It is no easy task.

As I pore through the mass of writings that I have accumulated on Rosenthal, I find the following two quotations, which elegantly summarize, for me, the juxtaposition of what I see as the core of Rosenthal's being, deeply interlocked psychologically and artistically—a methodical, disciplined life and a legendary, glamorous biography.

In a recent interview Rosenthal told Alexandra Grilikhes, "My life is so orderly. I love the feeling that everything is in place, that I know where things are and how they will be. My animals love order and routine and my life revolves around the routine of my animals. . . . The reason or the result of how I lead my life is that I have the work which is very, very, in a sense, frightening. When I work on my pieces I go through a lot of pain, a lot of fear and real crunching kinds of episodes. Yet all of it is within a very orderly structure. I think I can stay sane and on an even keel because my work is framed within this structure. My animals keep me sane because they take me for walks, they own my van; when it's time to go, we gotta go. And no matter how much work I do, how tired I am . . . at six o'clock in the morning we're at the park. And we go back to the park two more times that day because I don't have a yard and they have to go out and run and be in grass." [1]

In her essay "A Cosmography of Herself: The Autobiology of Rachel Rosenthal," Bonnie Marranca writes, "In an early piece, *Grand Canyon* (1978), Rosenthal transforms into a vampire who flies over the canyon on a snowy winter day. She reads it like a topology of her life. The canyon's faults, erosion pattern, plateaus, and rocks act as signs of her life in this personal journey of metamorphosis: a geological fault is for her a matter of guilt. As narrative strategy, the journey is both real and symbolic in her work. Rosenthal's family fled Hitler's Europe, first to Brazil, then to New York during World War II, and so she became a refugee, a traveler, homeless, an immigrant. Rosenthal, who lives in Los Angeles and speaks English with the New York City accent of someone who once spoke another language, has always made geography—which is to say, walking across the earth—her subject. She brings the feeling of travel into performance."[2]

A Tale of Two Cities: Pre- and Postwar Paris, 1926–1940 and 1946–early 1950s

Rachel Rosenthal's two Paris experiences collectively have provided her, psychologically as well as intellectually and culturally, with the contents of much of her early performance work, the discovery of Antonin Artaud's notions of theater, and a certain lifelong modus operandi—the combination of which is strikingly novel in America. Unusual and intriguing in this country is the French nature of Rosenthal's theater experiences, expertise, and goals; and this—together with the exoticism of her upper-class French childhood, a major source for much of her early performance work—fascinates American critics and American audiences alike. In reviews and newspaper accounts of her work and persona, one often encounters an awed tone in the descriptions of her life and personal style: all too frequently there is a litany of the same predictable biographical highlights, leading to a great oversimplification of Rosenthal's complex biographical saga, let alone the artistic character of her work.

Rachel Rosenthal was born in Paris on November 9, 1926, and lived in the city until June 1940, when the Rosenthal family left hurriedly to escape the Nazi invasion of France. Rachel was thirteen at the time. "The afternoon that we left, the swastika was hanging on our villa in the south."[3] They lived briefly in Rio de Janeiro, Brazil, and then in 1941 moved to New York City. Rosenthal's childhood Paris was thus the city of the years between the two great Wars, seen from the vantage point of a child of a wealthy and cultured Russian émigré family.

In 1946, at age nineteen, Rosenthal returned to Paris while her parents remained in New York. This postwar Paris was that of the older Artaud, the younger existentialists, and the theater of the absurd. Between 1946 and 1954, Rosenthal traveled restlessly back and forth between Paris and New York, an independent, curious, and lively student in search of a self-designed, wide-ranging education.

It was an education already set in motion by the peculiar circumstances of her childhood, one that Rosenthal has often described in interviews and in performances as a childhood of privilege, secret traumas, and theatricality.

In actuality, her childhood was distinctly unconventional. Her parents, Leonard and Mara Rosenthal, both Jewish but totally assimilated, did not marry until Rachel was around seven years old. Leonard, a Russian émigré multimillionaire importer of Oriental pearls and precious stones, had settled in Paris in 1888, at age fourteen. He was married at the time of Rachel's birth and so built Mara Jacoubovitch, his mistress—a woman twenty years younger than he and "a professional beauty" (according to her daughter)—a little townhouse near the Bois de Boulogne. Mara had emigrated from Moscow and was well connected through family members with the theater; Rachel later recalled that Mara, "although she never pursued a real career, possessed an incredible contralto."[4]

Her parents lived in a house decorated with Chinese rugs, a four-poster bed with a gilded baldachin, Baccarat cut-crystal glasses, Sèvres and Wedgwood sets of china, and paintings (including a Claude Monet); they employed some six servants, a governess ("All my life I have been trying to undo the damage that this woman did"),[5] and Julie, a Cordon Bleu cook. They surrounded themselves with artistic and political friends, whom they entertained constantly with lavish multicourse dinners and parties.

Rosenthal once wrote that she could never regain this Paradise Lost. "I dream of having things brought to the table; beds made; clothes washed; the car brought around. I long for the magic of being served spectacular foods on lovely china. Politically, of course, the kiss of death."[6] She also told an interviewer that she always felt "on show for for my parents, because I was brought up by nurses and governesses."[7]

She remembers performing from age three for her parents and their friends, especially on her birthday, which coincided with her parents' wedding anniversary. Apprehensive before the event, she greatly enjoyed the performance and the applause but always retreated to her room afterwards. "So in my relationship with people, there was no intimacy, just the love that an audience gives a performer and a performer gives back to an audience. This is what my real temperament wanted to do. It started very early."[8] As a child, too, she seriously studied ballet and played with her puppet theater for hours at a time.

Three of Rosenthal's autobiographical performances—*Charm, The*

Head of Olga K., and *My Brazil*—are drawn from these childhood experiences, which ranged from the enchanting to the deeply disturbing. There was a perpetual and dramatic contrast between the lavish material splendor and glamorous lifestyle of the household, and the undercurrents of emotional and psychological alienations and tensions. The characters at the heart of Rosenthal's childhood were her much-loved father; her mother, with whom Rosenthal had a more overtly troubled relationship; an older half sister, Olga; and a half brother, Pierre. Pierre, whom she adored, died in Africa during World War II; in the 1970s, Olga and Rachel severed all contact with each other.

In 1977, Rosenthal set the stage literally for a re-creation of her early Paris experiences in *Charm,* subtitled "A Sonata in Three Movements," each corresponding to a floor of her family's Paris house. Four months later, she presented *The Head of Olga K.,* in which she played both herself and her half sister, Olga, who was then living in Africa. Two years later, in 1979, Rosenthal created *My Brazil* based on her seven-month stay there in 1940, a time of sexual awakening in the context of exile. At the time of its first presentation, Rosenthal explained in an interview, "I take aspects of my life that I feel were useless and worthless, and through performance redeem them. It's a means of understanding and re-creation. Putting them in an art form has a mythmaking quality. It is also an order making. Although these things happened in the past, my way of observing them makes them become what they were not before." [9]

Order making? Mythmaking? Re-creation? Redemption? Therapy? Voyeurism? Art? Spectacle? These are among the many strains mixed together in Rosenthal's early performances, often causing audience members and historian-critics alike to oscillate back and forth from detective work (is it true or not?) to immersion in foreign romances; and from psychological fascination and temporary identification with the narrative and its heroine, to sheer delight in Rosenthal's brilliant theater skills that made one see her as a child rather than what she was then in the 1970s—a woman in her fifties.

Antonin Artaud and Paris Theater, 1946–1950s

Paris was the site of Rosenthal's childhood; it was the site, too, of her early encounters in the later 1940s with French experimental theater, especially with Antonin Artaud.

In the Paris of 1926 (the year Rosenthal was born), Artaud tried his hand at directing his short-lived Théâtre Alfred Jarry. That year he wrote, "The spectator who comes to our theater knows that he is to undergo a real operation in which not only his mind but his senses and his flesh are at stake. Henceforth he will go to the theater the way he goes to the surgeon or the dentist. . . . He must be totally convinced that we are capable of making him scream." [10]

When Rosenthal returned to Paris in 1946, she did not meet Artaud (who, prematurely old and just out of a long, painful period of hospitalization, was to die two years later at the age of fifty-two), but she did discover his *Theater and Its Double,* which she later described as "my theater Bible." [11]

Artaud's ideas made it possible for Rosenthal to focus her energies. Until encountering them, she had felt not only scattered geographically but threatened by a rather painful sense of dilettantism: "I was always flitting between one thing and another thing, because I just couldn't decide where I wanted to alight finally." Art, music, dance, theater, and literature competed for her attention. Now she was inspired by Artaud's denial of the supremacy of the text in theater, his fascination with visual spectacle, and his experiments with sound and acting. "The kind of theater that he envisaged was an integration of all the things that I loved, and that it can be done through the medium of theater. . . . and that was for me a tremendous liberation and a tremendous opening up, because it led eventually to my doing Instant Theatre and all my performances." [12]

Resolved that theater would be her métier, Rosenthal began to study in Paris with the actor-director Jean-Louis Barrault, a great admirer of Artaud, and with Roger Blin (who had spent a considerable amount of time with Artaud in the final years of his life), the director of the first production of Samuel Beckett's *Waiting for Godot.*

Four weeks before Artaud died in 1948, he wrote that the duty of the poet, the writer, is not to shut himself off from the world:

> but on the contrary to go
> into the world
> > To jolt
> > to attack
> > the mind of the public
> > otherwise
> > what use is he?
> And why was he born? [13]

Rosenthal, too, deeply believes in the purpose of art as being one of intervention in the world. Like Artaud, she wants to jolt the public. Like Artaud, she conceives the theater as an all-embracing spectacle. Like Artaud, hers is a fanatical and visionary commitment to theater. She was fascinated by his concept of "the Theater of Cruelty," but unlike Artaud, she did not go mad nor did she die relatively young. Yet once in a public lecture when I projected slides of the young Rosenthal and a movie still of the young Artaud as a monk in *The Passion of Joan of Arc,* the audience and I were struck by their dramatically similar androgynous beauty and obsessive gazes. Although Rosenthal is older now than Artaud was at his death, one sees in the frequent photographic images of the bald-headed Rosenthal—as in the last photographs of Artaud in 1948—a face imprinted by a life of deliberate intensity. Perhaps the most dramatic of the photographs to record this is the series of studies by Annie Leibovitz of Rosenthal, buried up to her neck in a sea of sand, reminding one of a rock eroded by centuries (see frontispiece).

Unlike Artaud, however, Rosenthal's passion has always been tempered by wit—sometimes acerbic and cool, at other times beguilingly comic; integral to most of her performances is a self-mocking attitude toward her own intensity. Also, unlike Artaud, Rosenthal chose not only to live in America but to open herself up to American as well as French influences.[14] And finally, she opted to live in Los Angeles rather than New York, and for years has been deeply enmeshed in certain aspects of California New Age thinking.

All this has enormously tempered the "Frenchness" of her thinking and style.

New York Avant-Garde Circles and the Aesthetic of Indifference, 1949–1955

Around 1949, Rosenthal began to be slowly drawn into the circle of John Cage, a virtually all-male gay world.[15] Just as Rosenthal has often spoken of her childhood, she has frequently told of her friendships with Merce Cunningham and John Cage (both of whom she met originally in Paris), Jasper Johns and Robert Rauschenberg—and of her time with them in New York in the early 1950s, when she appeared intermittently in the Cage circle.[16] It was a loosely formed community, with certain shared aesthetics and attitudes that coalesced during the McCarthy period of 1950–53. Theirs was a cool aesthetic deeply interspersed with irony, a set of values that I once named in an *Artforum* article as "The Aesthetic of Indifference." [17]

In the interview with Grilikhes, Rosenthal recalled Cage's apartment and its atmosphere at that time, "a corner walkup next to the Brooklyn Bridge . . . [where] the only thing in that apartment was a big piano with green plants on it. . . . The music's sound waves, people's thoughts and speech all seemed to flow. What was circulating was so powerful, it became my model for an image of power." [18]

In New York, Rosenthal also continued to study and move in theater circles (including working with Erwin Piscator, the German director, and Heinz Condell, set designer of the Metropolitan Opera); and she also danced in Cunningham's Junior Company. She introduced all these new friends to her parents' "Russian" parties, and remembers that "it was a strange mixture of worlds." [19] Surely, in future histories of this period, Rosenthal's role as a catalyst will not only be more studied but will be more acknowledged as contributing to the evolution of ideas in this ambience.

In 1954–1955, Rosenthal lived in the same building as Johns, who at the time was producing his first flags and targets; he made a cast of her head for one of his wonderful early constructions. [20] She made art, too. "I did a bunch of sculptures that were made of metal, wood, glass, and tar . . . black . . . kind of elegant . . . conceptual and sensuous, very much like Bob's [Rauschenberg] objects were." [21] One gets a vivid sense of these young, unknown artists as they first emerged on the New York art scene from the review of a group show of some eighty artists in the Third Annual Exhibition at the Tanager Gallery. The reviewer, identified only as "F. P.," writes, "Exhibitors who are new to this reviewer are: Johns, showing something like a music box; Rosenthal, who shows a tall tarred object like a construction beam on end, in the jaws of which hang brass wires." [22]

This confluence of the ideas of the young American artists, dancers, and composers with those of the French theater of the absurd and Artaud was simultaneously exciting and deeply disconcerting to Rosenthal. Approaching her thirtieth birthday, she remembers feeling that she had never produced a body of work, "because I could never stay long enough with what it took to make one." [23] She recalls, too, her total sense of male identification with its resulting alienating effect on her as a woman artist; there were few women among her circle. ("I remember three: Sari Dienes, M. C. Richards, and Fance Stevenson.") [24] In retrospect, she recognized that she had not been temperamentally suited to the solitary life of the studio, yet had equally been unable to commit herself truly to theater.

Her father was vocal in his strong opposition to a theater career for his daughter, and she had internalized that sentiment. The result was that she "was afraid of getting into theater . . . [and yet her] real talent was as a performer."[25] It was only in 1955, when her father died suddenly of a heart attack on a visit to Los Angeles—his death for her was to be both a great loss and a great liberation[26]—that she felt confident to make a heartfelt commitment professionally. That year she moved to Los Angeles and began a career in theater.

Instant Theatre, 1956–1966

The Los Angeles of this period was brash and liberating and Rosenthal thrived in this new environment. Within a year she had created Instant Theatre, which lasted from 1956 to 1966. "It's only when I started Instant Theatre that I began to feel that I was beginning to put out some of what I was capable of putting out."[27] In 1960, she married King Moody, an actor, who became her partner in this enterprise, and by 1963 they had moved Instant Theatre into a professional theater, the Horseshoe Stage Theater (now the Zephyr) on Melrose Avenue in Los Angeles, which held ninety-nine seats. She and Moody mortgaged their house to finance this, and they "lived there, virtually, for three years."[28]

Finally, in Los Angeles, Rosenthal had become a leader rather than a gifted follower; a teacher rather than a student; and an expert in theater techniques rather than (as she had still seen herself in New York) a dilettante in the arts.

Recollecting this period in an article in 1974, she writes, "I was fleeing from a vortex of supercharged energy made up of Jap [Johns], Bob [Rauschenberg], John Cage, Merce Cunningham, Ray Johnson, Cy Twombly, M. C. Richards, and others, that was threatening to engulf and destroy my still-immature soft center. Greater L.A., in those days, was quite practicable. There was visibility and room to roam, and innocent palm trees that were not yet 'Ed Ruschas.'" Briefly, she taught acting and dance at the Pasadena Playhouse, where she "brought a much-watered-down version of N.Y. avant-garde to the academic curriculum."[29] Finding this situation confining, however, she quickly developed the concept of Instant Theatre.

In an interview I did with Rosenthal in 1989 for the Archives of American Art, she described how Instant Theatre evolved and its innovative nature of an "assemblage sensibility . . . a collision [a concept she credits to Artaud] of totally disparate things put together as two ideas that created a resultant."[30]

She had begun by giving workshops, requiring people to come prepared with scenes.

> But then, you know how lazy people are, and they wouldn't come prepared, and so I gave them exercises and improvs which I would think up. And these were so fascinating to them that after a while nobody was bringing in scenes and they all wanted to do my exercises. And this is how little by little the work became Instant Theatre. . . . We used all kinds of objects and things that we found in the garbage in the alleys . . . and the use of objects was not like props. They were really like extensions of ideas and conceptual ways of handling everyday objects. The look of the work we did became the parallel of the sensibility of the visual arts of the period, which was assemblage and collage and all that stuff. More and more I got into costume and, again, people would donate scraps and with these scraps we would take safety pins and assemble these things on ourselves. Again, creating the most extravagant costumes and then just taking off the safety pins and going back to scraps, and using the same things over and over again, but never the same way twice. . . . We worked a lot with records, and with found sounds, just noise sounds and really pushing the form. And we created a dream world on stage, which was really magical and astonishing.

Rosenthal invented new ways of handling lighting, with people carrying lamps "and being integrated with the action. And then I started to color the lamps with gels, which nobody did at the time. It was always straws and pinks and blues and, in a sense, I did the first psychedelic lighting."

Jack Hirschman described an evening of Instant Theatre in 1963, lauding it as "one of the most exciting experiments in theater poetry on this or any American coast. . . . To say that Instant Theatre possesses something of surrealism, something of Dadaism, something of the puppet theater and the opera is to approach its meaning, which, to my mind, is poetry itself."[31] The theater was situated in a storefront in Ocean Beach, amidst "old stone hotels . . . cheap dress shops, Italian grocers, Yiddish in the windows, storefront studios, crutches and eye patches, wine bottles holding up the buildings, filth in the street." Hirschman evokes the brisk tempo of this intermedia evening of music, gestures, and words that formed vignettes lasting ten minutes or less. In one set, for example, Rosenthal appeared in a black dress, battered red hat, and red shoes, using the no-glass door in the back of the stage as a mirror, as well as a glass to look through and a door to enter.

Years later, Diane Calder reported on her memories of a visit to Instant Theatre: "The prop rooms backstage of Rachel Rosenthal and King Moody's Instant Theatre might be the envy of many a gallery owner or performance artist. Rows of masks line one whole wall, lacking only the little white cards stating 'Collection of . . .' that accompany comparable displays on folk art in certified craft museums. Sculpted pedestals are pulled on stage in full view of the audience and set up to structure space optimally for whatever action occurs next. Bits of matched and mismatched costumes hang like soft sculpture waiting to transform actors' images." [32]

Young Hollywood actors—the most notable included Anthony Perkins, Dean Stockwell, and Vic Morrow—as well as young artists studied with Rosenthal; and in the first years members of the Ferus Gallery attended the performances regularly, artists such as Ed Kienholz, Wally Berman, Billy Al Bengston, John Altoon, and Ed Moses. The three Horseshoe Stage years with Instant Theatre were exciting but exhausting with its shifting personnel, nightly workshops during the week that ran from seven until after midnight, and two adult shows and four children's shows on the weekend. There were major problems over Equity rules and money, and Rosenthal experienced her first debilitating attacks of osteoarthritis in her knees, which made it increasingly hard for her to move with any fluidity on the stage.

Finally, Moody and she decided reluctantly to close Instant Theatre, which in its first incarnation (it was briefly reopened in 1976–77) had lasted exactly a decade. "When I emerged from that in 1966, I felt like Methuselah because for me life had stopped. For years I did nothing but Instant Theatre. I hadn't seen any art. I hadn't seen any shows. I hardly ever read the paper. I didn't know what was going on. I was reading fairy tales continually in order to prepare for the next fairy tale that we did. When I emerged, I was forty, I think, and it was like, where's it all gone? But it was an extraordinary period, and the work we did was really amazing." [33]

Clay Sculpture, 1967–1975

Rosenthal turned to visual art again and for a number of years immersed herself in this (including studying ceramics with the well-known southern California ceramist John Mason) rather than in theater work. She was fairly successful in this new career as a sculptor, but restless. Later she was to comment that when Instant Theatre stopped in 1966, she had no choice but to try to succeed as an artist, yet she felt these sculpture pieces were mainly characterized merely by their good taste and salability. "They did not blaze trails and they did not satisfy me."[34]

Over the next few years she exhibited this clay sculpture frequently. In 1969, Thomas Albright, art critic of the *San Francisco Chronicle*, wrote admiringly of her combination of "fancifully functional shapes and rich glazings with a heady theatrical scene."[35] Albright was right— there is, indeed, a theatricality to these pieces, together with an organic vitality. (When exhibiting, Rosenthal customarily placed the sculpture in sand piled into wooden crates, as in her one-person exhibition at the Grandview Gallery in 1974.) Rosenthal consciously pushed the limits of associations with both nature and ancient history and myth. In 1974, she described her pieces as "evocative of hair or colonies of parasites,"[36] and said that her pieces, based on natural and early architectural forms such as a beehive and rounded stele, were named after ancient cities of the Amazons: Mytilene, Amastris, Salmanoe, and Clete.

In hindsight, she seemed to be active and artistically busy, but waiting for something. A new community? A way of returning to theater?

Rosenthal and Early Los Angeles Feminism, 1972–1975

On January 21, 1972, hundreds of women arrived from all over California and from the Midwest and the Southwest for the West Coast Conference of Women Artists (held under the auspices of the California Institute of the Arts in Valencia); Rosenthal was among them. For three days, the women attended the now-legendary installation and performances of Womanhouse, saw innumerable slide shows, and listened to lectures.[37]

Rosenthal was bowled over by the barrage of information and by the presence of so many women artists. "I was astonished because I was still under the very sexist notion that there were no women artists. I was still going round and round with my own insanity. 'What am I? Am I an artist? If I'm an artist, I can't be a woman . . .' I began to question all my notions. I began to read all the feminist literature— Betty Friedan's *The Feminine Mystique,* Adrienne Rich, Susan Griffin, Mary Daly, and Deena Metzger."[38]

For the first time, Rosenthal began to meet and talk primarily with women. She started a consciousness-raising group in Tarzana, where she was living at the time, and attended one of June Wayne's famous Joan of Art seminars, where between thirty and fifty women artists were trained in strategies as to how to present themselves successfully to a gallery, a museum, a director or critic, and so on. (Rosenthal remembers the great delight of once flamboyantly playing the role of the New York art dealer Leo Castelli in a meeting.)[39] She participated in a discussion group led by Miriam Schapiro and Judy Chicago in which everyone agreed that there was a pressing need for a woman-only, collective-run alternative art space.

The result was the creation of the lively, short-lived Womanspace; eventually Rosenthal became co-chairperson of its board of directors. (Later Rosenthal would also be instrumental in creating another women's art space in Los Angeles, that of Grandview.) She learned to work in the early feminist democratic mode of consensus, and to give up what she once described to me as her "fascistic" directorship style of operation.

Like so many of us at that time, she responded to the philosophy of the famous early feminist slogan, "The personal is the political." There were endless conversations between women about our lives: we listened hour after hour, not only patiently but eagerly, to each other's experiences, and we all became surprisingly adept at talking about them vividly. Early feminist performances in Los Angeles abounded with these tales, which had great resonance for their feminist audiences. Though Rosenthal was often critical of the rough-shod and amateur nature of the performances' style of presentation, she would seek them out, realizing that "the meaning of the piece and the politics behind it were indeed revolutionary and totally new."[40] These were heady years. I myself was deeply involved in this world, teaching first at the University of California–Irvine, and later at the UC–San Diego campus (together with David Antin, Eleanor Antin, and Allan Kaprow), and beginning to write on the subject of California performance.[41]

Not only did Rosenthal become inspired to perform through feminism, but also in 1975 she decided she must get help for the degenerative osteoarthritis in her knees. She began to seek out medical advice—with a certain amount of success. This meant that she now was able to move with more physical ease in her performances, just as psychologically she was to move with more daring into arenas of emotionally laden material.

In 1975, too, Rosenthal's mother died. As with her father, the death of her mother gave a permission to Rosenthal.[42] In 1976, she wrote, "My father had been dead a year when I created I.T. [Instant Theatre]. Mother never quite understood or approved of it. She liked the fairy tales but I knew I wasn't satisfying her. And satisfying my parents while, on the surface, seeming to rebel against them, was the name of the game. Now that Mother is dead, many things are beginning to emerge from the fog. Things about myself I wasn't at all aware of. And the trip back to Paris after twenty-two years was an eye-opener also: you really can't go home again."[43]

It was only following the death of her mother that she began to explore in an art form the contents of her childhood and her relationship to her parents—framed in the permissive and encouraging ambience of southern California feminism and the new medium of feminist performance art. Performance possibilities led to psychological insights. "I was able to do in my performance work what I had never been able to do in my life, which is to reveal myself, to disclose, to air, to put out all this garbage and turn it around and make it into art, and in a sense reveal all the dark secrets that I had kept locked up all these years. It was redemption and exorcism. And this was the direction that I took during the first part of my career as a performance artist."[44]

By November 1975, when Rosenthal created *Replays,* her first performance, southern California had become the main scene of performance art, including work by male performers such as Chris Burden, Guy de Cointet, Allan Kaprow, Paul McCarthy, and John White. Among the female performers were Eleanor Antin, Nancy Buchanan, Leslie Labowitz, Suzanne Lacy,[45] Barbara T. Smith, and a host of young feminist artists, many of whom produced performances, both individual and collaborative, in the context of the Woman's Building in Los Angeles, which had been established in 1973.

Letter Exchanges with Barbara T. Smith, 1975–1976

In the summer of 1975, Barbara T. Smith, one of the most original and risk-taking of the early southern California women performers, created *A Week in the Life of . . . ,* which was part of a series of performances to benefit a local artists' co-op. A professional auctioneer, assisted by Allan Kaprow and Peter Lodato, auctioned off "interactive time-based events"[46] with Smith to an enthusiastic audience, and Rosenthal bought three, including a correspondence exchange.[47] Rosenthal gravitated toward Smith because, at the time, "a lot of my work was very visceral and theatrical and sensual and was not sufficiently conceptual. . . . I learned a lot from her [Smith]."[48] This is an influence that has not been discussed so far in critical writings on Rosenthal, which have focused for the most part on Rosenthal's theater affinities and influences, together with her later involvement in scientific and cultural theory.

This exchange with Smith provided Rosenthal with a novel performance-framed epistolary space in which to discuss her notions of life and art—a fascinating and original opportunity at an important moment of transition in Rosenthal's life. The first two letters were written just before Rosenthal created *Replays* and *Thanks* in November of that year.

On June 19, 1975, Rosenthal wrote her first letter to Smith, exploring at length the origins in her childhood of her weight problem and her obsession with food. (Food was to become a recurring theme in her performances, beginning with *Charm* in early 1977.) In a poetic, richly detailed letter, she describes the meals served by Julie, the family cook, in the context of the sumptuous lifestyle of her family.

In her second letter to Smith, written on August 12, 1975, she begins by recounting the saga of a recent "Frankish invasion" by her Parisian cousin and cousin's family, the debilitating flare-up of her degenerative arthritis, and more generally of her attitudes toward her body, beginning in childhood. "Since we talked at length about our families, I [have] decided to write you about Pain—or rather to start with that and see where it takes me. . . . It seems that as far back as I can remember, I had a dichotomous relationship with my body. On the one hand, a tremendous confidence, comfort, and exhilaration in the way it moved . . . the way it enabled me to express my feelings in dance, my love of life, in athletics, my strength and individuality in tomboy games; on the other hand, I was ashamed of my body because I knew it wasn't svelte and beautiful."[49] Rosenthal analyzes the connections between attitudes toward her body and eating patterns: "All my life, I've believed in salvation through right eating, and all my life I was addicted to food!" She ends, confessing to Smith, "You have no idea how hard it was to write this kvetchy letter. . . . I wrote and rewrote, read and reread, wondered if I shouldn't just tear it up. What do you think?"

First Performances, 1975, and the Revival of Instant Theatre, 1976–1977

In quick succession on November 14 and November 25, 1975, Rosenthal presented her first two performances (solo pieces, each performed only once): *Replays* and *Thanks*. Edie Danieli reviewed both of them for the article "Rachel Rosenthal: A Life History," in *Artweek*,[50] in which she describes her excitement when Rosenthal appears to announce that the audience had been summoned under false pretenses: there would be no performance. *Replays* then begins.

In *Replays* the audience is told the history of Rosenthal's painful degeneration of her knees through texts and slides—interspersed with memories of her Parisian childhood. In an unpublished interview I did with her in 1977, she recalled the feeling of "exorcism" that she had derived from this performance, which she credits with the lessening of the swelling in her legs.[51] Less than two weeks after *Replays,* Rosenthal performed *Thanks*. Audience members were asked to volunteer as surrogates for various people in Rosenthal's life whom she wanted to thank—including a family maid and Rosenthal's father. In her review, Danieli describes a young man who volunteered to play the latter role, but whose daughter refused to let go of his hand; thus "as he became Rosenthal's father, the little girl became Rachel."[52] The piece ends with each participant receiving a box containing a small collage or assemblage.

What were the next steps for Rosenthal? To continue in this direction with solo one-time pieces, or to be inspired to return to theater? Or both?

In Rosenthal's third letter to Smith, dated July 17, 1976,[53] she announces the decision she and her husband, Moody, had made a week before: to attempt to revive Instant Theatre in the context of "reviewing my life and the various tensions that developed at different stages, as a result of the pull of conflicting energies that always quartered me between theater and visual arts." She comments, slightly dismissively, about *Replays* and *Thanks:* they were well received, "which at least took away what would have been a tremendous amount of doubt about still being able to perform." She had also just visited Paris for the first time in twenty-two years, lamenting that one cannot "go home again." Rosenthal writes frankly, too, of her fears of failure. Yet, she ends this letter, "We may be doing something extravagantly crazy, but at least we'll try. And as we're trying, there will be such fun! And fun is something I prize highly. It's also something I've never fully felt otherwise than standing on a stage, under the lights, laying it out there for the people."

For several months in 1976–77, Rosenthal ran an intensive workshop at her house in an attempt to revive Instant Theatre, and members of her workshop participated in her next two performances—*Charm* and *The Head of Olga K.*—both of which still employed improvisation. The experiment with Instant Theatre, however, was not a commercial success; it was hard to attract audiences and financially it became unbearably stressful. After a few months, Rosenthal reluctantly closed it for good.

What was she left with? Performance. What would she make of it? Something uniquely her own. Between 1975 and the early 1980s, Rosenthal produced eleven performances [54] that directly related to episodes in her life. "If you put all my performances together, then you will have my life done in the form of an artwork." [55]

Charm and *The Head of Olga K.*, 1977

Rosenthal's *Charm,* performed on January 28, 1977, [56] by herself and Moody with workshop members who represented the servant and "Nightmare Figures," contrasts the "charm" of her parents' glamorous public life to the upper regions of their Parisian house, where Rosenthal lived with the servants, experiencing nightmares, facial tics, and oppressive treatment from her governesses. Toward the performance's end, greedily consuming one pastry after the next, she confides in the audience about childhood memories. "The servant enters, blowing cigarette smoke into Rachel's face. He slaps a tray of very fancy pastries down on top of the other cakes. He gives her disgusted looks. 'My Father and Mother weren't married! My father *bought* my mother from Gordeyev! (Gorges on the pastries.) Shura committed suicide in Mother's boudoir because he loved her.' . . . The servant enters [again] slowly, carrying in a huge chocolate cake topped with whipped cream and cherries. Rachel immediately dives in, gouging the cake with her hands and stuffing her face. She has whipped cream all over her mouth and chin. 'I don't want to be strange!' " [57]

In an interview from this year, Rosenthal spoke about the contrast between her techniques for performance and those in Instant Theatre. [58] Ironically, reversing the conventional notions of what constitutes theater versus early performance art, she had consistently worked with improvisation in Instant Theatre, whereas now in performance she resorted to a much slower, more deliberate process. (It was only in 1978, however, that she scripted a performance for the first time, that of *The Death Show.*)

How did she create a performance? "It's like a secretion that goes on for about two months before I put it out, like building a cocoon or a bower."[59] In preparation for *Replays,* for example, she had not only written at length to Barbara T. Smith about the contents, but had presented a version of it in the form of a slide show to a friend. *Charm,* too, evolved slowly as Rosenthal drew its contents from the emotions stirred by the death of her mother in 1975, the discussions in her June 1975 letter to Smith, together with her visit to Paris in 1976 and her reimmersion in 1976–77 in the ambience and techniques of Instant Theatre.

Smith herself attended *Charm* and wrote a review based on the particularities of her own interest in performance—that it was *not* theater.[60] Smith begins her long text by addressing this issue of performance versus theater. "One distinction I require is that in some sense the performer is not acting, that is, pretending, but is here, now, what he or she is. And that what we are witnessing (in the old-fashioned sense of *attesting to,* not enjoying in the entertainment sense) is a step in this living artist's personal growth and actual experience." She then elegantly describes the sequences of this piece and asks herself, Is this a contrived story? Did Rosenthal make it all up? Smith answers no, and then comments, "And here is where the question of where theater ends and performance begins arises. At first the piece is much more theater . . . but gradually it becomes the real Rachel. . . . To us, the privileged witnesses, she reveals clues permitting us to penetrate and assist in reconstructing and releasing her."

In April 1977, a few months after *Charm,* Rosenthal staged *The Head of Olga K.* for the first time. (Up until this point in her performances Rosenthal had maintained resolutely that they should be presented only once.)[61] Originally planned as a slide show with a voice-over, she eventually invoked her Instant Theatre workshop group, elegantly costumed, to perform improv, with Rosenthal playing both the role of herself and her sister. *The Head of Olga K.* presents the extraordinary tale of Olga, Rosenthal's half sister, who earlier on was a Resistance fighter during the war and is now a glorified civil servant living in Africa and surrounded by black servants (whom she hates). The tale is told through live acting, slides, and a "Reader"

(King Moody) who quotes from correspondence between the two sisters. (In the performance's unpublished script, Rosenthal tells us that the spoken material is "taken verbatim from a 1975–76 correspondence the artist carried on with her half sister, Dr. Olga Klein.") [62]

This was the first piece of Rosenthal's I saw [63] and I remember feeling restless. It seemed to me that it was too straight theater, too scripted, and too consciously a piece of acting. At the time, I had just been commissioned by *Arts Magazine* to write a two-part essay, "Toward a History of California Performance," [64] and was beginning my research. My taste was for something different at that time. I had been involved in early northern California performance, and was now trying to come to terms with a very different aesthetic in southern California. Rosenthal was part of that different aesthetic, and it would take me a while to become accustomed to it. In my second *Arts* article, which sketched out early performance in the south, I attempted to characterize some distinctions between the two parts of the state. I spelled out three main differences: first, in the south there was much more of a relationship with the East Coast than in the north; second, feminism played a more central role; and third, "there has been a consistent thrust toward the theatrical aspects of performance art." [65]

Yet from this point onward, although somewhat resistant, I began systematically to attend Rosenthal's performances, indeed to seek them out. I became increasingly fascinated—like so many others in her audiences—by the novelistic way her autobiography was unfolding; it had a strange parallel to those nineteenth-century novels that came out in serial form. I began, like a reader of a Dickens' serial, to be impatient for the next installment. Over the next few years, I saw all her autobiographical works, a genre that came to a halt around 1981, when Rosenthal "realized I didn't redeem anything really. That I just had a body of work. However, the doing was still very healing, in a sense, because my life stopped haunting me after that. And that was the big result, the big benefit that came from it." [66]

Grand Canyon, The Death Show, The Arousing (Shock, Thunder), and *My Brazil,* 1978–1979

In 1978, Rosenthal was living alone for the first time in twenty years. At the beginning of the year, her marriage had collapsed and she fled from Los Angeles to spend a week in the Grand Canyon. "When I'm depressed, I go to spend time by myself in the Earth." [67]

Upon her return she created *Grand Canyon,* in which she materializes into the Fat Vampire and flies over the canyon, which becomes for her a topographical map of her life; her encounters include discovering in the deepest gash of the canyon the Dead Vampire's body—that of Rosenthal's mother. Rescuing the body from the river, she stabs it in the heart, and then weeps for hours over the body.[68]

Later that year, the Fat Vampire returned as her "demon" in *The Death Show,* which begins with an "icon" made up of a photograph of Rosenthal's fat self, surrounded by a foot-wide "funeral wreath" of cakes, doughnuts, and Danish pastries sprayed with black enamel paint.[69] Rosenthal once stated that the performance was triggered by the end of her twenty-year marriage and a fifty-pound weight loss; it was "about loss, and the need to allow things to die."[70]

The following year (1979), she continued to address notions of change and awakening, first in *The Arousing (Shock, Thunder)* and later in *My Brazil.* This performance revolved around the dramatic change in her life as a young teenager when she and her family lived in Brazil after their escape from France.[71] Its narrative veers from romantic memories of lush tropical landscapes, to apprehensiveness about her family's refugee status and Nazi power in Brazil at this time, to mourning over the death of her half brother, Pierre.

Rosenthal structured *The Arousing* around an I Ching hexagram *(chen)* about the awakening to power through fear. The five-segment piece starts with a video of her face, after which Rosenthal appears with her face masked; underneath the mask are bandages, which she slowly unwraps, revealing her face decked out with a beard and mustache—she pulls these off with a "mighty roar." Later she applies makeup while explaining the meaning of these transformations to the audience.[72] The performance concludes with Rosenthal talking about her new freedom and power, and in the final section, "Moving On," Rosenthal, sitting on a bench and smiling at the audience, points to an old trunk, which magically explodes in fire and smoke.

At one point in *The Arousing,* Rosenthal quotes from an Adrienne Rich poem:

> No one who survives to speak
> new language, has avoided this:
> the cutting away of an old force that held her
> rooted to an old ground
> the pitch of utter loneliness

where she herself and all creation
seem equally dispersed, weightless, her being a cry
to which no echo comes or can ever come.[73]

The Transformed Body, 1978–1981

What Rich had described as "new language," one that inevi-
tably demands the abandonment of "old ground," became an increasingly urgent goal for Rosenthal in both her art and her life. What
"baggage" from the old trunk, so to speak, must she relinquish to
achieve it? For the next few years she was to struggle with this. The
most literal struggle (but a profoundly metaphysical one also) was with
her body—certainly already a central theme from her earliest performances and already pivotal in 1978 in *The Death Show* and *The Arousing*—and the impact of aging.

Between 1980 and 1981, Rosenthal consciously transformed her
physical appearance, both as a woman in private life and as a performer, from that of a middle-aged attractive woman into a bald-headed
androgynous being, verging on the masculine. In 1986, it is this
Crone—a term Rosenthal often uses to describe her current self—who
begins to deliver prophetic warnings to her audiences about the destruction of the earth and who becomes the enraged protector of Gaia
and of animals.

In 1980, in *Bonsoir, Dr. Schön!*[74] Rosenthal has herself displayed
nude for the first time in a performance; assistants unravel the gauzes
that conceal her body, pointing out to the audience all the physical
defects of the performer. In 1981, in *Leave Her in Naxos,* which she
performed with her company, Rosenthal has her head shaved onstage
(she has continued to shave it regularly ever since). This follows earlier
scenes, including an erotic encounter between young lovers, and a
narration with slides by Rosenthal—in which she tells the audience
about her earlier love affairs, concluding with a recent sexual rejection
by a young, strikingly handsome man, whose slide had just appeared
on the screen (he then joins Rosenthal on the stage). At the end, as a
reviewer noted, Rosenthal looks "like a lama, ascetic and spiritual . . .
[appearing] very masculine with her bald head, but . . . still absurdly
dressed in her garish, spangled costume."[75]

Two months later in 1981 Rosenthal started off *Soldier of Fortune*
with a luxurious seven-course meal onstage served by a waiter. Drink-
ing a magnum of champagne, she sits elegantly attired in a Nile green
gown with a tiara on her elaborately coiffeured wig. The performance

concludes with her swaggering off the stage, bald-headed and wearing fatigue pants, jacket, and boots, as she declaims, "I've changed—no longer the plump Tarzana housewife who used to make art on the side. I am a hustler, a soldier of fortune."[76]

In the summer of 1981, a photograph of Rosenthal appeared on the cover of the *L.A. Weekly*,[77] a strangely elegant figure, bald-headed with a piercing gaze, her beloved rat Tatti perched on her raised hand. "It was one of those weird things, you know, where the image just jelled. I felt for the first time that I looked like how I felt inside, and it was immensely liberating. So that whole period, the gestation between 1978 and 1981, which was the severing from my life as a married woman, had finally culminated in my divesting myself of all my money[78] and starting completely new, not only with no money, but also with a look which was totally different from my past look, and which created an identity and an authenticity for me that I never had, and that was also commensurate with the kind of work I was doing, and it helped me in the direction that I was going in in my work."[79]

This "old" androgynous image has clearly not only helped Rosenthal herself in the new directions of her work, but also has strangely legitimized her increasingly shamanistic role for us, her audience. She now literally "looks the part."

This old prophet is not a figure who appeared from nowhere. We had known her already (either witnessed in reality or from hearsay) in an earlier, younger, and more personal incarnation—in Rosenthal's autobiographical pieces (and, indeed, she continues to use, on occasion, autobiographical references in her current work). Thus, she is, so to speak, a prophet with a past, a prophet with known human frailties. For me, and I suspect others, that has always been an oddly compelling—one might say a humanizing—aspect to her body of work of this past decade or so. It tempers, together with Rosenthal's perennial caustic humor, the authoritative tone of the fierce new works.

In a fascinating 1994 issue of the *Performing Arts Journal*, which features a section entitled "Ages of the Avant-Garde," Rosenthal is among those artists who discuss their aging. "I was in my early thirties when my knees started to go bad. . . . Since my suffering had been uniform for upward of thirty years, I didn't feel the flow of time. . . . In 1986, however, the year I was to turn sixty, it suddenly hit me. SIXTY! I became aware for the first time that I was no longer young. This realization made me old. . . . That year, I did my piece, *L.O.W. in Gaia,* and the Crone emerged for the first time in my work."

By a fortunate synchronicity, this statement by Rosenthal on aging is the final text in this book. Thus not only does Rosenthal literally have the "last word," but appropriately, as she celebrated her seventieth birthday on November 9, 1996, these words are about aging and endurance. "I have huge reserves of energy during performances. Everybody remarks on that. But my endurance isn't what it was. . . . Then another performance comes along and I am like a race horse at the gate. . . . I can walk my dogs without pain and move about the stage without looking too ridiculous. Isn't that a miracle?"[80]

A Decade of Performances, 1982–1992

I have selected a number of reviews for this anthology that respond to Rosenthal's main performances[81] between 1982 and 1992. With two exceptions *(KabbaLAmobile* and *Was Black),* these 1982–92 works became part of Rosenthal's traveling repertoire in her regular national and international touring of these years. They are scripted performances, sometimes solo, sometimes presented with other performers/participants, but almost always accompanied with slides and tapes. Not only their content but their repeated presentation makes them profoundly different from Rosenthal's Instant Theatre and earlier performance work, which were so often "a one-time-only situation. . . . It was like a sumi drawing, you know, you couldn't retouch it. . . . But then starting in 1982, 1983, I began to tour, and so the pieces had to be repeated over and over again. And how to keep them fresh and real and in the moment, and how to keep up the magic and the ceremony aspect of performance and not fall into an 'acting' mode . . . that was a real effort and focus at that period, and I'm still developing that capability."[82]

In her review of *Traps* (1982), Sally Banes interprets it as a "global exorcism,"[83] a description that could apply to many of the other works of this decade. Alisa Solomon cautions her *Village Voice* readers that although "Rachel Rosenthal makes performances to mend the world . . . knowing that her works center on ecology, the protection of animals, and the preservation of the earth can hardly prepare you for the brutal way they grab at you."[84] What so often grabs one in this decade of spectacles is, I believe, the formidable combination of Rosenthal's passionate politically and intellectually informed convictions and intelligence together with her new "old" physical appearance, her array of personae, theatrical skills, and surprising wit. And, very important, she speaks to a public that is already frequently deeply concerned with the same issues of ecological survival.

Chameleon-like, Rosenthal springs and glides from persona to persona, character to character. In his lengthy examination of *Gaia, Mon Amour* (1983), Fidel Danieli describes Rosenthal's various characters—from a bespectacled bag lady with a false nose, to a ceremoniously robed young Year King, to Mother Earth—and the finale of the piece. "Establishing a sacred spot front-center, she drums and chants as pictures of arid but voluptuous rock formations are projected behind her."[85] Jacki Apple reports on the first appearance of Rosenthal in *KabbaLAmobile* (1984): "Dressed in a billowing white costume with red and black quilted sections and yellow sash . . . her face made up in white with black and yellow lines. . . . Arms wide open, palms up, kimono-like sleeves flapping in the wind . . . [she] climbed a scaffolding platform, facing the audience, like a sorcerer."[86] *KabbaLAmobile* was a work that involved stunt car drivers and the cabala. *The Others* (1984) addressed animal rights and cruelty to animals. In it, Rosenthal shares the stage with forty animals and their owners and in her review, Sylvie Drake lists some of these "stunning animals—a gorgeous Appaloosa mare, regal snakes, a pygmy goat, dogs, cats, rabbits, rats, hamsters, squirrels, doves, parrots, monkeys, macaws, and a turkey."[87] In *L.O.W. in Gaia* (1986), a solo piece, Rosenthal roams back and forth between her three personae, whom Donald Karwelis characterizes as "the fortieth-century monster, not of woman born; Gaia—the Death Crone (the Greek earth goddess); and Rachel as Rachel-the-tourist."[88]

Sasha Anawalt narrates the succession of images that move through *Was Black* (1986), a piece responding to the nuclear disaster at Chernobyl: Rosenthal as a Russian cabaret singer, clothed in a long black gown with white-powdered face; the fleeing nude white-powdered figures who later dress themselves in cocktail party attire, pour salt on Rosenthal's head, and bind her, leaving her, "wrapped in blinking Christmas tree lights that trace her body in the darkness"[89]—which suggests not only the dangerous radiated Chernobyl area but implications of a future fate for the whole planet. Martin Bernheimer sets forth the artist's scenario of *Amazonia* (1990) as "fervently protesting ecological waste. . . . She invokes geological and biological history, recounts myths, and stacks metaphors."[90] For Ross Wetzsteon, *Pangaean Dreams* (1990) demonstrates Rosenthal's message, delivered, for the most part, "with Whitmanesque vigor, stunning theatricality, and a cave-painter's mastery of prehistoric imagery—that the more we immerse ourselves in the natural world, the stronger our sense of self becomes." [91]

Erika Munk points out the irony of *Rachel's Brain* (1987) being performed on the day that the United States sent its *Discovery* astronauts into orbit, while "Humanity, says *Rachel's Brain,* should get down, should reverse its attempt to escape the body and the earth." [92] Rosenthal starts off this performance as a singing Marie Antoinette, whose wig is topped by a model of a frigate, and moves through the roles of both the signing-gorilla Koko and her trainer, to end perched on an airlift, screaming, "What the hell am I doing here! Put me down!"

For Rosenthal, *Rachel's Brain* [93] was "a culmination of all that I had been thinking and feeling and reading about in terms of what are we doing. What are we doing as a species? What is happening? How are we affecting the Earth? Well, we are affecting the Earth very badly, and where does it all come from? It comes from the human brain, so let's look at the human brain." [94]

What will happen, Rosenthal asks, to this world of ours in the future? In going through Rosenthal's archives, I found an unpublished 1990 manuscript, "Letter from the Future," which I decided to publish in this book, partly because its text strongly reminded me of Doris Lessing's wonderful science fiction and her old, pessimistic, enduring females. Rosenthal's letter is written by a tough survivor, too, who lives on an earth now inhabited by very few people, whose brains have shrunk as have the resources. "The machines don't run. . . . We can't bathe or sail. The water is too dangerous for the health. . . . We have come to believe in a subterranean deity who is very angry at us. We see her as a frightening being who is out to get us for what the old people had done." [95] This woman is clearly a descendant of the narrator of *filename: FUTURFAX,* a work, performed for the first time in 1992, which Alisa Solomon has described as a "terrifying yet hilarious . . . seventy-five-minute monologue." [96]

filename: FUTURFAX, *San Francisco, April 8, 1995.* Tonight, in the context of a weekend of feminist events entitled "Utopia/Dystopia" at the Yerba Buena Center for the Arts, Rosenthal stages *filename: FUTURFAX.* After many months of working on this book, absorbed with such tasks as getting reprint permissions and proofreading, I am dazzled by the physicality of Rosenthal's performance style, vitality, and agility—she roams around the stage, twists her torso this way and that, sometimes dancing exuberantly—and by the mobility of her face, gestures, and body and her bald-headed, harsh, androgynous, old beauty. Equally she is possessed of an incredible vocal range—by turns soft and harsh, chiding and mocking, anguished and offhand, guttural and high-pitched, enraged and debonair. She constantly engages the members of the audience, makes asides to them, jokes, and appeals to their sense of justice.

filename: FUTURFAX takes place in the year 2012, after the Great Calamity. Outside are young marauding gangs—together with disembodied recorded voices, male and female, young and old, and ambience sounds that intrude into the space. Rosenthal's character has retreated to the precarious safety of her home, sparsely furnished by a few chairs, a table, and a ladder. She celebrates her eighty-sixth birthday, munching on a few limp carrots, which she then vomits out. At one point, the phone rings and she speaks briefly in French to Nicole[97] in Paris before the phone is abruptly disconnected. Halfway through the piece she notices a pile of fax papers, fallen on the floor from the machine, sent by people who are living at the end of the twenty-first century. Rosenthal picks the sheets up, commenting, "A fax from the future. Some people actually made it." And then, suddenly paranoid, "How did they get my number?" This sort of moribund wit enlivens the dialogue throughout her seventy-five-minute monologue. At the end of the performance Rosenthal assumes an increasingly shamanistic persona—speaking with an impassioned voice—only to be suddenly shot at by young thugs offstage. The fax continues to spew out its pages as she writhes, dying on the floor.

In an exchange with the audience after the performance is over, Rosenthal, sitting casually on the edge of the stage, acknowledges her increasing pessimism about the future. She agrees with a questioner that, yes, she is deeply pessimistic and we are indeed an accursed species, yet one must act as if change is possible. As solace, she tells the audience that chaos theory teaches us that there is no way of predicting absolutely and accurately what will happen.

I feel oddly encouraged by Rosenthal's not totally cheerful assurance, and realize that that is the effect her work often has on me these days.

"La Prise de Conscience" and "Autobiology"

In a 1991 exchange with Suzanne Lacy, the performance artist, entitled "Saving the World," Rosenthal states, "There are levels of action, but there is only one level of consciousness, what we call in French, 'la prise de conscience.' I don't know how you can translate it except by saying, 'being grabbed by consciousness.' "[98] For her the notion of such consciousness is coupled with giving up the personal.

And, "in giving up the personal" she enters a new realm, one that Bonnie Marranca has brilliantly named "autobiology." Marranca's essay, "A Cosmography of Herself: The Autobiology of Rachel Rosenthal," offers a wide-ranging set of references for a reading of the later work of Rosenthal, which Marranca describes as constructed "around body, biology, and gender. . . . In effect, Rosenthal fuses the controversial Gaia hypothesis, the view of nature described in chaos theory, and the perspective on geology described in the study of plate tectonics to trace the autobiology of her life. Drawing on issues raised by these scientific ideas, her performances are oriented increasingly around ecological themes and animal rights. But more than that, the face of the earth has become a metaphor for her own physiognomy."[99] And this takes place, as Marranca writes, in the context of "the ecological condition of contemporary life at the end of the twentieth century."

No longer content with history that merely spans her own lifetime, for the past ten years or so Rosenthal has roamed back and forth in a grand history, that of the future and distant past. Alexandra Grilikhes begins her exchange with Rosenthal with a discussion of the 1988–90 *Pangaean Dreams,* in which the artist personifies Pangaea, the supercontinent of 250 million years ago. Rosenthal responds, "Having felt connected to the Earth for such a long time, it was interesting to me that the same year I worked on *Pangaean Dreams* and studied about plate tectonics was the year that all my bones began to break. I wondered if there was some connection on a psychic level. . . . I used the connection as a means to structure a piece that would somehow, through identifying with me as a human being, bring an audience into identifying with the Planet."[100]

In their 1991 discussion, Rosenthal informs Lacy that there is no time left, that nature is dying and will soon be dead. "The question is: Are we going to get the 'prise de conscience' early enough so that we can somehow manage that demise and then the transformation that will enable life to continue in a managed way on Earth?"[101] Animal life and animal rights are at the heart of Rosenthal's "conscience." In the evolutionary development of animals on this planet, Rosenthal sees warnings and a parable for humans. At times, animals appear as "consciences," shamanistic "guides," and inspirations; at other times, they are creatures whom she must nurture against human invasiveness and brutality.

Always a voracious reader, Rosenthal has over the past ten years or so plunged herself into an even wider span of research. Each piece is meticulously researched: "Usually it is a mixture of personal stuff, books I read, and what's happening in the world—in equal parts. . . . In preparation for *The Others,* I read Tom Regan's *The Case for Animal Rights* and Peter Singer's *Animal Liberation,* and a whole bunch of other books and articles in animal publications. For *Traps,* the main book was Lyall Watson's *Lifetide,* and at the time I was also reading Gary Zukav's *The Dancing Wu-Li Masters,* and Ilya Prigogine's *From Being to Becoming.* Generally I read a lot of Prigogine anyway, as he has become very important in chaos theory." [102] She has also studied shamanism, in both reading and workshops (and in 1985 created a piece entitled *Shamanic Ritual* for the Woman's Building in Los Angeles). Key to the content, resonance, and success of her newer work is such research in the context of her growing fascination [103] with science.

In 1992, she told Denise Meola in an interview that "the separation between art and science is going to disappear completely. . . . Quantum physics has shown us something wonderful: everything we touch and observe changes for the reason of being observed; our input actually changes the world. . . . Artists have a calling, a responsibility to understand these new scientific paradigms and create work that reflects that understanding, that disseminates these paradigms on the human level. . . . I had a proposal to work with seismological instruments that are in place all over the world. The sky's the limit!" [104]

What keeps this grand, optimistic vision from being realized? The answer, simply put, according to Rosenthal, is humankind and human culture. It is a theme Rosenthal constantly returns to in her performances, interviews, lectures, and life. Marranca maintains rightly that "one of the profound themes in Rosenthal's work is the understanding that the ecosystem is inseparable from the cultural system of a people." [105] Rosenthal returned again to try and grapple with this topic in *Zone,* a work that attracted a lot of public attention prior to its performance in Los Angeles at the beginning of 1994, and a wide range of critical responses, private and public, afterward.

Zone, 1994

In her review of Rosenthal's *Zone,* Amelia Jones writes, "Living in fin-de-millennium California, I, like Rachel Rosenthal, have felt threatened by the seemingly random, vicious violence of contemporary life and have found myself obsessing about chaos, death, and human evil."[106] Rosenthal explains in her program notes that *Zone—* whose narrative and imagery circle around the Romanov family (represented by five cast members and Rosenthal as the tsarina) in their last days, surrounded by a "Throng" (of some sixty performers, primarily of color)—was conceived as "a metaphor for patriarchal Western civilization and its demise." She intended it to be "a siren alarm calling on all of us, of all colors, beliefs, ethnicities, nationalities, etc. to recognize that we are truly on the edge of chaos and to choose between life and death."[107]

This grand and costly epic, with its dramatic costumes, sets, sounds, and lighting, and superb choreography by Mehmet Sander of nondancers in the undulating, surging, restless, threatening "Throng," appeared almost filmic in many of its scenes. It was staged briefly only once—at the University of California's Center for the Performing Arts in Los Angeles on the weekend of February 11 and 12, 1994—and it was immediately and harshly criticized in the *Los Angeles Times.*[108] Indeed Jones herself, basically an admirer of Rosenthal, read it as an ambitious but flawed piece—a sentiment shared by many in Los Angeles—whose conflation of "environmental disaster with colonialism, the Cold War, patriarchy, and a generalized notion of human depravity . . . reduces each specific instance of oppression and destruction to a vague category of 'human evil,' defusing the potential for resistance."[109]

It seems to me that, in many ways, *Zone* is a Janus-like work in Rosenthal's career, that it faces two directions, past and future. It was developed out of the contents and style of the over a decade-old scripted performances, many of them spectacles. Equally, it looks forward, in its collaborative process and networking, toward a return to improvisation and intimacy.

Whether one admires the work or not, *Zone* necessarily stands currently at the end of the spectacle genre in Rosenthal's work because—uncharacteristically—so far she has not begun (as of the winter of 1996–97) to work on another piece of such magnitude. *Zone* was an astonishing work, but even for me—despite its almost overpoweringly inventive and stunning imagery and narrative moments—it did feel like a grand finale of a certain stage in Rosenthal's work. On the other hand, Rosenthal and its performers bonded through the experience of working together. (On April 2, 1994, I traveled to Los Angeles to attend a remarkably open and fascinatingly rich exchange about the *Zone* experience among many of its performers.)[110] More than half her current company is drawn from the *Zone* participants. Thus, especially in hindsight, *Zone* became a catalyst for one of the returns to small scale in Rosenthal's cyclical swings between improvisation and script, between intimacy and public grandeur.

The DbD Experience, Espace DBD, and the New Rachel Rosenthal Company

Rosenthal has a long history of working with groups and teaching. She likes to work with others, and is drawn to the imaginative possibilities of collective invention. Teaching workshops and running a company profoundly satisfies the strongly didactic part of her. I sense, too, that these activities provide her with a community, one that is supportive and meets almost daily, yet is not demanding on her psyche in quite the same way as a family or close personal friendships. Teaching also provides, of course, ongoing and reliable financial support in contrast to her large costly productions.

First there was the long experience of Instant Theatre, in its early ten-year manifestation, and its brief second reincarnation. Rosenthal recalls in the later 1970s talking to a woman—an earlier participant in Instant Theatre—who suggested that Rosenthal teach theater workshops. Each would offer "a curriculum that stems from the Instant Theatre exercises, but . . . would be a workshop a little bit like EST in the sense that people would come not necessarily because they wanted to do theater, but simply for the experience."[111] Thus, in 1979, as part of her conscious redirecting of herself, emotionally, artistically, and financially, Rosenthal invented "The DbD Experience," an intensive thirty-five-hour weekend workshop divided into three days—Origins, Connections, and Power—which she has been running intermittently ever since. She named it after her much-loved paraplegic cat, Dibidi, and the word also stands for "Doing by Doing."

Like her earlier Instant Theatre, The DbD Experience acquired a large Los Angeles following for Rosenthal among artists, dancers, and theater people—as well as many "nonprofessionals" who took it for its innate experience. In 1984, Linda Burnham, then editor of *High Performance*, published an article-interview, "The D.B.D. Experience:

Rachel Rosenthal's Mind/Body Spa: A Bath for the Soul." Rosenthal told Burnham that its art making made the workshop different from California New Age workshops, although it has certain resemblances to them with its guided imagery and meditation. "It's different from psychodrama in that we don't use language and we are not trying to play out psychological problems. The work is much more spiritual and abstract and artlike, often on a mythical level."[112] By now Rosenthal estimates that she has run over fifty strict DbD Experiences and many more workshops using different formats.

For three years, between 1980 and 1983, Rosenthal housed these DbD workshops in her building, which she had just acquired. She also created Espace DBD there. Sponsoring the work of a wide range of established and emerging performance artists, this space could accommodate an audience of fifty, and averaged two performances every weekend until city parking ordinances brought it to a halt.

In December 1994, The Rachel Rosenthal Company (established in 1989), now with its new cast of sixteen performers, put on *DbDbDb–D, An Evening* in the newly reopened Espace DBD. In the following year, Rosenthal and an ensemble of her best students presented *Five Easy Pieces and Then Some* at the California Center for Performing Arts in Escondido. In the spring of 1996, she and her company of ten members began a new production, *Tohubohu!* at Espace DBD. In the publicity for it, Rosenthal writes, "A long time ago, I had a dream. It was a dream of a kind of theatre that would create itself; without a script, without rehearsals, with no director, simply by bringing together a group of well-trained and inspired people who would spontaneously and collectively carve a work of art out of the raw materials of theatre: time, space, action, text, sound, gesture, lights, objects, costumes, masks. . . . Such a theatre could never be pinned down or repeated."[113]

Yet despite the endless improvisation and differences in each individual performance, Rosenthal and her group base their work on a core of cohesiveness: indeed she views as the biggest pitfall of improvisation, "the mere creation of disconnected images, information and ingredients." Instead, she aims for the expression of a "spontaneous and collective ordering of chaos (multiplicity) through a very disciplined art form." The members are in a state of "continual workshopping," as Rosenthal wrote to me recently, in order to develop and maintain an underpinning of "formal, structural and thematic ordering" on which all the nonlinear improvisation is based. She says that the most frequently asked questions by audience members after an evening of improvisation are: How did the ensemble decide on certain themes? How did they decide to bring out one prop rather than another? "People are incredulous when we say none of the above was planned because they sense the order very strongly and have trouble believing that such order can arise without predetermination. Yet this is, of course, the central philosophy of my workshops, and now the core of our Company's agenda in this process."[114]

Los Angeles, Rosenthal's Studio, June 1, 1996. I arrive almost late and sit on a cushion on the floor to see *Tohubohu!* As the other performers[115] (strikingly young and ethnically diverse) move props—a large opaque glass container-object, a big basket perched on a dirty white box, a broom with green brushes, a hanging bright textile—onto the informal stage, Rosenthal talks about improvisation. She introduces the musician/composer and his percussion assemblage (there will be taped music and sounds, too) and tells us that "Tohubohu" is a French word, derived from Hebrew, which means chaos, confusion, and hubbub.

Silver foil that rustles noisily clothes the first performers . . . silence except for the sound of a flute . . . an eccentric couple dart around, squashing imaginary fleas . . . a woman walks along carrying an empty gold frame . . . Rosenthal moves across the floor, totally absorbed and intense, exclaiming in a guttural voice, "I love watching fights to the death". . . a man, nude to the waist, and wearing a helmet, bandages her whole body and head with a roll of toilet paper . . . two performers in a long orange Martha Graham-like tube crawl along the floor, brushing by my feet. . . an African American male performer, his back to us, shits marbles onto the floor . . . he and Rosenthal argue over territory with threats of lynching and rape, resolving their differences with his gift of imaginary sugar . . . a white male performer, juggling marbles, inquires if the audience has all of its [i.e., marbles], and then rolls the marbles along the floor, one by one . . . a haunting duo of an Asian and a white man sing and shake Australian musical rain sticks as they dance . . . Rosenthal pushes a wheelchair containing a huddled patient, who winks and grimaces madly at the audience . . . the song, "You've Got to Accent-U-Ate the Positive" is played . . . Rosenthal reassures a performer, who comes anxiously running onto the stage, "not to worry, we have to find new ways" . . . finally, wrapped in a red cloth and looking like an androgynous emperor in exile, Rosenthal, glancing at her watch, informs us abruptly, "That's it, the end."

A discussion with the audience follows, during which different readings of the pieces are suggested. Rosenthal talks of migration, exile, and displacement. She describes one vignette as being about "viral and bacterial invasions and the tables-are-turned business of us humans, top predators, becoming food for the infinitely tiny." The wheelchair episode responds to the current Dr. Kevorkian suicide debates. At one point, in response to a question, she tells us that these intimate improvisations with her new company, rather than her earlier spectacle work, make "the autumn of my career and life so enjoyable."

I sit mulling over this remark, not really listening to the further exchange but rather thinking about Rosenthal's long career . . . her birth in Paris in 1926 and her childhood there . . . Artaud's thoughts on theater and the theater of the absurd . . . the dance experiments of Cunningham and the music experiments of Cage . . . Instant Theatre . . . Rosenthal's early autobiographical performances . . . the later fierce grand spectacles. . . the repertoire of gestures, movements, and vocal plays that she has developed over some forty years . . . the dramatic counterpoint between Rosenthal's movements and those of her young, agile, new company members . . . that this current collaboration has dislodged (up to a certain point) her almost predictable thematic trajectories . . . that the new performers have not only their own styles but their own trajectories, too . . . and how all this has come together to create such radiantly fresh theater on this evening in the early summer of 1996.

Notes

1. Alexandra Grilikhes, "Taboo Subjects: An Interview with Rachel Rosenthal," *American Writing: A Magazine,* no. 10, 1994–95. (Reprinted below.)

2. Bonnie Marranca, "A Cosmography of Herself: The Autobiology of Rachel Rosenthal," in *Ecologies of Theater* (Baltimore: Johns Hopkins University Press, 1996). (Reprinted below.)

3. Moira Roth, Interview, Los Angeles, September 2 and 3, 1989, Archives of American Art, Smithsonian Institution, Washington, D.C., p. 11. Hereafter I refer to this 115-page transcription of my interview with Rachel Rosenthal, available at the various branches of the Archives of American Art, Smithsonian Institution, as Roth, Archives of American Art Interview.

4. Rachel Rosenthal to Barbara Smith, July 17, 1976. (Reprinted below.) This long letter outlines the connections of Rosenthal's family to theater. See also Rosenthal's first letter to Barbara Smith, June 19, 1975, which contains a remarkably vivid account of the decor and food of her childhood. (Reprinted below.)

5. Roth, Archives of American Art Interview, p. 2.

6. From an unpublished manuscript, circa 1983, by Rosenthal entitled "3,000 Words about Myself," in the artist's archives in Los Angeles.

7. Denise Meola, "Interview: Rachel Rosenthal," *Omni,* August 1992. (Reprinted below.)

8. Ibid.

9. Ruth Askey, "Exoticism and Fear in Rio," *Artweek,* November 17, 1979. (Reprinted below.)

10. Antonin Artaud, "The Alfred Jarry Theater," in *Antonin Artaud: Selected Writings,* ed. Susan Sontag (New York: Farrar, Straus, and Giroux, 1976), pp. 156–57.

11. Rachel Rosenthal, "Rachel Rosenthal," *Journal: The Los Angeles Institute of Contemporary Art,* February 5, 1974. (Reprinted below.) Concerning the date of Rosenthal's first discovery of Artaud's *The Theater and Its Double*—it was originally published in French in 1938 and translated into English in 1958—she has on various occasions assigned different dates, ranging from 1947 to 1949. In a recent interview with me, however, she settled on the year 1948.

12. Roth, Archives of American Art Interview, p. 20.

13. Antonin Artaud to René Guilly, quoted in Frances Morris, *Paris Post War: Art and Existentialism, 1945–55* (London: Tate Gallery, 1993), p. 66.

14. One must remember that it was John Cage who introduced many artists and musicians in his New School for Social Research class to Artaud's work, when it was translated into English in 1958.

15. Rosenthal has continued throughout the rest of her life to be attracted to this circle and her memories of those early days. For example, she placed a Cage text as a pivotal one in her 1994 performance, *Zone.*

16. Rosenthal had a brief affair with Jasper Johns in the summer of 1954. See Roth, Archives of American Art Interview, pp. 23–24.

17. Moira Roth, "The Aesthetic of Indifference," *Artforum,* November 1977.

18. Grilikhes, "Taboo Subjects" Interview. In the interview, Rosenthal tells Grilikhes that she refers to this experience of Cage's apartment to represent "power" in her 1980 performance, *Bonsoir, Dr. Schön!*

19. Roth, Archives of American Art Interview, p. 26.

20. For illustration of this "Untitled" 1954 piece with Rosenthal's head, see Max Kozloff, *Jasper Johns* (New York: Harry N. Abrams, 1967), Plate 8.

21. Roth, Archives of American Art Interview, p. 25.

22. F. P., "Third Annual," *Art News,* January 1955, p. 48.

23. Ibid., p. 27.

24. Rosenthal to Moira Roth, June 21, 1996.

25. Roth, Archives of American Art Interview, p. 27.

26. Ibid., pp. 27–29.

27. Ibid.

28. Ibid., p. 36.

29. Rosenthal, *Journal: The Los Angeles Institute of Contemporary Art.*

30. Roth, Archives of American Art Interview, p. 46. The quotations in the following paragraph are all drawn from this interview, pp. 32–33. For an extended study of Instant Theatre, see William Dwight Peterson, *A History of Instant Theatre* (Ann Arbor, Mich.: UMI, 1991). This published dissertation from the University of Texas–Austin contains an Instant Theatre Chronology together with a section on Instant Theatre curriculum and exercises, and a series of transcribed "talks" by Rosenthal to workshop participants.

31. Jack Hirschman, "Instant Theatre," *FM & Fine Arts* (May 1963). (Reprinted below.) The quotations in this paragraph are all drawn from this text.

32. Diane Calder, "Instant Theatre," *Newsletter on the Arts VII,* no. 6. (This was found in the artist's archives in Los Angeles and there is no notation of date of publication. Ed.)

33. Roth, Archives of American Art Interview, p. 36.

34. See Rosenthal's July 17, 1976 letter to Barbara Smith.

35. Thomas Albright, "A Look at Stone Sculpture," *San Francisco Chronicle,* June 30, 1969.

36. Rachel Rosenthal, "Coiled Sculpture," *Ceramics Monthly,* March 1974, p. 34.

37. For a discussion of those events and the overall feminist scene in Los Angeles in the 1970s, see relevant sections in *The Power of Feminist Art: The American Movement of the 1970s, History and Impact,* ed. Norma Broude and Mary D. Garrard (New York: Harry N. Abrams, 1994).

38. Roth, Archives of American Art Interview, pp. 39, 41–42.

39. Ibid., p. 54.

40. Ibid., p. 57.

41. See my writings on performance, including: "Toward a History of California Performance: Part One," *Arts Magazine,* February 1978, reprinted with a new introduction as "Bay Area Performance Art," in *Reflections,* San Francisco Art Institute, 1981; "Toward a History of California Performance: Part Two," *Arts Magazine,* June 1978; "A Star Is Born: Performance Art in California," *Performing Arts Journal* 12 (Spring 1980); "Autobiography, Theater, Mysticism and Politics: Women's Performance Art in Southern California," in *Performance Anthology: Source Book for a Decade of California Performance,* ed. Carl E. Loeffler and Darlene Tong (San Francisco: Contemporary Arts Press, 1980, new edition 1989); "Character, Costume and Theater in Early California Performance," *Living Art Vancouver* (Vancouver, Canada: Living Art Performance Festival, 1981); "Cross Currents and Crossroads in Contemporary American Performance Art," *Alles und noch viel mehr* (Bern, Switzerland: Kunsthalle Bern, 1985); and "Performance Art," *Studio International* (June 1982). Much of my research culminated in 1983, when I edited *The Amazing Decade: Women and Performance Art in America, 1970—1980, A Source Book*

(Los Angeles: Astro Artz, 1983), a book based on an exhibition of women's performance art curated by Mary Jane Jacob in New Orleans in 1980 under the auspices of the Women's Caucus for Art.

42. On March 8, 1979, Rosenthal organized a "Dinner Party" for a small group of friends, including Barbara T. Smith and Betye Saar, as their contribution to The International Dinner Party by Suzanne Lacy—in itself a response to the opening of Judy Chicago's *Dinner Party* at the San Francisco Museum of Modern Art. Each artist spoke about her mother for a few minutes and the session was videotaped. The event inspired Rosenthal to write an interesting yet unpublished essay on her mother and her unresolved ambivalent feelings about her. See the artist's archives in Los Angeles.

43. See Rosenthal's July 17, 1976 letter to Barbara T. Smith.

44. Roth, Archives of American Art Interview, p. 42.

45. See the conversation between Suzanne Lacy and Rosenthal in "Saving the World: A Dialogue between Suzanne Lacy and Rachel Rosenthal," *Artweek*, September 12, 1991. (Reprinted below.)

46. For a contemporary account of this piece by Barbara T. Smith, see Melinda Wortz, "Art Is Magic," *Artweek*, August 9, 1975. In a fax correspondence between Smith and Roth on May 27, 1996, Smith wrote, "This was an auction during which various structured events to be carried out between the buyer and myself at a future time were sold. Conceptually, the piece was about making performance *(i.e., time)* equivalently valuable with objects."

47. Paying a sum of $32.50, Rosenthal received a formal written agreement, signed by herself and Barbara T. Smith, that read "During the month of June each will write three letters to the other. The buyer will begin the exchange and wait for a reply before sending the second letter and so forth." (In fact the exchange of letters took place over a year.) Copies of these three letters from Rosenthal to Smith (and Smith's answers) are in the artist's archives in Los Angeles; the first (June 19, 1975) and the third (July 17, 1976) are printed in this book.

48. Roth, Archives of American Art Interview, p. 45. It is significant to note that Smith had earlier created a series of performances around food, its symbolism, and meal rituals, beginning with *Ritual Meal* (1969), *White Meal* (1970), *Celebration of the Holy Squash* (1971), and *The Longest Day of Night, Feed Me,* and *Pure Food* (all in 1973).

49. Unpublished letter to Barbara T. Smith, August 16, 1995. The quotations in this paragraph are all drawn from this text.

50. Edie Danieli, "Rachel Rosenthal: A Life History," *Artweek*, December 13, 1975. (Reprinted below.)

51. Moira Roth, unpublished transcribed interview with Rachel Rosenthal, November 23, 1977, in Roth's archives in Berkeley.

52. Danieli, "Rachel Rosenthal: A Life History."

53. Rosenthal's July 17, 1976 letter to Barbara T. Smith. The quotations in this paragraph are all drawn from this text.

54. In chronological sequence, these eleven autobiographical performances are: *Replays, Thanks, Charm, The Head of Olga K., Grand Canyon, The Death Show, The Arousing (Shock, Thunder), My Brazil, Bonsoir, Dr. Schön!, Leave Her in Naxos,* and *Soldier of Fortune.*

55. Rachel Rosenthal, quoted in Roth, *The Amazing Decade,* p. 126.

56. *Charm* was only performed once, but in 1986 Rosenthal re-created it as a radio piece, produced by Jacki Apple with the Los Angeles radio station KPFK and *High Performance.*

57. Rachel Rosenthal, *Charm,* unpublished script (which had been later transcribed from a recording of the performance), the artist's archives in Los Angeles.

58. Roth, 1977 unpublished transcribed interview. Also see discussion in Eelka Lampe, "Rachel Rosenthal Creating Her Selves," *TDR* (Spring 1988), in which Lampe places Rosenthal in a performance/nonperformance scale (complete with diagrams). See also Lampe's earlier unpublished M.A. thesis, "Theatricality in Performance Art: The Work of Rachel Rosenthal" (Department of Performance Studies, New York University, 1985).

59. Roth, 1977 unpublished transcribed interview.

60. See Smith's review of *Charm.* (Reprinted below.) All the quotations in this paragraph are drawn from this text. Also see an interesting interview by Elaine Barkin, in which Rosenthal discusses her notions of "performance," theater, and audience, together with extensive comments on Artaud. (Reprinted below.)

61. Roth, 1977 unpublished transcribed interview.

62. Rachel Rosenthal, *The Head of Olga K.* in the artist's archives in Los Angeles. Also see printed description of the piece by Rosenthal, "The Head of Olga K.," *High Performance* (June 1978).

63. I saw *The Head of Olga K.* when it was performed at the University of California–San Diego on May 1, 1977.

64. Roth, "Toward a History of California Performance, Parts One and Two," *Arts Magazine,* February and June 1978.

65. Ibid., Part Two, June 1978, p. 114.

66. Roth, Archives of American Art Interview, p. 71.

67. Ibid., p. 60.

68. *Grand Canyon* was only performed once (in 1978) but there is an audio-cassette of this performance and a radio interview with Bill Hunt for the Los Angeles radio station KPFK.

69. See accounts of this by Rachel Rosenthal, "The Death Show," *High Performance* (March 1979); and Ruth Askey, "Rachel Rosenthal Exorcises Death," *Artweek,* November 18, 1978. (Reprinted below.)

70. Quoted from an unpublished text by Rosenthal on her performances in the artist's archives in Los Angeles.

71. See review of *My Brazil* by Ruth Askey, "Exoticism and Fear in Rio."

72. Rachel Rosenthal, "The Arousing (Shock, Thunder)," *High Performance* (September 1979), pp. 22-23.

73. Ibid., p. 23.

74. See description of *Bonsoir, Dr. Schön!* in Ruth Weisberg, "Autobiographical Journey," *Artweek,* November 22, 1980. (Reprinted below.)

75. Ruth Weisberg, "Reaching for Revelations," *Artweek,* March 14, 1981. (Reprinted below.)

76. See a description of *Soldier of Fortune* in Melinda Wortz, "Los Angeles," *Art News,* October 1981. (Reprinted below.) Toward the end of 1981, in *Performance and the Masochist Tradition,* Rosenthal presented herself gagged, her hands bound together, and asked the audience to pierce her wrists with fishhooks. See a description of this performance in a review by Emily Hicks, "Examining the Taboo," *Artweek,* November 14, 1981. (Reprinted below.)

77. This cover accompanied an essay by Richard J. Stayton, "Rachel Rosenthal Confronts Her Beasts," *L.A. Weekly,* July 3–9, 1981.

78. A major turning point in Rosenthal's life was when she was defrauded of all her money in January 1981 by a financial manager. In April of that year, she turns this experience into the subject of *Soldier of Fortune.*

79. Roth, Archives of American Art Interview, p. 82.

80. Rachel Rosenthal, "Rachel Rosenthal," *Performing Arts Journal,* no. 46 (January 1994). (Reprinted below.)

81. The chronological sequence of this decade of performances between 1982 and 1992 is as follows: *Traps, Gaia, Mon Amour, KabbaLAmobile, The Others, Foodchain, Shamanic Ritual, L.O.W. in Gaia, Was Black, Rachel's Brain, Death Valley, Zatoichi, Amazonia, Pangaean Dreams,* and *filename: FUTURFAX.*

82. Roth, Archives of American Art Interview, p. 91.

83. Sally Banes, "Rachel Rosenthal: As the Egg Turns," *The Village Voice,* December 6, 1983. (Reprinted below.)

84. Alisa Solomon, "Worm's Eye View," *The Village Voice,* August 18, 1987. (Reprinted below.)

85. Fidel Danieli, "Gaia, Mon Amour," *Visual Art* (Summer 1984). (Reprinted below.)

86. Jacki Apple, "The Romance of Automobiles," *Artweek,* September 29, 1984. (Reprinted below.)

87. Sylvie Drake, "Rachel Rosenthal Puts on the Dog at Japan America," *Los Angeles Times,* December 21, 1984, Calendar. (Reprinted below.)

88. Donald Karwelis, "Speaking to the Enemy," *Artweek,* September 5, 1987. (Reprinted below.)

89. Sasha Anawalt, " 'Was Black' Overshadows Other Visions," *Los Angeles Herald Examiner,* June 28, 1986. (Reprinted below.)

90. Martin Bernheimer, "Rachel Rosenthal Guides E.A.R. Unit on an Amazon Safari," *Los Angeles Times,* May 18, 1990. (Reprinted below.)

91. Ross Wetzsteon, "Stand-up Shaman," *The Village Voice,* August 6, 1991. (Reprinted below.)

92. Erika Munk, "Brainchildren of a Lesser God," *The Village Voice,* October 11, 1988. (Reprinted below.)

93. The script is reprinted below.

94. Roth, Archives of American Art Interview, p. 104.

95. Rachel Rosenthal, "Letter from the Future," unpublished manuscript, 1990. (Reprinted below.)

96. Alisa Solomon, "Rosenthal Performs *FUTURFAX* for Whitney in New York," *Los Angeles Times,* April 25, 1992. (Reprinted below.)

97. Nicole Landau, a cousin, is the relative whom Rosenthal is closest to these days in real life. Landau visits her in Los Angeles and they keep in close contact.

98. Lacy and Rosenthal, "Saving the World." What follows in the next few paragraphs of my text is drawn heavily from an earlier essay I wrote, "The Passion of Rachel Rosenthal," *Parachute* (January–March 1994), p. 21. The *Parachute* issue was one of two (the first appeared in October–December 1993) devoted to the theme of "le Bestiaire, endangered species."

99. Marranca, "A Cosmography of Herself."

100. Grilikhes, "Taboo Subjects" Interview.

101. Lacy and Rosenthal, "Saving the World." (In Rosenthal's statements in *Artweek,* lowercase was used for "earth." However, as it is her deep conviction that "Earth" should always begin with an uppercase letter, this has been changed in the book whenever Rosenthal uses the word. Ed.)

102. Roth, "The Passion of Rachel Rosenthal," p. 25.

103. Even in the earlier autobiographical performances, it should be noted that there are many scientific references. For example, the title of *Charm* not only refers to the "charmed" life of Rosenthal's parents, but to an account in an article in the *Los Angeles Times* of that year which Rosenthal had read, describing a theory about subatomic particles and quarks, one of which had been named "charm" by a whimsical scientist. She refers to the many-worlds theory in *My Brazil* and in *Traps* to evolutionary biology.

104. Meola, Interview.

105. Marranca, "A Cosmography of Herself."

106. Amelia Jones, "Rachel Rosenthal: UCLA. Center for the Performing Arts," *Artforum,* April 1994. (Reprinted below.)

107. Rachel Rosenthal, "Program Notes by Rachel Rosenthal," *UCLA Center for the Performing Arts 1993–1994 Season* [brochure], n.p.

108. Lewis Segal, "Apocalypse Adrift: Rachel Rosenthal's 'Zone' a Flat, Predictable Satire," *Los Angeles Times,* February 14, 1994.

109. Jones, "Rachel Rosenthal."

110. This taped discussion about *Zone* among its performers and Rosenthal was transcribed and the transcription is housed in the artist's archives in Los Angeles.

111. Roth, Archives of American Art Interview, p. 78.

112. Linda Burnham, "The D.B.D. Experience: Rachel Rosenthal's Mind/Body Spa: A Bath for the Soul," *High Performance,* no. 26 (1994). (Reprinted below.) (In rereading her statement in this text concerning the lack of language in DbD, Rosenthal recently told me that she had intended to stress that it was only "verbal" language that was not used. Ed.)

113. The Rachel Rosenthal Company News Release, April 11, 1996, n.p.

114. Rachel Rosenthal to Moira Roth, June 12, 1996.

115. Franc Baliton, Tad Coughenour, Rochelle Fabb, C. Derrick Jones, Imesol Moreno, Michael Morrisey, and Mike Sakamoto, with live videotaper, Leslie Purcell.

I Conversations and Interviews

Elaine Barkin

Excerpts from Part 1, "Conversation in Two Parts

with Rachel Rosenthal"

EB: How would you describe your activities as a "performance artist" and in what ways do those activities differ from those of a "performer"?

RR: Mainly the difference is that I perform in an art context. A lot of people believe that I'm too theatrical. I can't help that because I come from a theater background. The other big difference is that I have control over the entire production. I conceive of the piece, I write the text, I perform it, I take care of the visuals, I do everything, you see, and I think that's probably what separates performance art from other performance functions. In most theatrical functions you have separation of tasks between playwright, actor, and so on, between creators and interpreters, whereas in performance art you're everything. Also, I think performance art is highly conceptual; it is based on concept, on metaphor. In terms of content, mine is probably more narrative, linear, textual, and literary than is the work of other artists, but even though it's based on personal experience and autobiography, it is still highly conceptual and deals with metaphors on many levels. Mine are also theatrical in the sense that I usually present a persona, whereas many other artists work from what they believe is their own self-image: they don't put on a costume, or put on a mask, or put on a voice (although some of them do, you know). The thing about performance art is that it's almost impossible to precisely delineate because every artist has another way of presenting a performance, and emphasis is put on different areas—some on sound, some on visuals, some on text. A person like Guy de Cointet is heavily based on text; he plays with

Originally published in *Perspectives of New Music* (Fall–Winter 1982/Spring–Summer 1983), 567–81.

language; he also has actors and actresses performing his pieces, so in that sense he is probably even more theatrical than I am. However, he is also considered a performance artist. Laurie Anderson's emphasis is sound, voice, music; her work is strongly involved with equipment, machines, and technology. Gary Lloyd is also involved with technology: he works with computers and satellite video. So it's wide open. And a lot of it is context: if you do it in a museum, they think you're an artist; if you do it in a theater, you're an actor. What it is really is artists expanding their area of involvement, and taking on the vast opportunities our society offers in terms of technology and areas of inquiry. They get involved in politics, in science, in music, and in technology, and yet they do it from the point of view of an artist. That's why I think the field is so fascinating and rich and much more exciting in its capacity than static art sometimes can be. . . .

. . . **EB:** Presumably you have an audience in mind, that is, you don't conceive of your work as private, as removed from a social environment, do you? How do you wish to affect your audience?

RR: *Profoundly.* I'm very interested in communication. Many artists are not; their work is opaque. I try to make my work reasonably transparent, reasonably accessible. Most of my past work has been autobiographical, using my own experiences and trying to affect an audience by reaching the universal through the very deeply personal. And so I have exposed a lot of things about my past, my self, my feelings, and have always put it on a broad metaphorical level that people could tap into. The pieces have affected people most profoundly on an emotional level as well as on an intellectual level, something I'm interested in. I don't like "cool" art. I'm more interested in "hot" art, something dealing with ritual, in a sense, participatory ritual. And although the audience is not actively participating, they still are empathizing in the event, and the event itself is very often a kind of exorcism or a rite of passage or a magical moment, where a moment of crisis comes to its apex and then bursts. Many people would come up to me after most of my performances and state that I touched them in ways that they can really understand. They have been through similar experiences or they can see correspondence between their experiences and mine, and through that process of sympathizing they also get the catharsis that I'm offering. I'm interested in art that may be beneficial to a society. . . .

. . . **EB:** You've said that some of your ideas are conceptually rooted in some of Artaud's ideas. The ritual connection is clear, yet he had a mistrust of the text and of the projection of the personal, both of which you've involved yourself with.

RR: When I read Artaud (I was probably twenty or twenty-two), he opened up for me the possibility of what the theater can be in terms of the physical theater. At that time, most theater that you saw in France was *theatre de boulevard,* comedies of mores and bourgeois drama and problems of love and money and a lot of talk. What he introduced was not only a wave of exoticism to the theater, taking ideas from African and Oriental theater, but he also brought metaphysics and the cosmic realm onto the stage. This cracked the thing wide open for me and quite a few others, for we then began to see the stage not just as a box within which texts are read or memorized but also a box of a whole universe of sounds, colors, gestures, and movements, a space within which all kinds of physical, visual, and audio events could take place and communicate ideas without the use of text. You see, I really operate on two tracks. One is the strictly performance art track and the other track is the kind of theater I've been doing since 1956, which used to be called Instant Theatre and now I call it DbD ("doing by doing"), and that is very much closer to Artaud's ideas than my art performances are. However, in that mode I work improvisationally, which is contrary to his ideas because he was interested in finding a kind of scientific alphabet of the theater.

EB: How do you feel about nonretrievability, of not being able to do something again?

RR: When you do what I call the "pure form," you can never try to re-create anything and you must always be off-balance, you must always surprise yourself. It's as if you're setting your own traps and then you fall into them and you have to work your way out of them. It's as if you have a field that you mine; you put all those mines in that field and then you decide to walk across it and you never know which one is going to explode. You set yourself up and you bring who and what you are at the moment, but you also have those mines that may explode, so it's both you and the outside working together. . . .

Linda Burnham

Excerpts from "The D.B.D. Experience:

Rachel Rosenthal's Mind/Body Spa:

A Bath for the Soul"

LB: What would you say if somebody said, "Oh, DbD is nothing but another California touchy-feely workshop?" What makes it unique?

RR: The art making. It's different from psychodrama in that we don't use language and we are not trying to play out psychological problems. The work is much more spiritual and abstract and artlike, often on a mythical level.

LB: Can you talk about DbD in terms of building blocks?

RR: I'm still working on it but it's a pretty good curriculum. It works. What I try to do is separate people from their everyday lives. It's like taking a bath in Lethe, the River of Forgetfulness. That's done through exercises of relaxation and awareness of letting go. Guided imagery and guided meditations. Beginning to put consciousness into the body instead of being like a disembodied head, so that there is no blockage between the intention of the imagination and the transmission of that intention through every part of your body.

When that begins to work, I try to open it up so that boundaries begin to disappear, internal as well as external. We go then into the boundaries between yourself and the space you are in, so that you become part of that space, like a fish feels the ocean, the medium in which you live. Then I try to dissolve the boundaries between human beings, so that the work we do as paired-off people or as groups is also designed to develop the sensibilities or feelers the way certain microorganisms have sensory organs all over their bodies. So the whole

Originally published in *High Performance* 26 (1984), 48–51, 90–91.

body begins to come alive to awareness of energies coming in from other people.

Then we go into freeing the voice, which is very, very tricky. Actually, it's quite amazing that the exercises achieve so much so fast. Most people have no voice! The voices are either swallowed back or they're caught in the throat or they're garbled and there's no support under the voice. In a very short amount of time with the kind of work we do individually with each person, the voices are released. Then the voice is put to use creatively. And what we try to do is to relate the vocal output to the entire being so that it's no longer an instrument or just a means to transmit certain information, but really becomes the personification on airwaves.

So then we start using the tools of art. That means we do exercises that enable us to learn a common vocabulary to do the kind of work that needs to be done. We work with sets, with lights, with sounds; we do our own music.

Saturday night there's a very important exercise, the object exercise. It's pivotal in the weekend. When we get to that point they're usually at a low ebb because they're exhausted. It's late at night and it's very demanding. It's not flashy, it's not done for art, it's the only exercise of the weekend that's purely done for the individual who's doing it, but with the complete attention and support and concentration by the rest of the group. And it's one person, one object. That particular exercise is usually a big breakthrough. It opens up whatever block is there.

LB: How did you discover it?

RR: By accident! Intuition. Trial and error! So each person gets what he or she really needs to get out of it, particularly now.

LB: But their specific needs are not necessarily revealed to you, are they?

RR: No, nothing's revealed to me. Before the workshop I have the people write me a letter and that gives me a hint. But you know each person is like a walking Rorschach test or a fingerprint. You get a feel for what a person is, how he or she functions. Body language. Being very open and in a kind of semitrance myself, somehow I get a sense of what's going on. But usually the exercises and the energy of the group do the work for me. So after the object exercise we have a big wonderful group improv and everybody kind of blows it out.

The three days have names: Origins, Connections, and Power. In the second day those connections are established. The third day, what I call power takes place, which is the connection to the cosmic power, to the energy of the universe. It's something that just happens particularly strongly in the Climbing the Mountain exercise. It seems to be a revelation to a lot of people of their own power and the power of the group.

After that there's a great deal of very strong and beautiful performances that are done in twos and threes or larger groups. There's a lot of feedback from the group. The individual gets a sense of what it is that people receive when they put something out. The critiques are not really critiques in the sense of I didn't like this or you should have done it that way, but rather, this is what I got from it. It helps you get a mirror of who you are.

And then at the end I show slides of the cosmos, just to music. We don't talk about it; it's just like a last meditation that connects you to those beautiful galaxies and nebula and clusters and all those lovely things that we have up there. By the time the weekend is over, because of everything that's happened, you get a bunch of people that are welded together into a family that's more loving and more close than people who have lived together for twenty years. And they know nothing about each other, unless they talk at the lunch breaks. You don't even know what a person does for a living, but you know the core of that person, you touch that core. You have communicated with that core. That's something very precious. You get a sense of communicating with other human beings in a way that usually doesn't happen in the world because of all the masks we put on.

LB: Do you see a healing quality in the workshop?

RR: The healing quality comes from a larger context, not so much from the individual psychological knots that have to be untied. That you can do yourself. It's not even assuming that anybody is sick or has problems or blockages. It's assuming that, as human beings in this society, this day and age, everybody is in the same boat; we all have this unassuaged hunger and thirst, we all have these locks, we all have these knots inside of us.

Sometimes the connection that you see onstage is so . . . unpsychological! It's like two bodies beginning to move together magically as if they've learned a choreography that they've rehearsed a hundred times, yet it's totally spontaneous. They are doing it for the first time, but they are beginning to vibrate together. When those things happen you can't describe them in words. You can't say, well, there was a scene in which this guy goes to the grocery store and the store owner is angry with him—it's nothing to do with that. It has to do with colors and shapes, movement, putting on a costume. Somehow you've got four people in a piece and they don't watch each other get dressed, yet they come out and they're all wearing white and black, those marvelous, synchronous moments that are sacred moments that create the art-work collectively.

You know, it's like a primal feeling where I imagine in the days of primal culture people would get that connection without words. They would all come together and make art together, create those moments that are sacred moments and are absolutely filled with the creating juices, where you can really feel the power of creation, not only the individual but the whole schmear, the whole number. Those are the things that happen in the workshop. It's like a weekend of collectively trying to go beyond, to resolve things with a good massage, to soften all these hard strings that we have inside us and to make us vulnerable.

LB: After five years, can you state the central idea of DbD, what makes it work?

RR: It's about erasing the borders, the demarcations between life and art. I do believe that whatever it is that you are will be transmitted into the art in one way or another. What is more the acme of behavior than art? You give form to something that didn't exist before; you are really fashioning your soul, an extension of your spirit. If you start tampering with that form, which is the materialization of your spirit, you can really reach to the deepest level of where your creativity lies, the whole source of your being. That's what it's about.

Now when I say that, people really get scared. They're thinking, oh boy, here comes this woman and she's going to tickle the core of my being! This is terrible! What if she tickles it in the wrong way? To that I can only say that we are always good and bad, we are always yin and yang, we are always black and white, a mess of opposites. I bring to the workshop my very best qualities and only my best qualities. For a weekend, two and a half days, I am a saint. My aim for that one weekend is to really take the spirit of the people who are there and give a bath to that spirit. I call DbD now the mind/body spa. You go there and you clean out your body and your spirit, your imagination and your art making. It's all taking this terrific bath and it's coming out clean. Then you go out and you get soiled again but you have had the experience of this real purity, the creative drive that brings the best out of you, not only as an individual, but as an individual who is part of a group, in society. So for that weekend, I am really there only and purely to be at the service of these individual spirits and I do what must be done. After the weekend I go home and I am still old Rachel, with all her weaknesses and stupidities and pettinesses, like everybody else. But for that weekend, I am a saint, or whatever you want to call it.

Suzanne Lacy and Rachel Rosenthal

Excerpts from "Saving the World: A Dialogue between Suzanne Lacy and Rachel Rosenthal"

SL: It seems that the effort to reach people and involve them is where the real challenge lies. It doesn't have to do with "Now we're ready to help" but rather with "How do you bring a truly mixed ethnic socioeconomic group together?" I think if we knew how to do that we'd be halfway there.

RR: Yes, reaching people is the hardest thing. I have a real problem because my work is seen by people who are already converted. Some of them are a little *less* converted, so maybe they become a little more converted. . . .

SL: I don't find that a problem in your work. I think that you have a particular eloquence as a writer and speaker and seer, and we have to have those kinds of people. My work is very different; in fact, I focus on the bringing of people together. But I don't find a contradiction in our intentions. You, by the way, reach a much more populous audience than most performance artists. But even if you didn't, the clarity with which you speak is important.

RR: I feel I need to take my work out to other communities that are less primed for it. I think I could reach and communicate with them. My concern at this point is how to do it. If I have to take a cut in my fee, I have to be booked much more often. So my concern is that I have to conserve energy. I can't scream myself out. If I'm also going to do a certain amount of work, either as a teacher or as a performer, with communities that don't have the means to hire me, then it's a

Originally published in *Artweek,* September 12, 1991, 1, 14–16.

balancing act. I have to balance my own energy and time and health, and still manage to get the word out. Because I feel at this point an urgency that has been building over the years in my work and in my life. Now I feel that, God, if we don't do it now, it's, you know, ta ta. And so it has to happen. . . .

. . . **RR:** I'm always musing about the business of how effective this is—how can we really move people to change their ways, change their thinking, to see what I call "The Big Picture." I find that when I do perform for an audience of a certain level of education, knowledge, and sophistication, they respond with a tremendous amount of enthusiasm. Perhaps I'm not slated to change my work in order to speak to people who don't have the background references. It's difficult for me to use another kind of language or approach. However, I *can* do that through teaching.

In the next year, I'm going to be teaching a whole bunch of talented ethnic youngsters in a workshop. We're going to get a piece together to show at Highways.

So, it's happening. But what is really bothering me—the reason I don't sleep at night—is seeing the graphic unraveling of our planet. It's been happening for quite a long time now, but not in a way that has caused people to stand up and take notice. It's only going to get stronger and stronger, like a real tidal wave. And it's going to happen on every level—ecological, economic, emotional, political, you name it. And it's happening because there are too many people. And I'm getting more and more worried that we're creating a subhuman—you know, a world where through overpopulation, through the lack of responsible curtailing of breeding, more and more people are being ground out who are at the lowest common denominator of the potential of human beings, and what that means, not only for our species, but what that means for the rest of the planet.

I know exactly how to fix everything. You know what I'm saying? The first thing you do is provide free abortion and contraception, making it totally available globally with a huge educational blitz from every country. Then you have to completely change the whole educational structure. You start Earth Studies in kindergarten, and they get more and more sophisticated as you grow up. You make Earth Studies the major function of education. You teach people where they live. They live on the Earth. And what does that mean? What kinds of responsibilities, what kinds of problems? What is the profile of the planet on which we live? Unless you can begin to reach people from the earliest years with the consciousness of the planet and what it means to be a human being, one of many species on this planet, we won't survive. We are indeed a species that can alter nature so that it becomes no longer nature, but a completely man-made artifact.

SL: Okay, but when I hear all this, my mind starts going into a fog. I'm sure that I'm not a lot different than many people. The issue is not the grand solution—and who's to say from our perspective what that is—but what incremental step does each of us begin taking in the right direction? I'm concerned with consciousness and consciousness change. I see how hard it is to change my consciousness—I've been working on it for years. How do you actually change people's perceptions of, for example, older women, or black people, or teenagers? How do people make a shift, and once they shift, does that shift really motivate them to act? . . .

. . . **RR:** There are levels of action, but there is only one level of consciousness, what we call in French "le prise de conscience." I don't know how you can translate it except by saying "being grabbed by consciousness." "Prise de conscience" is like a satori. You suddenly get the whole picture. You know, you get it. And then there are all these different levels of action. Everybody is at a different level because of their position in the world, because of their financial situation, their emotional situation, whatever. Each person, at whatever level she is, is going to do whatever she can do or is able to do. In my case, I'm definitely more and more aware of what I call "The Big Picture." I see this perspective and I see the horizon, and I see this whole mess and the dichotomy between those who are messing it up even more and those who are swimming against the current so to speak, the current of a polluted stream. Trying to help and trying to do. Those people (you're one of them, and there are many others) are extraordinary people who are putting their lives on the line, inventing new ways of affecting, new ways of trying to stem the tide. I'm always filled with admiration for such people.

So where I am right now—you keep warning me that we're going to talk about the personal, right? What I can say about myself is that more and more I don't have a personal. It's not important anymore. I think that you come to a certain age, you know, and who cares anymore about that? At the same time, I can't function at certain levels of detail as younger people can. So, if I have a vision, if I see "The Big Picture," I feel the tremendous urgent responsibility to put it out. Then let others come and say, Okay, we can approach it from this side or that side. Now I may be totally wrong. I'm not saying that I'm right and the whole world is wrong. But my instinct says that this is how it is and this is how it should be. . . .

. . . **SL:** Every ten years or so, I seem to take some time to sit back and wait for a shift in the form of my work. Your language has developed and become more sophisticated, but it has stayed fairly consistent. You work within a theatrical presentational mode. I operate in a very different way. I'm infinitely more interested in designing a new shape. I don't have any skills at acting, for example. I am not interested in skill development as much as I am in the notion of creating a new way of framing conversation, or framing life activity.

RR: Well, you see, I think the difference between my modus operandi and your modus operandi and how you're feeling these subjective things is that when I have a concept, I impose it on the people who are contracted by me. I have total control. I put it out and I write it and I have somebody working with me on the musical level and on the visual level. And then I book it. It's different for you, because you need to worm yourself into people's good graces one by one, and create a very large community of people who think your ideas are great and they want to partake of them. I could never do that in a million years. . . .

. . . **SL:** What is frustrating for both of us is that once you have a global picture and if you are fairly cynical about artists' potential influence within that, it's going to present a problem: what we do compared with what there is to be done. In my work, I may only address the consciousness of a very few thousand people on the planet.

RR: What about me? I mean it's the consciousness of even less, probably.

I'm very conscious of numbers. And numbers at this point have to do with the urgency of time. Because there is no time left. A lot of people feel that it's already the point of no return. At this point, the way I see it, nature is dead, or at least dying and will be dead very soon. The question is: Are we going to get the "prise de conscience" early enough so that we can somehow manage that demise and then the transformation that will enable life to continue in a managed way on Earth? Will we be able to minimize the catastrophes that are imminent to the point where even though some will be eliminated, at least the amount of extinctions will not be as catastrophic and the societal upheavals will not be as catastrophic as they could be? It's really a question of degree, as I see it now. I see things very apocalyptically at this point, and I live a very strange dichotomy because, on the one hand, I have a continual subtext of ghastliness and horror about the world, and, on the other level, I've never been happier in my whole life.

SL: That has to do with making art.

RR: It has to do with making art. Once you hear that call, if you don't answer it, I believe you can get terribly punished. You can get sick on an emotional level, on a mental level, on a physical level; you can have accidents—you know all kinds of terrible things can happen.

It also has to do with being free. I feel free of things that used to be my prisons. I'm free of pain because I have a new knee, and my leg, which was in pain continually for decades, is now no longer hurting. It's changed my life. Then I'm free of relationships that are obsessive. I have very pleasant relationships with friends and with my co-workers and all of that, but they're not obsessive, and I can take it or leave it. My relationships with my animals are always at a great high, and so that's wonderful. I'm also freer of my obsession with food, which has been the bane of my existence. Those are the things in a life that were the ropes that were holding me down—and they are suddenly loosened. I'm sixty-four. . . .

. . . **RR:** When I was teaching at Santa Barbara recently, somebody in the audience asked about that [Rodney] King tape. Here some person comes along and does a videotape of a police beating that will have far more of a repercussion politically than any of the art around.

I said, yes, on a certain level you're absolutely correct. On the level of day-to-day politics, these are things that function. But art operates on a totally other level that you can't really measure. Because when you think about all the people who are doing "the right thing" today and who are involved in such deep and conscious works, who knows but that these people at some point may have been touched by art?

Maybe they don't even remember, are not even aware of it. Just looking at the Piero della Francesca in a museum and seeing the kind of idealized structure that it is, the kind of clear, pure, diaphanous mind work that is involved in creating that work of art—it touches you on a level that you can't really explain or measure. And somehow it changes you, transforms you in a way. So, in that way, I think that art is of the utmost importance.

Even if you are not a great artist and are not going to be able to contribute on a professional level, you are aligning your energy field with the energy field of planetary creation. You are feeding that field, instead of feeding the field that destroys and kills. On that level also, art is extremely important. Again, this is not something that you can measure. Art, because of the nature of what it is, is not something that you can approach with a study group to ask, "Is this effective and what does it really do?" You can't do that—it's like a psychic phenomenon—when you look at it, it's gone. And yet, on the spiritual level, I think that it is doing its work and it has to continue to do its work. So that's where I'm optimistic. . . .

Denise Meola

Excerpts from "Interview, Rachel Rosenthal"

DM: You've performed since you were three?

RR: Yes. We had a fun family and were always having theatrical presen-
tations. I had puppet theaters I'd manipulate for hours on end. I always felt as if I were on show for my parents, because I was brought
up by nurses and governesses. So when we actually faced each other, it
was an event. I would be on my best behavior, well-dressed, well-
combed, clean, and cute. I felt like a little pink poodle, a Shirley Tem-
ple-like person. At six, I began ballet classes and felt like a dancing
bear. Every year on my birthday there was a huge celebration because
it was also my parents' wedding anniversary. That's when I performed
for 150 people.

   I'd go through agonies up to the performance—just like now. I'd
enjoy performing and enjoy the applause. I never stayed downstairs
afterwards but gathered up all my presents and went upstairs to my
room to be by myself. So in my relationship with people, there was no
intimacy, just the love that an audience gives a performer and a performer gives back to an audience. This is what my real temperament
wanted to do. It started very early. . . .

. . . **DM:** Why are women drawn to this kind of art [performance art]?

RR: It's simple: They were barred from almost everything else. Hordes
of women made visual art but few had a gallery representing them.
Performance art was a way for women to make a dent in the art world
without passing through the art structure—the gallery scene, muse-

Originally published in *Omni*, August 1992, 57–60, 74–75.

ums, collectors, the whole schmear. This way they could be who they are. Also, somehow women have a knack for performance.

Women were very revolutionary in the 1970s, going into taboo areas. Men did taboo things, but most of what they did had to do with body and pain. Many men worked on the masochistic level, doing ordeals, shooting themselves, and so on. Women were usually more interested in telling their story. This was a perfect vehicle, an art way of making personal and political statements. This was more effective than going on a soapbox, writing an article, or giving a lecture. For women, this was a fabulous way to get out of the closet and be who we are. . . .

. . . **DM:** What is the role of an artist in today's culture?

RR: The separation between art and science is going to disappear completely. More scientists realize their work is art and not hard science and vice versa. Art is like research and development in science. That's why it's so hard to assess if it's "good" or "bad." Quantum physics has shown us something wonderful: everything we touch and observe changes for the reason of being observed; our input actually changes the world. There's a tremendous movement of Earth-oriented philosophies and political awareness among artists. If artists read science and connect with the most contemporary realizations about the universe and reality and then work that knowledge into a form readily understood, that will go far in creating a new reality. Artists have a calling, a responsibility to understand these new scientific paradigms and create work that reflects that understanding, that disseminates these paradigms on the human level.

DM: How has the evolving technology changed the ways in which artists communicate?

RR: In every way. Artists are working with computers and video. I had a proposal to work with seismological instruments that are in place all over the world. The sky's the limit! Whatever science and technology has to offer in creating a collaboration concerning metaphor and statement should be explored. . . .

. . . **DM:** Are computers capable of having a soul, a consciousness—a mind?

RR: Since civilization began, people have longed to create intelligent objects. There's the myth of Galatea, the Golem, Frankenstein. Now technology makes that myth possible. I'm a bit of an animist. I think everything has a mind, consciousness, and soul, but what type of souls, and what degree of consciousness?

DM: *Rachel's Brain* begins with a quote by Arthur Koestler that the evolution of the brain not only overshot the needs of prehistoric man; it is also evolution's only example of providing a species with an organ it does not know how to use.

RR: There is something in the genetic structure of our brains that created a total imbalance between object making and our ethical sense. So we've developed this attitude that if it's there, it has to be examined, used. If one can do it, it ought to be done. This is the scientific view, and we came to it not as a quirk of history, but because of the way our brains are shaped. And so we muddle on in our evolution. . . .

. . . **DM:** What is consciousness?

RR: Consciousness is a gift. We've taught ourselves we're the only ones who are conscious. Many other traditions talk about universal mind, a pervasive consciousness of all creation. We don't do that in the Western world. We have to learn to be humble. There is good and bad, creation and destruction, violence and peace. I'm not saying the whole human race has gone bad, but that we are in free fall and can't remain aloft. A universal and very sudden shift in consciousness could save us if everyone realized "The Big Picture" of global interconnectedness of all life. You'll understand why I'm rather pessimistic. . . .

DM: Are the gods laughing at us?

RR: I hope so. I'd hate to think they were on our level of angst.

Alexandra Grilikhes

"Taboo Subjects:

An Interview with Rachel Rosenthal"

AG: The way you conceive of yourself onstage is striking. Like anyone else, you're a person full of chaos and inner contradictions, ready to boil over into volcanic eruption at the same time that you're a vast other version, a cosmic persona. Going back and forth easily between the two, you embody them both. In your piece, *Pangaean Dreams,* you personify Pangaea, the supercontinent of 250 million years ago, Earth herself, comparing your own history of bone fractures with the breakup of Pangaea, and playing yourself and the Earth interchangeably as one entity.

RR: Since I'm at the center of what I put out, I don't reflect on or conceive of myself in any specific way. I've always been more identified with animals than with people. The pain of animals was and is so real to me that I feel it physically in my body. From that place I went to the rest of the Earth; to plants, to minerals, to air and water, and gradually I realized I was connected to the whole Earth. I'm completely identified with the Earth because the Earth is my deity, so to speak. It's not really a religion; it's a veneration, a spiritual approach. I want to give the planet a voice because I feel that she's in great trouble and she will make a lot of trouble for us—in fact, she already is, and it will only get worse. The problem of the individual body is a microcosm/macrocosm situation; as above, so below. Everything is connected. Because I am identified with the Earth as well as being a human being, if I were to conceive of myself as anything, it would be as a go-between.

Originally published, in slightly altered form, in *American Writing: A Magazine,* no. 10, 1994–95, 10–26.

Having felt connected to the Earth for such a long time, it was interesting to me that the same year I worked on *Pangaean Dreams* and studied about plate tectonics was the year that all my bones began to break. I wondered if there was some connection on a psychic level. Pangaea, the supercontinent of the Triassic, broke up between 200 and 180 million years ago through tectonic action.

I used the connection as a means to structure a piece that would somehow, through identifying with me as a human being, bring an audience into identifying with the planet.

The idea of plate tectonics is that the Earth creates her own flesh and then devours herself at the same time. She produces her flesh at the bottom of the ocean in the ocean ridges; then the plates move away from the ridges. At the other end, the plates dive in this subduction trench under the continents and go back into the mantle where that whole crust is destroyed, and then, through convection currents, slowly it comes back at the surface and moves out through the ridges again. So Earth is able to produce and give birth to herself and at the same time destroy herself in this continuous cycle. What is happening really at the surface with the biota is a reflection of this deeper life-and-death process. We are more concerned with the biota because we are part of it, but in reality, we're sort of like the frosting on the cake. Because what is happening deeper down is even more spectacular, and it has to do with the body of the Earth itself. What actually motivates or engenders this extraordinary dance of life on the thin layer of biota between the planet and the cosmos is the engine that drives the way life works.

In *Pangaean Dreams* I do a dance where I say, "Under the sea a dragon lives coiled around the world. How did they know, the ancients, how did they intuit? Well: they knew the dragon lives; they were right, the dragon loves—we are her Andromeda chained to the rock of life."

I created the image of a dragon because when you see maps of the interior of the ocean with all the water gone, the ocean ridge looks absolutely like a dragon coiled around Earth. It has its paws out, its head is Iceland, and its tail goes up the gulf of California. It's 46,000 miles long. When you look at the shape it's totally amazing. What we call St. Helena, Ascension Island, the Galapagos, Tristan de Cunha, Iceland are all points of the ridge that have broken water. I have this notion of a dragon holding Andromeda—the living part of the biota, of Earth—prisoner attached to the rock. If plate tectonics were to grind to a halt, all of life, little by little, would grind to a halt. It's astonishing how the planet works in this dynamic and extraordinarily powerful way. On every level it's the same principle, the cycling of life and death.

AG: I was intrigued by your line in the piece where you say, "The rate of motion of the crustal plates is the same as that of my fingernails' growth. When one plate moves, all move. Every hurt on Gaia's body will hurt on ours." That's a particular consciousness I find unusual in an artist. Have you felt this way for a long time?

RR: It's hard to say at which point I developed that consciousness. I have transformed myself, or I have been transformed so thoroughly over the decades that it's difficult for me to say at which point on the continuum I became who I am today. I was a late bloomer anyway, and I suffered so much from being who I was for so long that I worked on myself every which way I could. Over the years little by little I've changed every atom in my body.

AG: You've had a lot of trouble all your life because of who you were? Can you elaborate?

RR: It started early. I was born into a class that didn't bring up its own babies, but gave them to professionals to rear; servants, nurses, and governesses were my immediate nurturers. My parents were around, but when we were together I was on show and we were all on our best behavior. I was very much aware of two sides, the underside and the surface. My parents adored me and my governesses were mean to me. I grew up with this dichotomy—that I was totally wonderful and totally horrible at the same time.

I had the sense of superiority and power that I was better than anybody and at the same time I felt that I was a fraud. Because on one hand I was successful at making people admire me yet I knew all along that there was no substance underneath. I was afraid that if I stayed in one place people would find me out so I kept moving; that was one thing. Another was economics. I was born into an affluent family and realized early on that not everybody lived as we did. And I felt very guilty. The other guilt came from the fact that we were able to leave France while so many of our people were killed in the Holocaust. My very big guilt was that we were saved.

I was thirteen when we left and fourteen when we came to New

York after spending a year in Brazil. Twice the Nazis were at our heels, in Paris and the south of France. A lot of the family were sent to Auschwitz and the rest went through a great deal of horror. We left at the absolute last moment.

The final issue was that I always wanted to be an artist and that I was very male-identified. I had bought the message that came with the territory: you can't be a woman and an artist. That was a big conflict in my life. For decades I wasted a great deal of energy on the question of whether or not I was an artist because I was not a man. A lot of it also came from the feeling that I was shallow—a scintillating front with nothing behind it. These were all issues that took me a long time to work out, to be able to come to the point where I feel I'm still shallow but much less so. For a long time I hid those shameful secrets. In 1975, when I started to do performance, for some reason I did a flip-flop and began to use myself as material for performance and began to air those shameful secrets. I realized they were also everybody else's shameful secrets. That was a big liberation for me and a way of reaching people.

AG: Your sense of self allows you to give such power to your work that you become it. Everything else falls away when you speak either about the Earth or yourself. Artists need space, you say. That if they have to repress what they do, enormous dis-ease results. You make the connection that artists in their actions are like nature is in hers.

RR: I recently revived a piece called *L.O.W. in Gaia.* It's a sort of meditation on a trip I took in the Mojave Desert by myself in a rented van. It's about the Earth, about aging and waste—toxic, nuclear, and personal waste. One of the personae in that piece is a fortieth-century monster, our descendant, who is completely irradiated because he lives atop a burial site for nuclear wastes, and so physically degenerate that he has no lips. In order to do it I dry my mouth and my lips disappear; my jaw is fused open. My hands no longer have prehensile thumbs, and I'm completely bent over like a bird. I emit bird sounds; it's a poor, pathetic creature.

The piece was inspired by an article I read in 1986 about how the government was trying to figure out ways to dispose of nuclear waste in such a way as to warn future generations not to dig up what's there. They figured they would do a kind of Stonehenge with monoliths and symbols that future people would understand.

My piece shows that people in the future are incapable of under-standing because they've so degenerated that they have no mind to grasp anything. The poor monster is rummaging for food on the ground and he finds these plates on which are the little triangular symbol for nuclear power. He's so excited that he picks up a plate and wants to pick up another but he has no prehensile thumb so he has to drop one plate in order to pick up a second. The first plate breaks and he is devastated. He starts screaming with anguish because he's broken the plate. He's obviously rummaging in irradiated ground and it's to-tally pathetic. Then I slip into being myself and play myself in the desert, and I'm excited and romantic and sentimental about being in nature and alone; it's beautiful and wonderful. Then the Death Crone appears and she is so spooky.

AG: You play her also.

RR: Yes. She comes in with two monologues that are very frightening. And the audience becomes frightened. I end up as myself, getting so spooked in the desert that I can't take it. So it goes from arriving and feeling alone in the wonderful silence and solitude to finally getting so spooked that I have to leave.

I wanted to show the frightening side of nature. When the Death Crone comes out the first time she says, "I'm the third aspect of the triple goddess, the one you fear the most; I am your death." She goes on to say how she functions and that she is not sentimental, that alive or dead is the same to her. Her power is frightening.

The year I wrote *L.O.W.* I turned sixty. In the piece I make it a point to say that I turned sixty, and I take out some lipstick and write 60 on my head. Later there's a section where I talk about the burning times, the witch burnings, and I say I've lived in those times although it's a sort of theatrical trick because I'm not sure I believe in reincarna-tion.

But I say that I feel I was burnt as a witch. And still feel it in every caged animal and every trapped paw. I go on enumerating all the things that are being done to animals and I end up in such a state of fury and violence that I take a big candle that's been burning onstage all this time, and pour hot wax on my head. And then the Crone comes out again.

In the spring of 1994, two weeks before I revived *L.O.W.* there was a big article in either the *Los Angeles Times* or the *New York Times* about how to bury nuclear waste and inform coming generations about its presence; it was exactly the same thing I had read in 1986. Dammit, the piece has not aged at all; it's simply not obsolete in terms of the issue!

My pieces are always up to date though I wish they would become obsolete. We don't seem to learn as a species. The more I live and observe what's going on the more I see that the Earth is developing ways to try to force us to understand and learn and desist. And we don't.

With each year I become more anxious and feel more pressured to put out this information. When I put it out people say "Uh huh, Uh huh." As a whole the population is not exposed to this information because it's kept very quiet.

AG: Maybe it has to do with the way people—the government—can feel separation from the rest of nature, which is the beginning of their drying out, of dying. "It's not us," they think, so they're able to bury nuclear waste "over there." They don't recognize the Earth as part of them, or themselves as part of Earth.

RR: My piece, *filename: FUTURFAX,* deals with that separation and with the consequences of that mind-set. In the past few years I've been studying chaos theory, a science that completely turns on its head that whole reductionist paradigm we've been taught for centuries. Suddenly scientists are seeing the Zen connections in chaos theory—a butterfly at the equator, for instance, moves its wings and completely changes climatic events in the Northern Hemisphere.

The problem is that anthropocentrism and a mechanical-reductionist view of the world are ingrained in society, in our economy, and in our way of viewing ourselves. It's so connected with the Christian view that we're the top of the heap, the top of evolution, that it's hard to quickly transform that paradigm. I wish it would happen faster because if people understand and accept these theories, they will really change our view of our place in the cosmos. I've been incorporating chaos theory into my work. I hope that some of the scientists who are involved in this paradigm will make it available on a popular level. It's absolutely vital that we "get it" as soon as possible.

During the time I worked on *FUTURFAX* I was reading the book, *Ishmael,* by Daniel Quinn. It's a very good view of where we are in relation to the cosmos and our position in Western civilization vis-à-vis our paradigm and philosophy. Quinn divides the world of human beings into "takers" and "leavers." The takers are successful Westerners who have lived on the notion of growth, progress, and success and are now facing a big crash. The leavers are the people we "takers" have more or less exterminated because they're small, live in harmony with the Earth, and understand sustainability.

AG: Your work provides a path of recognition and acceptance into chaos. And celebrates it. In *Pangaean Dreams* when you recite, "I am the frenzy of bodies, rubbing, sweating, groaning, and farting," you take repressed feelings and bring them to the forefront of consciousness, letting the fissures inside and outside us show through. Which makes it less possible for us to bury nuclear waste "over there."

RR: Yes. Absolutely.

AG: At the beginning of *FUTURFAX,* there is a voice-over that announces, "We are exempt from the laws of nature." In both *Pangaean Dreams* and *FUTURFAX,* there is a return to a mythical state of life, a condition that participates in the powers of metamorphosis. Many people, mystics and artists among them, have imagined that nature could be influenced by ritual enactment and that mythical figures like Inanna and Persephone can restore what death has destroyed.

The Yellow Emperor's four thousand-year-old classic of Chinese medicine, the *Neijing,* describes how to survive by living according to the laws of nature and the seasons—a way of knowledge we have forgotten. Your work embodies the kind of ritual observance—the connection to the cycle of life and death—that occurs among many traditional peoples. Seeing your work, one is moved to tacitly acknowledge its ritual function for your tribe: disconnected and alienated urban people.

RR: I don't consciously set out to do that but it is, I think, the result of my work. I know these things have to be said and I try to know my audience—sophisticated, urban, self-centered, and self-serving, unaware of what I call "The Big Picture"—and communicate with them in a way they understand.

I was in Denver or Houston, and there was a woman in the audience—I always talk to the audience after a performance to get a sense of what they got from the piece—and she said, "You seem to be saying that we humans have done these terrible things and that what's happening is our fault. Can you explain how that is?"

I said, "Come on, you know the answer to that!" And she said, "No, I want you to tell me!" She was very emphatic. I am amazed there are still people like that who just don't get it, who don't know what it is we have done and are continuing to do. These are the people whom I feel compelled to touch somehow and communicate with.

Often, when I work on a piece, I think it's too simplistic, everyone's going to laugh at me, it's so obvious. Then I see that it's not that obvious and people still don't get it. It's always a shock to discover this.

There are many people who do get it and who are on the same wavelength as I am, but there are plenty who aren't, so it has to be put out there. The way it's received and how others perceive it is not my work. It's not my problem.

AG: Everything you describe is accomplished through ritual. What attracts you, like reading about plate tectonics, reaches you at your core; Earth's plate tectonics, which give her the ability to regenerate, relate to your own ability to heal and regenerate.

RR: The fact that it comes out as ritual is probably because that's the nature of the beast. If you align yourself with the fields of the Earth, you fall into cycling and repetition and renewal and eternal returns—all very different from the linear way we have perceived things.

And the handling of objects without reference to their utilitarian connotations turns ordinary things into ritual objects, and activities into rituals. In my piece *Rachel's Brain,* I used cauliflowers for brains because visually they're like brains.

AG: In your pieces, one gets the impression that the terrors and horrors of real life, the unrepressed, natural forces that threaten to break through, are the important ones for you artistically.

RR: Let me tell you something about the terrors and horrors. I think they are the reason people do drugs. I believe that drugs and the culture that stemmed out of the lure and seductiveness of Castaneda's books—as an example—come from the same thing, the call of the wild, the call of the horrors and terrors. There's a whole part of us—the glands that produce adrenaline among them—that we have very little use for most of the time. We go to big sports events, get excited, scream, become violent, and it's all vicarious. There is very little opportunity to go into the wild as people used to do, where they get really scared out of their wits. So we create artificial means to experience those feelings.

The first part of my history as a performance artist doing my own work spanned the years 1975–81, the second part from 1981 until now. From 1981 on it became less autobiographical and more involved in bigger issues. The first piece I did of this nature, which was in my repertory for two years, was about masochism. It was called *Performance and the Masochist Tradition,* part of a trilogy entitled *Taboo Subjects.* I used as an example of masochism the piercing of the flesh with hooks. My examples were the Native American sun dance tradition; Stelarc, an artist, who did performances in which he had many hooks in his flesh and was hoisted up in different positions; and a so-called sexual pervert I read about in *Semiotext(e)* magazine who did the same thing.

In that piece I used hooks on myself; it was the only time I ever did that. Although I did it in an ironic way, people just freaked. In the piece I tried to show that the need for this kind of penetration and for pain was the only expression people could find to connect with the sort of core terror which is, I think, the motor of the cosmos.

When you learn how the universe works, the kind of violence that goes on out there is really horrendous. We have been well shielded from the terrors of the universe, although now we are destroying our shield. But we don't go into the wilderness for vision quests or rites of passage as people used to do. We don't send kids out alone in the wilderness to go through this "real fear" thing in order to come out on the other side. There is hunger for extreme feeling and for that connection with the sense of awe. People express this awareness in slang when they say, "It's awesome." But awesome has lost its juice. You have a good ice cream sundae and it's "awesome." What it means is something you venerate and are awestruck by: nature. I think a lot of the joyrides and the violence for violence's sake and the use of drugs have to do with this need.

AG: If everything is awesome, there is no awesome.

RR: That's right. You could easily call it a lot of other things. I think nostalgia for awesomeness has put the word into our vocabulary.

AG: So the seeking after extreme feeling is part of the need to connect with the terror and horror of real life. That only through pain can transformation occur.

RR: And also ecstasy. People are addicted to sex in a way that is almost pathological. I think people feel that only through sex can they reach the sense of being out of their skin, outside themselves, touching the cosmos. So this is, at least, a pleasurable way of doing it. But a lot of people mix sex and pain and sex and violence. I think all of that comes from yearnings not satisfied in any other way.

AG: Your work evokes the uncontrollable; contradictions and chaos bubble up in it as we sit hidden and vulnerable in the dark, which allows us to recognize these things in a nonthreatening way. Your persona seems related to that of Coyote the trickster, who extends the boundaries of the permissible and interjects the spirit of disorder. The trickster puts us in touch with hunger, lust, pain, and injury—feelings hard to control—and gets us to experience more of the totality of life, something your work celebrates.

RR: I've said in interviews that I am a trickster, a sort of cosmic clown; I do absolutely see myself as that.

It's interesting because my life is so orderly. I love the feeling that everything is in place, that I know where things are and how they will be. My animals love order and routine and my life revolves around the routine of my animals. The framework has to include these things and then it works without being disruptive or destructive or threatening. The reason or the result of how I lead my life is that I have the work which is very, very, in a sense, frightening. When I work on my pieces I go through a lot of pain, a lot of fear and real crunching kinds of episodes. Yet all of it is within a very orderly structure. I think I can stay sane and on an even keel because my work is framed within this structure. My animals keep me sane because they take me for walks, they own my van; when it's time to go, we gotta go. And no matter how much work I do, how tired I am—even if I get sick, which doesn't happen very often—at six o'clock in the morning we're at the park. And we go back to the park two more times that day because I don't have a yard and they have to go out and run and be in grass.

AG: You have dogs?

RR: Two big dogs and two cats. They keep me absolutely sane and in good shape. Without them it would be very hard and very different because I would let things go. I would get sloppy.

Just the fact of being able to touch their fur, having my hands in fur is the connection. When I'm in the car I'm continually touching the fur. When I'm working or reading in bed, I've got my kitties and I'm touching their fur. And I realize it's keeping me sane and connected. That's the link somehow.

AG: You embody the Mistress of the Animals so much in your life. Many people have animals, but they don't speak of them in the way you do. In *Pangaean Dreams,* you say, "I am the Tyrannosaurus in your brainstem; you are part angel, part dinosaur, a Pangaean dinosaur ensconced in your brain." In your work you invoke the animal—or the feeling the animal represents—and remind us of the animal part of ourselves, which in Western society we tend to project away. Yet animal totems are still a powerful part of ourselves, the minotaur and centaur being late examples. Just as the Mistress of the Animals was always depicted with animals, animals are always with you; you express the myth in a conscious way.

RR: I did an installation, "Animal-Human Hybrids," at a branch of the Getty Museum in Los Angeles that dealt with exactly what you're talking about—the very early identification with animals on the spiritual level, and then the projection of the human onto the deity. This projection created animal-human hybrids—the animal with the human head, the mixes of different species, and so on. Little by little, due to patriarchal and monotheistic religions, the demonization of these hybrids as devils and monsters came about.

I went to Toys "R" Us and bought a whole bunch of toys—monsters and cutesies, little sirens and minotaurs, the beast from *Beauty and the Beast* and Batman. There's a huge mythology for children now that deals with the resurgence of the animal hybrid, except that it's been completely trivialized. My installation consisted of extraordinary old books full of amazing images, interspersed with these toys.

For the exhibit, I also wrote an essay on how these images have persisted throughout Western civilization. Animal totems have never really disappeared. Even the nineteenth century had demonized figures of vampires and werewolves. And there seems to be a resurgence of these as well.

In my neighborhood I feed all the birds and I've been adopted by a family of wild rats. I did twenty-nine rescues of them one by one with a humane trap, taking them to the wilderness near a stream and vegetation where they could meet each other. But the smart old ones never got trapped so I still have a little family of rats at home. The rats know they can come inside whenever they want, but now that there are cats, they don't. They have the courtyard and we can see each other all the time; of course it freaks out a lot of my students but, "c'est la vie."

AG: Tell me about your classes.

RR: I have two kinds of workshops. One is a thirty-five-hour intensive weekend—The DbD experience—doing by doing. It is for everybody and anybody, including those who are totally without art experience. It's a full performance curriculum with music, sound, sets and costumes, body work, voice work, and all kinds of exercises and improvisations. It works on two levels: one is the art, the other the personal through the art. Then I have an eight-week weekly class that goes from seven until midnight on Mondays, which is more of a "how to" performance class. When I go on residencies to other schools and universities I do an adaptation and mix of the two.

AG: You've been doing this for a long time?

RR: Whenever I'm at home in Los Angeles and not on tour.

RR: The critic Bonnie Marranca has described me as biocentric rather than anthropocentric.

AG: I think that's accurate. Seeing *Pangaean Dreams* reminded me of the Taoist approach to Chi Gong. At the beginning, the Chi Gong master tells you to be conscious of yourself as a giant standing between the sky and Earth, where you receive heaven's energy and Earth's energy at the same time. Taoists believe the two energies meet in you as they spiral on their path. In your piece, you were that giant.

RR: When I teach I make an effort to root people into the energy of the Earth. I give them imagery and guided meditations that have to do with visualizing going through the crust, the plates, the mantle into the core to the very center of the Earth and being able to tap into this huge furnace of power and bring it up again through the core, the mantle, the plates, the crust, then through the soles of the feet into the body, filling themselves with this power and then letting the power come out through the tops of their heads, and then, like a fountain, go back into the Earth with the circularity of a magnet.

Another part of my teaching is that this power is available to everyone, but that it becomes noxious when you think of yourself as powerful. You have to see yourself as power flowing; you are like a conduit or channel through which power comes, then you flow it out into the world. It's not a miserly thing, where you're hoarding it. You dispense it. That's my image.

When I became a teacher, and had my own performance gallery, I noticed a change in the way people treated me in that they were giving me power. So I had to deal with the new feeling of being a powerful person and being treated that way.

In 1980, I did a piece about power called *Bonsoir, Dr. Schön!*, in which I said that an image of power for me was John Cage's apartment in the early 1950s in New York. He had a corner walkup next to the Brooklyn Bridge. We used to go there often to hear David Tudor's concerts. It was an old building with floor-to-ceiling windows that looked out onto the river. The floor was covered with jute matting and there were no curtains or blinds. The only thing in that apartment was a big piano with green plants on it. At night it felt free, available, and open to all currents. Sounds and lights would come from the river and because there were no impediments, the air circulated freely around the apartment. The music's sound waves, people's thoughts and speech all seemed to flow. What was circulating was so powerful, it became my model for an image of power.

Fairy tales are my other image of power. The hero or heroine has to go through many trials to get to the treasure, but it doesn't end at the point where he or she gets it. The real task is to bring the boon back to society, so the return trip is the hard one. Usually there is a chase with obstacles, and the quest isn't finished until the boon is brought back. It's again an image of circularity, where you get the power but you have to bring it back and hand it over.

AG: So power is constantly moving.

RR: That's right. And I teach that there is more where that came from. People are afraid they will deplete themselves when they put it out, whereas it's just the opposite—what they're doing is making themselves open for more to come in. Since the energy of the Earth is boundless, and the self-renewal of the Earth is also, as children of the Earth we can tap into it any way or time that we want.

I try to give people this imagery so they will understand that power and energy are not something you gain over others or over nature— it comes straight from Earth as a birthright. The trick is to keep it flowing.

AG: You're saying there has to be a kind of emptiness within you or the energy is blocked from moving, which is a kind of death.

RR: We have in our culture a *horror vacui,* the fear of emptiness. I feel this is a grave mistake because—and I know this is very Eastern teaching—emptiness is not nothingness. Emptiness is simply the ability to be able to be available for whatever comes in, and if you are full, nothing can enter. We are so full of doctrines and theology we are rendered incapable of being open to new things.

AG: I noticed during the question period after a performance I attended, members of the audience seemed so engaged in their politically correct analysis of your work that they couldn't allow themselves to "get" what you were doing through their senses.

RR: I find that attitude very prevalent. Some people are deaf and blind—completely encrusted in their politically correct stance. I think I'm pretty politically correct myself, but people often can't hear because they're busy putting out their correctness; it's a power thing. If you're totally engorged with politically correct thinking, nothing can come out—or in.

In *Bonsoir, Dr. Schön!* I decided to start with a forty-five-minute videotape on which sixty of my friends, colleagues, and students would praise me. I had told them each to say something on camera that was true and heartfelt, something about me that they thought was absolutely fabulous. The audience stayed for forty-five minutes of compliments addressed to me, which I thought would have sickened them.

AG: It probably worked at a level below consciousness, like advertising does, and they thought, "She must be absolutely the best!"

RR: It's possible, though my idea at the time was that they'd be sickened. After this huge pumping-up of power, I wanted to give equal time to the other side by showing helplessness, vulnerability, and lack of power. The only thing I could think of was nudity. I was fifty-two at the time and taking my clothes off for just one person was almost impossible. To do it for an audience was so distasteful and horrendous that I kept saying, "Please goddess, don't make me do this, give me another idea!" But nothing else came and I knew I had to do it.

While the tape was playing to the audience I was actually onstage in a wheelchair with a white shroud over me, naked under the shroud and wrapped in a thick rope with a gold mask on my face. All the audience could see was the white shroud sitting there. They didn't know it was me because I wasn't moving. After I was wheeled in by two assistants, the shroud removed and the rope unwrapped, I was seated there, naked. There was a voice-over and a slide of the moon.

On the voice-over I speak about power and my childhood as they're unwrapping me. Under the mask I keep saying, "I don't want to do it," and as they take the mask off I keep repeating, "I don't want to do it." It's really painful.

They're showing the audience all my bad points. One assistant is showing the flab and the sagging tits and the cellulite. The other is taping red crosses on my body on those bad parts. So I'm covered with red crosses. They take little rubber vermin animals you can buy at magic stores, little snakes and tarantulas, and hang them on my body. I talk about the fact that when I was young I was like the moon, which is why I show a slide of the moon. Like the moon I always showed my front, and my front was always beautiful. All the bad little creatures were in the back, but I never showed my back to anyone. There was always this image of me of the wonderful front. These little creatures were burrowing holes in the back of my moon and eventually coming out the front. That was one of the sequences in the piece that was so painful and difficult to do. These are examples of how I decide to do it and how sometimes it decides for me. It was a mixture of the public view of what is good and bad, not only physically but morally.

AG: You've said that when you work on a piece, you go through "a lot of pain, a lot of fear, a lot of crunching kinds of episodes," as if you're doing this work for yourself as an artist, a person, and in the role of the shaman who makes the journey for the rest of the people who sit in the dark and watch you and are reminded of their own tasks not yet undertaken. Do you think these pieces are works that choose you because they are your next task? Is going through your own suffering to make the descent showing us one way to go about it? If you have so thoroughly transformed yourself, are these works then part of a continuing transformation, perhaps even the myth of your transformation?

RR: Yes. I have done more transformation through my actual art than through the techniques that are usually available, like therapy. I find that the rite of passage I propose for myself with each performance is what makes the real difference. Sometimes I initiate it in a willful manner and sometimes "it" comes and forces me. For instance, in 1984, when I did my animal piece, it was a willful decision because I was so scared. What happened at the time was that I felt I was getting a forum: because I was more visible. I decided to do a piece about animals to make people look at the issues.

I was worried, because in all those years of feeling such empathy for animals I had always sent money to organizations and told them not to send me their literature because I knew that reading the literature would make me ill. Finally I decided, "I have to look at this." For the piece I started to read the literature about the way animals are abused, treated, exploited, totally objectified—as if they are not sentient beings and lack feelings—and it had so strong an effect on me that I contracted myasthenia gravis, a disease which is the result of severe emotional shock. Right now the disease, which I've had since 1985, is in remission, thank goodness. Doing the piece was painful and difficult because it not only brought out all the ways we oppress and torture animals, but there is a whole section in which I become the animal. A lot of people really "got it." To this day, people come up to me and say, "You know, I changed my ways with animals after seeing your piece."

AG: You once said, "If you put all my performances together, then you will have my life done in the form of an artwork." Is this still true?

RR: It is, except that it's becoming harder for me to go into the personal because my personal is so dull. With *Pangaean Dreams* it was okay because in 1990 when I did that piece all my bones broke. That was a good hook with the personal. I live a very uneventful personal life and only really experience the excitement and adventures through the work itself.

In my last big piece that I did for UCLA called *Zone* I have a monologue where I go back to the past because what's happening to me now is so related to what's happening to the world that it's losing its personal content. There are many things I can pull in from the past; the things in the present are in the form of my interpretation of what I know is going on in the world.

AG: I've heard you were considering retirement from performing.

RR: Every so often I say "I've had it, I've had it, I'm quitting!" But of course I never will. I'm in great shape. Performing is not difficult. But I would like to have a few months off so that I could write my book. I never seem to be able to sit down and do it because I'm always working. I haven't been granted a Guggenheim and I need enough money to be able to stop working for a few months and write.

AG: An autobiography?

RR: No, a book about teaching, though, actually, the longer I wait the better I teach.

AG: Would a book about teaching be autobiographical? Isn't what you're teaching a distillation of everything you have learned, studied, thought, done, and metamorphosed into?

RR: It would, yes. And since I live a lot in the moment I have a problem with rehashing things, retracing my steps and explaining what I've done. In my pieces when I have to go back into the past it's very hard, so I think I've been hanging back about writing the book. But I should have the book out; it would help others.

AG: You've described improvisation as something that's always in the present; you can't be in the past or future, you have to be in the now. It's a wonderful description of being in the Tao.

RR: It's the same thing exactly.

II Writings on Rachel Rosenthal

Bonnie Marranca

"A Cosmography of Herself: The Autobiology

of Rachel Rosenthal"

Nowhere more evocatively does performance art express the ecological condition of contemporary life at the end of the twentieth century than in the works of Rachel Rosenthal, elaborating as they do the polemics of harmony and chaos, which so many seek to moderate in their lives and in the world around them. This antinomy is at the heart of her dramaturgy, and since performance art is primarily a solo form made on the body of the performer, it is, more significantly, a function of her physiology as a woman in her mid-sixties. What comes through in the performances of Rosenthal is her worldliness in the acceptance of natural history as a part of the history of the world and part of her history. Because performance art is not a tragic form, nor Rosenthal's nature tragic, comic irony is the mood of the all too human *commedia* that is the natural history of her own life.

All of these themes come together like fibers of a nervous system in the kind of performances Rosenthal constructs around body, biology, and gender. She transvalues the routinely autobiographical form into what I call the *autobiological,* making performance a life science. Her feminism evolves a profoundly philosophical system that impels feminine principles toward an ethics of performance. Then human ethics is made symmetrical with environmental ethics, opening up a historical perspective that moves beyond the merely personal to the more broadly global. The very precise spiritual focus of her work collapses human time into cosmic time, aligning art and science, poetry and performance.

In effect, Rosenthal fuses the controversial Gaia hypothesis, the view

Originally published in *Kenyon Review* (Spring 1993): 59–67, and revised for publication in *Ecologies of Theater* (Baltimore: Johns Hopkins University Press, 1996).

of nature described in chaos theory, and the perspective on geology described in the study of plate tectonics to trace the autobiology of her life. Drawing on issues raised by these scientific ideas, her performances are oriented increasingly around ecological themes and animal rights. But more than that, the face of the earth has become a metaphor for her own physiognomy.

In an early piece, *Grand Canyon* (1978), Rosenthal transforms into a vampire who flies over the canyon on a snowy winter day. She reads it like a topology of her life. The canyon's faults, erosion pattern, plateaus, and rocks act as signs of her life in this personal journey of metamorphosis: a geological fault is for her a matter of guilt. As narrative strategy, the journey is both real and symbolic in her work. Rosenthal's family fled Hitler's Europe, first to Brazil, then to New York during World War II, and so she became a refugee, a traveler, homeless, an immigrant. Rosenthal, who lives in Los Angeles and speaks English with the New York City accent of someone who once spoke another language, has always made geography—which is to say, walking across the earth—her subject. She brings the feeling of travel into performance.

Another one of her works named after a specific topography is *Death Valley* (1988). More metaphoric in name, this *J'accuse* solo is accompanied by dissonant violin and vocal work consisting of animal sounds, Jewish religious rhythms, speech-song, and chants. The operatic reach of the piece links it to the avant-garde arias Cathy Berberian was known for in Europe a few decades ago. In any case, music has always been an essential element in Rosenthal's performance style, based as it is so freely in the timbre of the voice. Her declamations often assume the character of song. In this piece she develops the theme of collaborator: "By being alive I have tacitly agreed to . . ." Dressed in a long blue, white, and black robe and long black gloves, wearing black lipstick and eye shadow, the elegant, bald-headed Rosenthal recites a litany of horrors that includes "obscenity of the food chain," "carnage of the earth," "stealing habitats," and "chemical warfare." At times Rosenthal takes on the cry of a coyote. She feels constant pain in her knees. The world is disjointed. Indeed, the year 1988 brought worldwide ecological turmoil.

A large-scale piece with live animals, *The Others* (1984), takes up the issue of animal liberation, a prominent motif in later performances. Here Rosenthal attacks the Cartesian view of animals as "thoughtless brutes" without consciousness. She speaks for their victimhood, or otherness, focusing their exploitation by science as a rights issue.

Some may find problematic Rosenthal's biocentrism because of its inherent antihumanist view. But it is at the core of her performances, the philosophical foundation of their "deep ecology" perspective. Within the ecologies of theater that I have been outlining in recent years, Rosenthal has affinities with the biocentric worldview reflected also in the works of Meredith Monk and Robert Wilson. These artists elucidate the utopian line of thinking in late twentieth-century theater, creating nonhierarchical performance worlds populated by human and nonhuman species. Even more than that, they share an interest in cosmology.

Biocentrism helps illuminate Rosenthal's interest in Gaia, the ancient earth goddess of the Greeks and the poetic essence of her personally revealing work *L.O.W. in Gaia* (1986). Here, in the true spirit of performance art, centered in the body as text, Rosenthal takes on the persona of Gaia herself. James Lovelock, whose two books on the Gaia theme draw on contemporary thinking in geology, geochemistry, evolutionary biology, and climatology, offers a view of the earth and the life it bears as a "physiological system." He regards it as a self-regulating organism rather than inert rock upon which plants and animals live. In this scheme of things the health of the planet matters more than that of individual species or organisms. If the word *theater*, like *theory*, derives from the idea of spectatorship, then the Gaia hypothesis is at the heart of Rosenthal's definition of the theatrical. I think of her as the Great Mother of Performance.

Lynn Margulis, Lovelock's colleague in first putting forth the challenging idea of Gaia, views symbiosis rather than the random accumulation of mutations as a source of evolutionary change and diversity. The reciprocal action between organism and environment—in sociological terms, a partnership society—is favored over that of competition among individuals. Margulis's contention that the earth is *autopoietic*—self-maintaining—sits comfortably with the contemporary psychology of self-actualization that Rosenthal affirms. This perspective on Gaia—its rebuke to the belief that environment dominates life, or humans the environment—is emphasized in Rosenthal's noncoercive dramaturgy, based not on the Aristotelian notion of interactive conflict but on a more process-oriented, open, nonhierarchical model. It is documentary rather than dramatic in nature, chaotic rather than unified. Scientifically based Necessity overrules Fate.

If in the earlier *Gaia, Mon Amour* (1983) she assumes the persona of the earth goddess in a series of interlocking monologues that catalogue human violence toward nature, the more expansive and dramatic *L.O.W. in Gaia* is a chronicle of a three-week vacation Rosenthal took in the Mojave Desert. In this work she shows color slides of herself there in a rented van and recounts her adventures hiking and preparing meals, even brief encounters with humans. She praises the beauty of the stars in the dry, silent night and the enchanting sound of a coyote concert. But Rosenthal is no sentimentalist. Little by little the haunting scenes of the desert landscape shown in the montage of slides give way to images of the desert floor littered with the detritus of the civilized world. Accompanying voice-overs and visual texts—by Gary Snyder, William Catton, Aldo Leopold, and others—provide commentary on nuclear radiation, pollution, technological profligacy, human irresponsibility. Here in the desert are the unmistakable allusions to ancient religion and myth and, in our own time, to nuclear testing and missile sites. The voice of the sagebrush whistles in the desert wind: nuclear crisis is one of metaphysical dimension.

One of the profound themes in Rosenthal's work is the understanding that the ecosystem is inseparable from the cultural system of a people. This insight returns to the ancient view of the world in which history, myth, religion, ecology, philosophy, and aesthetics were considered together in any reflection on human affairs. Rosenthal is simply forcing performance to accept its place in the history of ideas. The feeling for landscape is at the very marrow of the American psyche. Rosenthal's diaristic performance problematizes the town-versus-country theme—she is drawn to the desert but lives in Los Angeles—so familiar to nature writing and the myth of the sublime western landscape with its boundless resources. She brings into high relief the very real possibility of ecological catastrophe.

L.O.W. in Gaia, then, is no mere eclogue singing the praises of desert solitaire, but a cry of rage to Gaia, in Rosenthal's adopted voice of a Crone. A ritualistic mood transforms this performance conceived in part as a meditation, in the small altar of bones she constructs around her, close to which she places a candle, and sanctified by her incantatory language. Rosenthal's totemism also gives a feeling of the sacred to her performance, which is more of a rite. Her head, on which she will trace in lipstick the number 60 (for her sixty years when the work was created) as a kind of magical act, only serves to enhance her mystique as a woman of special qualities. Indeed, she is a Crone.

In prepatriarchal mythology, linked as it was to ecology, the Crone—

the force of life and death—formed part of the three-in-one unity that comprised Virgin, Mother, and Crone. Rosenthal weaves around the concept of time the condition of her own aging body, and that of the earth, her linkage emphasizing personally the importance given to the contemporary consideration of ecology as an aspect of biology. So human time is apprehended in the sweep of cosmic time, and myth joined to history. Furthermore, Rosenthal develops the theme as a cosmography of herself, drawing on this suppressed women's history to articulate an autoecology.

However appealing the Gaia hypothesis is as a way of explaining life on the planet, I am somewhat skeptical of Lovelock's recent book on the subject, *The Ages of Gaia,* in which he invokes comparison between Gaia and the Virgin Mary. Though she certainly regards the earth with a sense of the sacred, Rosenthal's own ethos is nondenominational, fully secular, even pagan.

In the ancient stone of Marble Mountain she sees an anthropomorphic likeness of the Death Crone. She reflects on death and dying. A sequence of slides is projected on the back wall of the performance space, unfolding in a series of portraits of Rosenthal in her own "Ages of Woman." While the autobiographical images unfold behind her she takes an electric razor over her bald head as if to fully erase history, and with it the seductiveness of youth, of woman, of victim. Then she speaks in one of her characteristic Euripidean women's voices:

I am the Crone
The third aspect of the Triple Goddess. The one you fear.
You can accept the Virgin,
barely stomach the Mother,
but me, you have attempted to destroy.
I am your death.
Not the glamorous death of battles, of heroism, of blood
spilled for a cause.
No, I am gout, ulcers, rheumatism, Alzheimer's, and cancer.
I am Nemesis of the Greeks.
Morgan Le Fay of the Cèlts
In India I am Kali the Black
In Scandinavia, Hel—Queen of the Shades
I am the Night Mare, the black mare-headed
    Demeter, Demeter Chthonic, the Subterranean.
Your culture turned me into a devil.
You reject me. You despise and fear older women.

If one of the most profound philosophical implications of theater is the moment-to-moment dying of the performer's body before the eyes of the audience, Rosenthal carries this thought to an extreme by making it the subject of her performance. Moreover, she then links this theme to the aging of the earth, of Gaia, and the desecration of the earth's body through the forces of commodification and relentless human destructiveness. In its compelling model of ecofeminist performance she brings together the exploitation of women's bodies and the body of the earth, that is, women's rights and biotic rights.

The origin of the universe at the Big Bang now seems certain, but Rosenthal sees its destiny as the Big Crash. Her nightmarish vision of the future is physicalized in the fortieth-century Monster she impersonates at the beginning and end of the performance: an androgynous creature who is bent over, jaw fused open, lipless, hands bereft of their tensile ability. The Monster will find in the ground bits and pieces of disks marked with a warning symbol announcing waste disposal nearby. The waste remains, but not the human race.

In Rosenthal's work, not only *L.O.W. in Gaia* but those pieces that address her grand themes of nuclear holocaust, pollution, consumerism, the forces of nature, the myth of progress, such as *Death Valley, Was Black,* and *Pangaean Dreams,* she condemns developments in history that have led to humankind's separation from the natural world. She evokes the opposition between nature and culture even as she humorously explores her own contradictions in the face of it. But Rosenthal is not anti-technological (her performances demand a sophisticated use of technology), she is not anti-Western (all cultures' wanton destruction of their land is acknowledged), and she is not antimodernist (her work sits comfortably in the century-long tradition of avant-garde performance). All of these positions have found a place in the environmentalist critique, but not with Rosenthal. In fact, she is more materialist than mystic, despite her conviction that the crisis of culture is a spiritual one.

Rosenthal offers a model of the performance artist who can imagine life-sustaining images amidst the imagery of extinction. She transforms the Death Crone into the creative force of the death-defying artist who can generate essential new myths for today. In a perversely classical sense, *L.O.W. in Gaia* is a public enactment of the myths of the community, a feminist satyr play to be considered alongside the classics.

Rosenthal dares to expose herself to the certain beauty in facing terror, the evil that is human, dreamed of by Artaud in his own radical autobiology. Singularly, she carries his disturbing chaotic spirit into American performance art, where she is author, director, spectacle, signaling through the hot air of global warming, if not its flames. Her bald head becomes a blank surface on which to reflect the history of the world, a mirror of its horror. The Crone is the ancient presence of the Other in her body: her double. The foreground of the performance is her own agonized body, now a theater where Artaud's "spiritual therapeutics" is acted out for the social body. Her body politics reaches out toward healing. Where else can one go with the final image of *Was Black,* a response to the Chernobyl disaster (and a literal translation of the Russian word), when the performers wrap around her torso and face a long cord whose tiny bulbs light up suddenly, reflecting in gruesome metaphor the radiated body?

Rosenthal projects from her body a special kind of performance knowledge, a womanly knowledge, the physiological understanding of images that is the powerful inner light of visionary performance. It is the spectacular autobiology of a performer one wants to know and to learn from, the very embodiment of the kind of illumination a body of knowledge bestows.

Yet all the while Rosenthal walks in the realm of myth she is demythologizing herself. A highly self-conscious performer, more theatrical and literary than most performance artists, she is forever finding "another self-made myth to explode." Among her favorite devices is the double or split self in dialogue, and the sudden about-face from a serious political diatribe on a social issue to a personal revelation of her own complicity in the problem. How to pursue further the possibility that the Great Mother mystique may unlock the possibility of a mother–daughter story?

The ironic play between masking and unmasking is nowhere more poignant than in Rosenthal's exposure of the very subject of performance art—the body—to laughter, even pity, and, more frighteningly, fear. Here is a performer confronting aging, one of the great taboos of performance life. Her body, she allows, is not the perfect instrument it is supposed to be *as a performing body.* "Why is every performance so hard? Why do I suffer like this?" Rosenthal personalizes the condition of chaos theory's fractal self in *Pangaean Dreams* (1990), a piece about motion: what could be more difficult for Rosenthal, with her decades-old knee problem (Wilson has his knee plays, she has hers). Osteoporosis is acknowledged as structural principle in the body of pain. With her wheelchair entrance and talk of plastic knees, back trouble, and fractured vertebrae, Rosenthal only underscores the lithe, puppet-like quality of her performances, in all its tragicomic implications. Rosenthal has a marvelously trained body, a mime's light-footedness and legerdemain, and one watches in performance a body struggling to act—the way one looks at aging dancers or listens to aging singers—with a heightened awareness of nature's competitiveness with art.

Given that performance is a function of the body, and with an aging, still-active avant-garde, it is surprising that this subject is not more important to artists, especially women, who stand to gain so much in the lifting of taboos on the aging female body/performer/image. The biological is the dangerous staging ground for the struggle between theory and praxis, or desire and experience. Rosenthal positions herself in this dialectic, creating for it a frame of reference full of poetry and panache. The performances constitute her own natural history.

If in *L.O.W. in Gaia* Rosenthal draws a metaphoric parallel between her own aging body and the earth, in *Pangaean Dreams* she considers the breaking apart of her body in the context of continental drift and plate tectonics. Again, the personal is extenuated to the global. As a resident of California, she can't help but anticipate the Big Rift. In this recent work, subtitled "A Shamanic Journey," Rosenthal descends into the underworld to search for answers to the mystery of existence. An accompanist beats the drum that induces her altered state of consciousness. Rosenthal chants and rattles to the four corners of the earth. Roaming around the bowels of the earth inside a video image, she discovers the workings of plate tectonics. It shapes for her an entirely revolutionary worldview.

Scoffed at for decades, Alfred Wegener's idea that the surface of the earth is divided into a small number of rigid, drifting plates on which continents, driven by hot, upwelling fluids, move and interact with each other, has become in recent times a fully elaborated perspective on the distribution of mountains, earthquakes, and volcanic activity. In fact, the earthquake in the Mojave Desert in June 1992 gave scientists a look at what they believe is a new tectonic system that is cutting California away from North America and moving it toward Alaska. In a development not without its cultural irony, the Baja region of Mexico is pushing northward on its Pacific plate, unnerving the San Andreas Fault. So Rosenthal's sense of continental drift has real repercussions in her life, as well as scientific legitimacy. She, Rachel Rosenthal, living at the end of the twentieth century, is part of a process that began about 250 million years ago, when the continents of the world formed a single mass, called Pangaea, which broke up into several continents that have been drifting ever since. As she reads the signs of her life in the earth itself, the semiological swells into the seismological. Nothing is what it seems. But now she has a radical understanding of time and space and personal upheaval. In another light, the discovery of the workings of plate tectonics was largely circulated during the period of cubist painting, which captured the fractured, shifting planes of reality on an unstable surface. It is this cubist vision, which in fact destroyed perspective as it had evolved since the Renaissance, that adds a metaphysical footnote to the scientific findings.

The knowledge that Rosenthal received about the earth on her underworld travels is presented in the form of the shamanic trance as "The Big Picture," a moving picture projected onto the surface of a long robe she wears, unfurled by sticks that stretch the robe wide as she opens her arms, unmistakably recalling Loie Fuller's grand gestures a century ago. It is a collage of dinosaurs, flocks of birds, ships, refugees, cowboys, Indians, cities, trains, factories, bridges: dislocation—a theme of the work—as life principle. Everyone is on the move.

If Rosenthal formerly longed for unity, rapprochement, now she accepts the way of the world as constant flux. Call her the Heraclitus of the performance world. Plate tectonics defines a state of mind, and Rosenthal considers all of its convulsive realignments "a learning experience." A simple event can turn into a groundbreaking perception. In a fantastic California-inspired image she sees the plate as a skateboard weaving around everyday activities. Even the structure of *Pangaean Dreams* seems to be affected by the idea of the plate: separate parts of the stage space act as plates (planes) in which different kinds of performance occur, the shamanic journey or Rosenthal as herself. The concept of the plate also evolves into the plane surface on which slides or video are projected throughout the piece. In this context, plate tectonics suggests a provocative interpretation of collage, which has always been the organizing principle of Rosenthal's work.

Added to this view are the lessons of chaos theory, which, in this context, allows for the comparison of human relationships to earth's tremors, magnetic fields, strange attractors. In other words, predictable turbulence is the law of nature. These scientific metaphors are joined to an all-embracing Gaia image to form a comprehensive ecosophy, which declares indivisible the ecosystem and the cultural, economic, political, and psychological systems of a people. The human body will share the same nervous system as Gaia, because nature and culture cannot be disjoined into separate environments. It is this split in "human nature" that Rosenthal's work addresses.

Themes of conflict and duality are explored in Rosenthal's dialogue with her male double, the personification of her pain, which she refers to as the Autonomous Being. He challenges her to account for her conflicting selves: Rosenthal is a worshiper of the Great Mother who disdains childbirth, a nature lover who cannot do without the amenities of conventional hygiene, a celebrator of womanhood who hates its biological imperatives. The most provocative exchange between Rosenthal and her Autonomous Being comes in a discussion about gender, in which he questions her feminism. Rosenthal answers that she is "a gay man in a woman's body." Autobiologically speaking, her identity crisis is a provocation of enormous complexity. "Men don't want me, because they sense something funny. Gay men don't want me, because they see me as a woman. Women want me, but I don't want them, because I want men—but not as a woman . . . !" Formidable seismologies erupt from the rhetorical body in this chaotic discourse of signs and shifting surface texts.

In another section of the performance Rosenthal talks about men and women and love in the style of a 1930s French film: taunting, seductive, pushing to extremes. Love is flaccid, feminine, amorphous; hate is vigorous, masculine, linear. Rosenthal is a feminist who can make feminists uncomfortable with their sexual position because she gives voice to the unmentionable subjects, as Carolee Schneemann has always done in her own pioneering autobiology. And, she is close in spirit to the mocking sophistication, even decadence, of Pina Bausch. These women eschew the frequently girlish, politically safe attitudes in performances by women for a more dangerous worldliness and womanliness where Eros and Irony share the stage.

What is especially engaging about Rosenthal is the great, good humor that characterizes her performances: quite simply, the comedy that is always attached to the biological in human drama. Rosenthal has a real earthiness and scatological sense that, when accompanied by the release from etiquette age can bring, leads to a decided freedom of expression. Who but she would worry about the methane content released into the environment by human beings? "From the Gaian perspective, we may be only as important as our farts," she confides to her audience.

Part of Rosenthal's "aura" is the multiple imagery of her own persona—the sense of glamour she exudes; the very sensual gestures of the long hands; her redoubtable femaleness, always flirting with androgyny; the drop earrings; the remnants of French sweetness in the voice. All of these qualities coexist with the bald head and deliberate dressing down, cross-dressing, at times in army fatigues; and the raunchy language and cutting through of taboos, the disturbing thoughts. Rosenthal is as much a personality as a performer, in the expansive modernist sense. Her performances stylize her desire for an out-of-body experience. Or is it Artaud's dream, still alive today, of the body without organs?

Dismemberment is part of shamanism, and in *Pangaean Dreams* this component of the journey is transmuted into Rosenthal's frequent digging up of bones and body parts throughout the performance. Bit by bit they are fitted together on an armature, until at the end of the performance the (partly) reconstructed body is hoisted about the performance space. Rosenthal has unearthed her own remains. The Autonomous Being had told her she was "part angel, part dinosaur," but most remarkably, part of the great chain of life since prerecorded history. It's the structure—the bones of a thought—that has always mattered to Rosenthal.

If, as Mircea Eliade has written, shamanism is a technique of ecstasy, then so is making art, following as it does the same trajectory of dismemberment and resurrection. The unmistakable allusion is that artists, like scientists, give themselves up to the quest for new worlds, and often they are ridiculed when they attempt to describe them. *Pangaean Dreams* is Rosenthal's *Tempest*.

For Rosenthal the new worldview is plate tectonics, which can, at last, explain her own body/continent of restless desire. Not for her the dance of death in the face of chaos. She prefers the tectonic boogie, one of the new *lazzi* for the twenty-first century.

> When one plate moves, all move. That's the law of chaos and I accept. I nod *Yes*. I will live my allotted time torn apart by my duality, kicking and screaming all the way. With the violent love of Gaia. With fear and trembling and loving care. With the Pangaean dinosaur ensconced in my brain. In the Earth. Of the Earth. In the world. Of the world.

Rosenthal's ecological testament reflects her profound understanding of the life force. In her search for enlightenment she discovers an ironic lesson: wisdom is insecurity. *Learn the tectonic boogie / Or you've had it, Baby.*

Jack Hirschman

"Instant Theatre"

Pier Street, Pacific Ocean Park: the most colorful street west of downtown Los Angeles. Old stone hotels (the Grand, the Metropole), cheap dress shops, Italian grocers, Yiddish in the windows, storefront studios, crutches and eye patches, wine bottles holding up the buildings, filth in the street, the continual slow patrol. . . . In one of the storefront places (crack-painted and with FIX IT lettered on the glass), there takes place every Thursday night one of the most exciting experiments in theater poetry on this or any American coast. Instant Theatre is its name and it is neither a happening, a psychodrama, nor a rehearsal. A small repertory gathers there to perform highly stylized improvisations (with a synthesized use of word, mime, and music) to an audience that for the most part comprises a handful of stray dogs mangy with nighttown rambling—and friends. No reviews in the morning papers. No tuxedos, men's rooms, cigarette machines. No price of admission either, but love, and everywhere is front row center.

The theater is an empty store rented for performing purposes by one of the actors, Sam Weinrib, who lives in the rear, makes his buck by oddjobbing, designing posters and silkscreens. Between his bedroom/studio and the theater itself is a john used by the actors for changes, and a narrow little room crammed with masks, hats, dresses, suits, shoes—the costumes of the Instant Theatre. Two doors (there are no wings) lead to the theater, a high-ceilinged, narrow room. Some dozen feet above the stone floor rope has been strung in the shape of an *N* from which scenery curtains and other instant stage designs are dropped or hung. Light sockets on each side of the wall are manually worked downstage by performers who are sitting out a set. Beyond

Originally published in *FM & Fine Arts* (May 1963), 7–9.

them, there are a few throw cushions and a couple of chairs for anyone happening in.

Next is the front window and its ledge. Here is just the place to begin because music sounds the opening note of the tapestries of Instant Theatre. On the front window ledge or, more precisely, within the one hard and the two glass walls, which in another day displayed manikins, spaghetti slivers, or used shoes, Stuart Miller sits. In most cases, he has just finished instanting the set with an improvisation of a garden gate, a tire, a masked manikin, an umbrella hung from a rope line. "Eyes out" has been called. (Since there is no curtain, everyone is asked to close their eyes while the performers emerge from the back room, give the set some thought, and then return to the back room for direct entrance or, perhaps, assume positions there and then.) At this point Miller announces the beginning of the performance by a musical overture. The overture, a couple of notes, is played on one of the many instruments perched up in his nook at the front window—bones, an untuned zither, a toy trumpet, a Kabuki drum, a children's music box, a wooden xylophone, a Chinese gong, wire plucks, lutes, various flutes—or by knocking on the window or by scratching the window or any combination of these.

The important thing is that the music is continued throughout the enactment of an improv, and that it is synchronized by such imaginative work by Miller as to pass beyond mere accompaniment and enter into the very blood of the spectacle itself. It becomes equal to the words and gestures of the performers. And in a successful improv the three languages are seen to be working in such miraculous harmony that anyone who never heard of jazz, calligraphic brush strokes—or of chance itself—would swear the whole thing was written in a script. Well, and so it is, but it is a script that no one in Instant Theatre has ever read *except* in the act of its being written.

Of the other components of Instant Theatre—the words and gestures. The sets usually run ten minutes—at least I have never seen one less than, say, seven minutes or more than fifteen. The "acting" performers are: the organizer and spiritual leader of the group, a Parisian-born actress and painter, Rachel Rosenthal; her actor-husband, King Moody; Weinreb; Lynette Wooliver; Camille Blair; and Anita Danchick. Two others, who specialize in dance, Dick Oliver and Claudia Hood, complete, with Miller, the repertory. But it would be unfair at the start to classify this one as actor and that one as dancer, for the dancers speak as well during an improv, entering the drama on two levels, just as all the "acting" performers are experienced in dance movement and mime.

With this in mind, let's have some improvs. The first time I went to Pier Street, I opened my eyes to find Oliver and Weinreb engaged in a set of . . . simulated Chinese music. The props are simple, a chair and cloth backdrop behind it; blue curtains thrown up and over the rope line above drape along the floor to give perspective to the scene. Weinreb enters from one of the doors. He is dressed in battered man's hat, gas mask, Mexican blanket-vest. He carries two, long bamboo-like sticks. He grunts from behind the gas mask as he moves the sticks back and forth, scraping the stone floor with them as if rowing or as a sign of nervousness or irascibility. Oliver enters from the other door, moving on tiptoe in a kind of catatonia, dressed as a woman, with veil, and carrying at the very end of his fingers a bird-cage netting. The contrast has been established. A kind of communicable noncommunication of hostility has been set up. Weinreb grunts on. He speaks. Oliver speaks. Their lines meet and do not. More grunting, scraping. Weinreb cries out, "What I want to see are objects that are static, that have no movement, that do nothing." At which Oliver, who has in the course of the improv climbed on the chair, drops the bird-cage netting.

This moment seems to me to be the essence of Instant Theatre, the point where many evocations of word, gesture, costume, and music (though I forget precisely the music at this moment) come together in what is as lucid a moment of poetry—a moment of illumination and enlightenment—as anything I have seen on the stage in many a day. And it must be emphasized that this kind of theater is concerned with the poetry of spectacle. Rather than purporting to be an illimitable outburst that would as well fit into a head-shrinker's office, its rigors, while expressed in what might be called spontaneity, come from deep areas of inner discipline. For the actor not only must play to the costume he wears, to the mask he assumes; he must also be more extremely aware of who is with him in an improv than the actor in a scripted play who, after three or four performances, ceases to react to the character on the stage in favor of the cues in the book.

In another improv—this one performed by Rachel Rosenthal and King Moody, who, it should be added, are the most experienced performers of the repertory—elements of grotesque and travesty were achieved that make realist-naturalist theater superficial by comparison. Picture . . . A door without a window. The actress is behind it as the music opens the eyes of the audience. She is dressed as (1) a coquette,

(2) a bawd, (3) a dame. Black dress. Battered red hat (later we'll see red heels as well). With her hand she turns the no-glass of the door into (1) a mirror, (2) a glass to look through, (3) no glass through which she can stick her head, while simultaneously monologuing on identity, on looking out, on going out rather than staying in. Enter the man. Black shirt, black tights. He goes to bench, stretches out, lifts his shirt. A small baby doll is lying, head under his tights, at his waist. The improv begins to develop into a dialogue of hostility and obsession (comic as only the grotesque can be) around the subject of contact, communication. The actress now coys, now taunts the air around the man. The man responds similarly. Their words, in short, do not make definite contact but are being set up for some action. This action turns out to be a touching of bodies, bringing them together in a grotesque mime in which, very slowly to the music, they spin downward and downward to the floor, the man crying, "I'm stuck," and the woman groaning in a kind of sexual desperation and frenzy. And as if to point up the instant beauty of the improv, a female manikin that has been placed backstage and, though not employed during the action (she stood like some evocation of conscience or sterility over the action), is "accidentally" knocked over as the man and woman reach the floor.

As in all theater, improvs work, and then they don't. There are good nights, and there are bad ones. But on a bad night of scripted drama where one can point, perhaps, to a bit of dialogue brilliantly spoken or a bit of setting that worked, in Instant Theatre such excellencies appear much more successful, partly because one feels that an invisible imagination is at work even in the weakest of improvs and partly because of the intimacy of the theater itself. In one improv, for example, as a kind of exercising that the repertory engages in, Camille Blair was to be a hoot-owl and Dick Oliver, the moon. But the connections were not made. Oliver, who decided to represent the moon by carrying a large round tinfoil on his back (he wore a harlequin mask up front), became the beautiful victim of chance. The garden gate that was used as a prop, struck by the theater lights, was continually shadowed on the back, as it were, of the moon. The effect was so visually inspiring as to forgive, if not completely, the lack of success of the improv at the dramatic level. These visual and musical insights are constant events at Instant Theatre; and it is no wonder to me that every time I've been there, someone in the audience with pen or pencil has been sketching away like mad.

To say that Instant Theatre possesses something of surrealism, something of Dadaism, something of the puppet theater and the opera is to approach its meaning, which, to my mind, is poetry itself. To see a man in a black hood, smoking an American flag and mouthing the most banal sort of political junk presents us with an image possible these days only in the world of Neo-Dada art. To witness the crawling mime—as in the performance by Lynette Wooliver—of an insect fatally doomed in its vegetarianism to an attraction for a roast of meat on a barbecue is the kind of experience all too often kept from the boards out of that obscene notion that theater magic belongs only in the crack-brained potions of theorists doomed to the pages of books. In Instant Theatre, which has been going on in Los Angeles for some seven years, we have, in my opinion, the only continuing contact with Theater Ritual and Theater Absurdity. This room full of masks ranging from bizzare old biddies to clowns to children; the sets that may at a whim open a world where absurd collisions of, say, torero hats, gas masks, Japanese umbrellas, periscopes, manikins, and also every conceivable type of human—these elements work together by working against each other. They offer us the kind of experience that extends the consciousness of theater as well as of this piddling and chancy life of ours—such theater, a theater of modest spectacle but spectacle nonetheless, is worth a hundred scripts from Ibsen to Miller for me. It has nothing to lose, and therefore every risk it takes is a victory. Aestheticians and critics can't cope with it because there is no text. It comes from the accidents in which we live, to which we all are prone; it puts on the dress of style to present us with those very accidents in heightened form; it passes back into the drabber world of accident. Recollection and paraphrasing won't help. There is such a thing as talking *about* magic. But for magic itself, you have to be there and see.

Edie Danieli

"Rachel Rosenthal: A Life History"

Encino/Los Angeles

Friday, November 14, 1975, 8:00 P.M., Orlando Gallery, Encino. We're all packed in the front gallery—there's not even standing room—and Rachel Rosenthal is standing on a small stage in front. She is all in white, exotic, pre-Raphaelite, but as the event unfolds the white becomes antiseptic, like bandages, and the purity or spirituality becomes clinical.

Rosenthal announces that this will not be a performance as was scheduled, and that we have been invited here under false pretenses. That moment is incredibly exciting; that is the phrase that breathes life into the event. She sits in a chair and slowly and very stiffly, like a marionette, begins to move her arms, and then, as if connected by string, her knees follow. She slowly rises and rotates her body to the sound of a dialogue between herself and her doctor as he examines her knees. We see slides of the X-rays, and she shows us her knees and draws in dotted lines the possible corrective surgery. She pours red liquid from a container to show us the amount of blood extracted from her knees in one examination. Now we see slides of all the activities she has had to give up: yoga, ballet, swimming, ti chi, bicycling, jogging. And to each one (outrageously staged) she says, "Of course, this is a simulation," and they are hilarious, and the situation is very sad.

The humor, the theater, the staging, all the acting skills that are innate to Rosenthal now, go hand in hand with the grim facts. A problem is the disparity between her logic and the doctor's findings, which indicate that she has congenitally troubled kneecaps. When she

Originally published in *Artweek,* December 13, 1975, 13.

was five she had a make-believe playmate who was crippled, and today she almost is. Rosenthal lists all the events and decisions in her life that could add up to crippled knees, and these are beautiful vignettes, not just of the past, but of Europe and wealthy parents in a beautiful home with spaces large enough for a young girl to give ballet recitals to guests. All the particular things in her memory, with their delicious details, seem like a fairy tale gone wrong.

The lights come on, and the distance between her mind and her knees seems like light years. But I know they are connected somehow. It is a mystery, the coexistence of opposites that are within her, but because she appears so strong (and I don't think that's an act), it's hard to believe they are unsurmountable.

Tuesday, November 25, 1975, 7:00 P.M., Wilshire West Plaza, Westwood. I am late and wondering as I frantically look for a parking space whether Rosenthal will start on time or wait for stragglers like me. As I drive past this glass high-rise, I see Rachel Rosenthal in the space, standing behind a table gesturing, and a semicircle of people on the floor already caught up in her magic. The scene is a mirage in this city context, and passersby wonder about it too.

To the audience of this piece, called *Thanks,* Rosenthal is conveying thanks to people in her life who have done something important for her or to her. As in the previous performance, the props are minimal and carefully chosen. Her immediate performance space doesn't go much beyond her body or approximate body space, but our relationship to her is almost the opposite of her last event. We are in a large, unfinished space, and are drawn around her to listen and wonder what is in all those little white boxes that nearly cover the top of an old redwood patio table. They are all the same size, each with an appropriate fold-out paper turkey on top.

"I would like Marthe to step forward," Rosenthal says, and immediately a girl responds. Rosenthal lights a long, slender orange candle, hands it to the girl who now personifies Marthe, and begins to tell the story of her mother's maid who had two irons, one on the stove that had filigree work around the sides and the one she used with a fancy handle. The cloth employed for steaming looked "toasted." Her mother's clothes had a particular smell, and she had a pleated skirt that Marthe would press precisely so that it was geometrically perfect. When Rosenthal finishes the story she hands the girl a box and so the performance continues until all the boxes and stories—important people and a noble cat—are told.

Coming in as I did just as the first person stood up, I couldn't tell if the people had been prepicked or not, and that mystery lasted until over halfway through the event, when I finally caught the phrasing, "Who will be my father?" And I thought, Volunteers! Which one will I respond to? No, not Picasso, that's too much. Rauschenberg? The Sunday painter? Her mother? The tall dark stranger? I should have held the light for Rosenthal's wonderful cat whose courage to live gave her the strength to go on. They were inseparable, a duality of existence. A young man volunteered to be her father, and his little girl refused to let go of his hand, so she stood at his side with her long blondish hair down her back. And as he became Rosenthal's father, the little girl became Rachel. It was indeed magic, and if you were a daddy's girl, you loved it. Something caught fire in the front row, midway through the performance; I saw the Sunday painter, represented by a little girl, sitting next to her mother who was beating at something resembling large ashes with glowing edges. I wondered if her paper turkey had been sacrificed. It was time to open the gifts, and you know that good feeling. All who had participated received a box that contained a little collage/assembled wall piece, each, of course, appropriate for the subject, and one as exquisite as the other. Now I was really sorry I hadn't participated, but, of course, I had, and I had a gift too.

Barbara T. Smith

"Rachel Rosenthal Performs *Charm*"

Los Angeles

I am reporting on a performance by Rachel Rosenthal, called *Charm,* presented at Mount St. Mary's College, January 28, as part of an excellent showing of women's work curated there by Rita Yokoi and continuing until February 20. I would like to address the question of theater versus performance, and in what sense this fascinating piece was a merging of both. I come to performance with a particular bias and expectation, looking for something that differs markedly from theater. One distinction I require is that in some sense the performer is not acting, that is, pretending, but is here, now, what he or she is. And that what we are witnessing (in the old-fashioned sense of *attesting to,* not enjoying in the entertainment sense) is a step in this living artist's personal growth and actual experience. Hence the qualitative value assigned to a performance depends to a large extent on my sense that this has been achieved. A good piece should lead us through and beyond the charms, the metaphors, the culturally conditioned ploys to some rare moments when the guard is down, the guises are not necessary, and we face reality unformed. It is a taboo-busting affair, the telling of tales not to be told, the risking of exposures or experiences not normally allowed.

With this clear, I can first guide you into Rosenthal's piece by a description of its elements. The overall form was that of theater, audience opposite stage. The piece was a "sonata in three movements" *(allegro ma non troppo, moderato cantabile,* and *con furioso),* developed partly through an offstage taped voice reading from George Alexander's description of the discovery and naming of subatomic particles.

Originally published in *Artweek,* February 19, 1977, 6–7.

With each movement so prefaced, we noted the enormous similarities between subparticles and human qualities. Indeed, some are called charms and others quarks, and so on. Each movement was punctuated by the reading of one of the three dictionary definitions of the word *charm,* and reference made to its central location in the book between *charlotte russe* and *charnel house.* The piece itself was a series of narrative vignettes, told by Rachel Rosenthal, in which each movement centered around the succeeding floors of her three-story childhood home in Paris.

Beginning, Rosenthal enters at our left, gorgeous in a dark brown crushed velvet gown weighted with heavy necklaces and pendants, her red hair a blazing crown—the high priestess of a social milieu she would now describe. Beside her chair is a small Louis XV marqueterie secretary; to our right the stage is bare. A woman of utmost charm and poise in manner, voice inflection, and presence, she captures our attention, our minds with wit, subtlety, facial expression, and gesture, now momentarily coy, then seductive, and again an intimate and revealing storyteller. All this is under perfect control, the control of one for whom skillful behavior is almost natural. She tells of her Russian parents, her mother's enormous beauty, her father's incredible wealth and playful exuberance, their superb French cuisine, the famous and wealthy guests, the elegant decor, all utterly unbelievable. We assume she is an amazing actress portraying a fantasy person with great skill. Periodically, our charmer is attended by an hilarious intruder, summoned by a silver bell to bring tray after tray of sumptuous pastries of all sorts. He is not completely unexpected in the setting; what is unexpected is what he wears—white gloves, a cutaway jacket, shirt, vest, a maid's white cap, and a tiny starched maid's apron, whose bow pokes rudely from between the cutaway tails behind. In front the apron covers perhaps-exposed genitals. We're not quite sure, and then realize maybe it's just a tease since he wears fishnet panty hose and is thus as sexy as a "Playgirl Bunny," yet male.

As the enchanting tales progress, many of them begin to reveal hints of the less-than-charming in such a life. Rosenthal is always beguiling, assuming our attention, but our eyes have been bewitched away! Pairs of figures in bizarre costumes appear. In slow and silent motion, they begin writhing and torturous interactions of gross seduction, rape, and orgiastic ecstacy, counterparts to Rosenthal's tales. They are impossible not to watch, hitting as they do our fascination with the unspoken and unexposed, the real and "dirty" secrets of the psyche, their actions magnified by the light play on their bodies that casts huge color-edged shadows on the walls. We see sordid exaltation, fucking, beating, biting, whips, garter-belts. A faceless, blinded bride enters to end each of the first two episodes. All the figures, including the butler/maid, are sexual composites and as such disturbingly unclear.

Meanwhile Rosenthal speaks out as if concerned for *us,* "Can you see me?" "Can you hear me?" Speaking of the house, she describes the first-floor public rooms, the parties and banquets, her father coming home, the search in his pockets for the inevitable gifts that were gems, pearls, tiny ivory elephants, and the like, the incredible high spirits, chasing around the dining table and the perfect, idyllic setting. On the second floor, the boudoirs, her parents' apartments, stories with sexual intimations and closure; no, she must not see the skin under her mother's breast! The constant message derived from these experiences was that real feelings and real curiosity were not to be felt, much less expressed: "could have no curiosity, I can't cry, I mustn't die, and I must lie and dissemble with an adored man."

The third movement deals with the third floor, where Rachel and the servants lived. There we realize the price, or obverse, of her unreality. We have been watching Rosenthal eat with increasing compulsion and less and less elegance, devouring dozens of napoleons, petit fours, strudels, pastries brought by the maid. (Eventually she rips into a whole cake with her bare hands and stuffs her face.) We hear of her insomnia as a child of three, the constant nightmares that she feared more than the wakefulness, the facial tics that were almost "cured" by her governess's ridicule and torture, the overheard gossip that threatened her stability and understanding of her family structure, the servants' expressed envy and hatred of the people they bowed to downstairs. This was her secret reality, which her parents never witnessed or protected her from. And we begin to ask what are *we* witnessing? Is this a contrived story? Did she make it up?

The amazing fact is that the stories are all true. While it seems incredible and thus an act, it is not. And here is where the question of where theater ends and performance begins arises. At first the piece is much more theater, for we see Rosenthal in a self-parody, enacting an extreme of Rachel, the charmer, with accomplished style, but gradually it becomes the real Rachel, constantly avoiding the ugly, being charming, perfect, and good at the price of inner turmoil. Her act has become second nature, so much a part of her that we cannot perceive the act. To us, the privileged witnesses, she reveals clues permitting us to penetrate and assist in reconstructing and releasing her. We see the eating in context, her inability to refuse sweets, the still present yet almost unnoticed facial tic, and as she chats, we hear a real tremble in the voice, the lowering register, the momentary haunted look in the eye, the rising rage that seems imminent, centered, and real, the absence now of the smile. And she really has gorged herself on sweets before our eyes. Now perhaps we know the basic reality that cuts through our barriers, too, going past metaphor and manners to the gut. We have also been watching her "demons," who by this final movement have grown in number until there is a Gordian knot of six writhing figures assuming a mass of intertwined chaos like a mythical Laocoon. The maidservant has developed into a salacious slut with red-painted lips and lascivious glances.

At last Rosenthal moves, exchanging place and manner with the nightmare figures who share her tea cakes while she assumes their demeanor with the childish plea of the Charmer, "Please, let there be no progress, no decay . . . and no pubic hair," only endless protection and bliss. How? She would marry her father and be ever yet little, adoring Rachel to him. At this point Rosenthal has taken a fixed position at our right. She is squatting as if defecating, her mouth open without sound or words, *empty;* her eyes wide open, *empty;* her hands reaching out as they once held the pastry tray, now *empty,* all *empty.* It is as if all this experience leaves her in an emotional bankruptcy, empty of all but charm, which is itself futile for the strength she needs. Frozen so, the lights go out on this horrifying, desperate, baroque image, haunted and still.

What can I say? It was superbly done, wonderfully rich, moving, and even entertaining. The best performance moments were when she revealed contact with long-denied feelings being allowed to come out, a reality breakthrough. And, of course, it was a complex and magic piece. In addition, this was the first exposure of her newly reconstituted Instant Theatre group, who became the orgiastic dancers in the piece so excellently. In its workshop this group is preparing for future performances as well. It is based on the original ideas and methods of Rosenthal's Instant Theatre group of the late 1950s.

Ruth Askey

"Rachel Rosenthal Exorcises Death"

Rachel Rosenthal's success as a performance artist is due to her considerable dramatic ability coupled with her talent for conveying gut-punching images.

In *The Death Show,* at Space Gallery on October 21, her solo performance was the final event closing Ed Lau's top-notch exhibition, *Thanatopsis.* A packed crowd sat on the floor around the "stage"—a narrow platform (with an easel at one end) covered in purple satin and set diagonally across the L-shaped gallery.

Rosenthal entered attired in clinging black pants and top, a head scarf, and long black gloves. (A metronome ticked throughout the performance. Beginning at a fast speed, it got progressively slower until the end, when it stopped ticking.) After passing crackers to the audience (we were told not to eat them yet), Rosenthal walked back and forth on the platform saying, "Death is ennobling / dying is punk / death is cathartic / dying is caca / death you hear about / dying is up yours / I can't live without death / I could do without dying / death is something else."

At times her undulating walk encompassed angular, awkward stances; yet she was keenly aware of her body and sharply in control of her audience. Traditionally autobiographical in her art, Rosenthal has documented other parts of her life in earlier performances. In *Charm* (Mount St. Mary's, January 28, 1977) we learned about growing up bright, rich, and psychologically battered in Paris; in *The Head of Olga K.* (UCSD, May 1, 1977) we learned about her relationship with her half sister.

Originally published in *Artweek,* November 18, 1978, 6.

In *The Death Show* Rosenthal explored her feelings about death, her denial of intermediate losses that caused her transfiguration into what she calls the "Fat Vampire," and finally her exorcism of that vampire. She moved us through forty-five minutes of intense drama, smoothly, effortlessly, and with great finesse.

First, Rosenthal spoke about the deaths of a beloved teddy bear in her childhood and, later, two adored cats. These three deaths become symbolic prototypes for different kinds of dying. Suddenly she took out a long knife, and pulling the ends of her gloved fingers with her teeth, she sliced off the glove tips and exposed bloodred claws. She clawed at her face, distorting it, and in the process became the Fat Vampire. Walking backward, she turned and faced a covered easel and took down the purple satin covering it. A color photograph of Rosenthal taken when she was fat and wearing vampire teeth was surrounded by a funeral wreath of cakes, doughnuts, and Danish pastries, all sprayed with black enamel paint resembling tar. "The Fat Vampire is fat from accumulations of countless botched up deaths not allowed to die," she said. Explaining how she killed the Fat Vampire, she beat herself, and pummeling her body, she said, "I could have killed the Fat Vampire long ago and many times."

A poignant ritual followed, called "Stations of the Fat Vampire," for which Rosenthal symbolically buried each previously ignored turning point in her life. She documented each station with a date, a compulsively eaten sweet food, and a crucial life event. The fourth station was "1955, Safeway Swirls; I refuse the death of my father and use my mother to avoid the path." As she recited each of the stations, she picked up a replica (same photograph as on easel) of the Fat Vampire and read from the back. Next she picked up a candle, placed the photograph on a cement base, spilled wax on it, and placed the candle over it. The ritual was repeated nine times. Then she turned and walked to the photograph/icon and slashed it with the knife. Putting vampire teeth in her mouth, she placed a vampire mask on top of her head and put a teddy bear between her legs. During this, a taped recitation of the *Bardo* (an adaptation from *The Tibetan Book of the Dead*) was heard, and we were instructed to eat our crackers.

Rosenthal mimed the vampire and lowered the mask on her face, then straightened up and lifted the bear from between her legs, cuddled it, put the mask over the bear's face, and leaned over to rest her chin on the bear's head. A totem pole of vampire faces appeared. Next she bit the bear's neck and the bear fell slowly from her hands onto the platform. Opening her eyes and mouth wide, she let loose with a horrifying silent scream. *The Death Show* was the tenth station of the Fat Vampire.

Ruth Askey

Excerpts from "Exoticism and Fear in Rio"

I rarely need a straitjacket nowadays, which was difficult to tie anyway since I insisted on doing it all myself. But I suffer from Life's
cramp. It's a superversion of writer's cramp. I am dying.

Rosenthal's most recent show, *My Brazil* (and they are shows because she brings her twenty years of acting expertise to each performance and often uses video, slides, and other actors), describes a
seven-month period, in 1940–41, when she and her family lived in Rio
de Janeiro as Jewish refugees. Rosenthal (age thirteen) and her mother
and father had left Paris hoping to make a new life in Brazil, but they
were urged to leave Rio, too, because "the 'dry war' had been brought
to this hemisphere [South America] by the Nazis."

On one level, her life in Rio appears to have been a long, tropical
vacation. She described diving through twenty-foot waves, choosing
between two dozen different kinds of bananas, and seeing forests stud-
ded with orchids like "millefleurs tapestries." She learned Portuguese
songs from *Carnaval '41* and told us of her youthful awareness of "exotic black bodies that rippled to audible or silent beats." Rosenthal
created lucid word pictures of the city and set up a mood so distinct
that I was able to smell it. On another level, we learned of her growing
fears about her family's refugee status and the wartime death (in Africa) of her beloved half brother.

The performance began with a taped male voice reading a *New York
Times* article written on July 16, 1940, stating that "the Nazi menace
in Brazil amounts to an undeclared war." Rosenthal, wearing a bright
turquoise gown and orchids in her hair, then entered with Anthony
Canty, who accompanied her on the conga drum. Canty, black,

Originally published in *Artweek,* November 17, 1979, 5–6.

stripped to the waist, and barefoot, wore white pants and Yoruba beads. Sheets of mylar, which hung behind them as they performed on a narrow platform, served as a second, unplanned viewing screen, their images refracting as they moved. At times Rosenthal's head disappeared, and she was transformed into a headless woman undulating to the drumbeat. At other times, a fold in the mylar made Canty's head into a double profile that was like a totemic image.

At regular intervals throughout the performance, Rosenthal stopped her recitation and sang Portuguese songs a cappella. The break in mood among her tales of a young girl in Rio, the mental probing of a mature woman, and her 1940s Latin songs had a jarring impact.

One song was about one of her father's business acquaintances who, in order to ingratiate himself, brought Rosenthal exotic animals caught in the jungle. An anteater died during a train trip, and an alligator was doomed, too, imprisoned in a bathtub. And then Rosenthal sang, *Eu Nesse Paso Vou Ate Honolulu,* which, loosely translated, means, "in the club where I dance the kangaroos dance too." All the songs dealt obliquely with the previous dialogue. Through these stories, we became aware of her current anxieties and visions. After stating, "I feel I am in the process of being sucked into a black hole . . . the oscillating tension between being a hero or an asshole is killing me," she sang *O O Opa! Que Danca Sopa!* The innocence of the song belied her wrenching psychological state.

After a final comment on a vision of herself becoming part of the universe—"so if one day you cannot find me, just remember: I will be missing in action"—Rosenthal lit two sparklers as the audience lit those handed out earlier. Only the sparklers were visible in the darkened room, perhaps offering a metaphor for hope.

In an interview with me in August, Rosenthal talked about her performance process: "I take aspects of my life that I feel were useless and worthless, and through performance redeem them. It's a means of understanding and re-creation. Putting them in an art form has a mythmaking quality. It is also an order making. Although these things happened in the past, my way of observing them makes them become what they were not before. . . . What a lot of people don't realize about an art performance is that it is happening right there before their eyes. No matter how much you work on the text, how much you prepare beforehand, the actual transformation is happening right there in front of the audience."

Ruth Weisberg

"Autobiographical Journey"

Those of us who witnessed Rachel Rosenthal's performance of *Bonsoir, Dr. Schön!* at Los Angeles Contemporary Exhibitions (LU-ACE) on October 30, had a rare evening of serendipity and catharsis. The performance presented a dense layering of idea, story, improvised music, and self-revelation. In retrospect, I realize how seamless and elegant the structure of the piece must have been in order to contain such stunning complexity. In addition, only a consummate actress could have guided us through such compelling autobiographical transformations. The dangers in autobiographical art are legion: solipsisms that interest an audience of one. In contrast, Rosenthal's exploration of self stripped away the ordinary meaning of symbols and images so that deeper connections might cause epiphany or catharsis. Along the way, she even made Halloween paraphernalia profound.

On the evening before Halloween, a large audience filtered into LACE, a TV monitor was casually turned on, and gradually the crowd grew quiet in order to listen to a series of short, spontaneous tributes by friends to Rosenthal's genius, courage, and beauty. Familiar art world figures looked handsome, cheerful, and intense on the TV monitor as they spoke eloquently of the artist's influence on their lives. Through their praise, they revealed themselves.

The audience gradually realized that a ghostly figure onstage was not a sculpture, but Rosenthal herself, in a gauze cocoon. Two assistants unwrapped her until her only covering was a contorted gold mask. She impressed an audience, casual about public nudity, with the terrible vulnerability of her nakedness. The assistants began to indicate various defects: the flab, the force of gravity, and the effects of age on

Originally published in *Artweek,* November 22, 1980, 3.

her body. Her voice-over spoke of a childhood governess who praised the cautious moon for its facade. Rosenthal commented that she was like the moon, appearing backless but with vampires and spiders hidden on the dark side. "Control of self is not power, but who knew then." A monstrous transformation began. Bats, spiders, and snakes were taped to her body, and she was coated with familiar orange Halloween frosting. Meanwhile, Cynthia Kastan, on the TV monitor, praised Rosenthal as an alchemist and as ennobling: "I love everything about you." Rosenthal didn't. Aware of the other side of the moon, she began to mutter, her pain so palpable and so extreme that I was grateful to be taking notes. Then came frantic self-abhorrence—in a frenzy of animal gestures, she rid herself of her gruesome covering.

Throughout this section, the random juxtaposition of adulation and praise from the video and the violent and pathetic image of Rosenthal onstage undermined our comfortable beliefs and perceptions. Underneath the artist's mask was another mask.

The next phase was Jupiter. Rosenthal, masked in silver, was dressed like a rich and dapper boulevardier. She spoke of her wealthy, autocratic, and adored father. Photographs of her as a child, in Paris with her father, flashed behind her. No one could have invented images more expressive of unconscious erotic power and precocious beauty. With her pet rat, Tatty Wattles, on her head, Rosenthal became Dr. Schön from Alban Berg's opera, *Lulu*. She seemed powerful, alternating charm and arrogance, smashing telephones and terrifying pet rats.

In the third phase, named for the sky, Rosenthal was dressed in her familiar overalls; her mask was white. She began to approximate the woman we hear praised by her friends on the TV. In an inspired sequence she radically altered our idea of pumpkins by carving three with gestures that transformed them from spheres into helixes, cutting them into long spirals as a European might peel an apple. In an image of great power, the three pumpkin spirals were decorated with gold, silver, and white masks, and hung on the wall with their entrails dangling.

In a section that bordered on the didactic, Rosenthal spoke of her need for a new role model for power; she chose the image of John Cage's room, empty of all but bed, piano, and plants, and open to sky and river—a conduit for power. She then described the spiral of her life and the manner of her anticipated "good" death. She saw herself as a beetle tied to a pole who will walk in circles until all the rope is used up. After describing this spiral with a joyous, celebratory dance, in an amazing final image she stopped at dead center, against a backdrop of stars in deep space, and emerged crowned with a huge, grinning pumpkin. She became the light, merged with the stars, and we were astonished to find that we had made the long, arduous, and triumphant journey with her.

Ruth Weisberg

"Reaching for Revelations"

Rachel Rosenthal's *Leave Her in Naxos,* performed on February 13 at the Museum of Art, UC Santa Barbara, was a strange sort of valentine, but a brilliant and disturbing performance. It made love, especially erotic love, seem like third-rate romance—barren, pointless, and dirty. The piece began with an ensemble of six actors muffled in raincoats and assuming stop-action caricatures of the pornographers of our imagination. Rosenthal entered wearing a dress so garish and vulgar that she evoked an image of Las Vegas in the extreme. Yet she did look ravishing and sexually attractive during the initial mock dialogue between the mythic figures of Ariadne and Theseus, in which she played both parts. Her tone was argumentative and neurotic, with an amusing use of the vernacular, set against the operatic melodrama of *Adriadne auf Naxos* by Richard Strauss.

As always in a Rosenthal performance, there were many levels of meaning and intention: the mythic, the personal, and the esthetic. This performance seemed to ride that edge between art and life more perilously than her work ever did before. However, the more revelatory the piece became, the better it worked, though the subtext of myth seemed a bit forced at the very end.

The visual and the auditory combined to create art of tremendous visceral power. In an early scene an orange-tinted woman and a blue-tinted man began the timeless erotic dance of courtship. The color of the dancers' bodies had just the right distancing effect, essential in making art distinct from life. Rosenthal intervened and covered the genitals of the woman with a diaper and of the man with a huge, fabricated phallus. The dancers then demonstrated a wide variety of

Originally published in *Artweek,* March 14, 1981, 6.

sexual positions; their dance was dispassionate, artful, and absurd. Again, there was a sense of stopped action as they froze in the traditional poses of Tantric Yoga.

Two other activities were also interwoven. Polaroids were taken of the members of the audience to heighten their sense of being voyeurs of this spectacle. Throughout, the camera was persuasively used as an agent of secondhand experience and pornographic intent. Meanwhile Rosenthal had begun a monologue about a nameless lost object. She began in an ordinary, very familiar way: "Did I have it when I unlocked the door? Let's see—I was carrying the groceries in my left arm and in my right." This juxtaposition of anxious dialogue and remote, careful sex evoked a terrible sense of loss—like a kind of extended postcoital sadness.

Rosenthal then recited a litany of her loves and lovers in response to the inane questions asked by another member of the ensemble whose costume was even more tawdry than hers. This woman's banality became an inspired counterpoint to Rosenthal's persistent self-revelation. We were presented with a vivid picture of beautiful, red-haired Rachel in Paris and New York, courted and bedded but never able to love unconditionally. Love had various aspects in this piece: frustrating, seductive, inane, cheap, and, ultimately, in a superlative monologue, terrifying. Toward the end, the performance became an exorcism of past love—Rosenthal, standing in a heart delineated by red candles, intoned: "Dead things in me, let these things die." Next her hair was gently and carefully shaved by a woman in red until we saw Rosenthal looking like a lama, ascetic and spiritual. She appeared very masculine with her bald head, but was still absurdly dressed in her garish, spangled costume. The shaving of Rosenthal's hair seemed an experience of death for the audience. It was fully accepted and even desired by Rosenthal; nevertheless, this gesture of loving violence appeared to be a violation and a denial. The result was an image powerful in its duality and its ability to disturb.

The end of the performance, which used the triumphant and streetwise music of Yoko Ono's "Kiss, Kiss, Kiss," was not able to supersede the image of the bald Rosenthal in her valentine setting. The quickness of the exorcism was unbelievable. In other performances, notably in her last one on October 30 at LACE, a profound epiphany melded actor and audience in the final moment. But this time the real catharsis for the audience was found outside the format of the performance. When Rosenthal took her bows, the audience gave her a standing ovation. There also may have been some ambiguity in the applause: Was it for Rosenthal's life, her act, or her art?

Among other praiseworthy aspects of this performance was the excellent ensemble-playing of the group. Particularly fine were the performances of Camille Bertolet and Jim Cathey, the dancers of Tantric Yoga, and Molly Cleator, Susan Kaplan, Stuart Miller, and Carl Miranda.

Melinda Wortz

"Los Angeles"

Rachel Rosenthal's performance piece *Soldier of Fortune* at Tortue Gallery was characteristically autobiographical in content. In a monologue she let it all hang out: the vast wealth as a child of a jewel merchant in Paris, the sensual delights, from Russian caviar to Belgian linen. And then the repeated financial disasters—her father's, her own, her "nest egg" in 1980 of $178,000 for which she felt guilty, and its loss in a swindle. This deluge of disaster was all delivered while devouring a seven-course meal, elegantly served, and a bottle of champagne.

Rosenthal's story is exotic, fascinating, and horrifying, as it has been in other performances, but now it is both topical and timeless. The fiddling (or eating)-while-Rome-burns theme is directly analogous to the Reagan administration—its most lavish inaugural ball(s) ever and its lack of compassion for welfare recipients. Rosenthal's plunge into the realm of the destitute and the suicidal and her triumphant emergence are what we would hope for our country and the world.

Throughout the dinner, Rosenthal wore a long, flowing caftan and a tiara perched atop her curls. Toward the end of the meal, staggering drunkenly off the stage, she described a nearly literal trip to Death Valley and her struggle to return to the living. Finally, in drunken confidence, she exclaimed, "I've changed—no longer the plump Tarzana housewife who used to make art on the side. I am a hustler, a soldier of fortune. Some people hate me for it, some love me for it—it's all the same, just a game."

In a dramatic finale, Rosenthal exchanged her elegant duds for a camouflage suit and boots, threw off her wig to reveal her shaved head, and climbed a ladder to the roof to shower the audience with coins

Originally published in *Art News,* October 1981, 189.

while teetering unsteadily on the edge, with great skill. Rosenthal's performances are always distinctive in their staging and acting. This one went beyond these attractions, enhanced by her exotic autobiography, to present the possibility for optimism in the face of great need, in both the art world and the world at large. The performance incorporated a blackout for the arts.

Emily Hicks

Excerpts from "Examining the Taboo"

It was fitting that for her first appearance in her own performance space, Espace DBD, Rachel Rosenthal transformed performance into a metacommentary on performance: *Performance and the Masochist Tradition.* This was one part of the tripartite *Taboo Subjects.* Appearing with her were Sue Dakin in *Insanity and Death,* and Italian performance artist Giuditta Tornetta in *I Hate Mondays.*

Analyzing the role of death in masochism, Rosenthal explained that the masochist courts, but rarely embraces, death. Remembering that the earliest actors separated themselves from the community by playing the role of the dead, we can see a continuity between ideas of death in the origins of theater and its function in contemporary performance art, in which death is a limit. It was Antonin Artaud who wrote, in the *First Manifesto of the Theatre of Cruelty,* "We cannot go on prostituting the idea of theatre whose only value is in its excruciating, magical relation to reality and danger." It was the deliberate putting of ourselves in a dangerous or painful situation that Rosenthal addressed. As Artaud tried to revive theater by attending to the taste of the audience for crime, erotic obsessions, and savagery, so Rosenthal rejuvenated performance art by confronting the audience with its role as sadist. She recalled the performance art tradition in which artists have been cut, bitten, shot, and nailed. In Dakin's and Rosenthal's pieces, there was a refusal of the ego/body to remain inviolate. Dakin described the penetration of her being by an alien form; Rosenthal dared the audience to pierce her wrists with fish hooks. In what only appeared to be a contradiction, Tornetta (Brenda Spencer) sought to

Originally published in *Artweek,* November 14, 1981, 16.

overcome her isolation, which she perceived as boredom, by shooting her schoolmates.

The audience entered to find the three performers seated at a table, as if in an academic conference. However, Dakin's wrists were bound high above her head and her back was to the audience; Rosenthal was gagged, her hands tied behind her back; Tornetta was gagged. Dakin freed herself and began her narrative. The others situated themselves against a wall. . . .

. . . Rosenthal's piece was structured as a direct address to the audience. She introduced the stories of three masochists: (1) Mr. M, whose condition came to the attention of French psychoanalyst Michel de M'uzan, (2) an Oglala Sioux, a pledger in the sun dance, and (3) Stelarc, an Australian performance artist who resides in Japan. All practice the suspension of their bodies by means of hooks inserted through the flesh. Rosenthal found the common motivating force to be a longing for the dissolution of the ego. Shifting from the lecture to a more direct approach, Rosenthal stood before members of the audience with fish hooks, gesturing them to insert them in her wrists. The reaction was one of horror. She had her technical assistant perform the task. Slides behind her showed Stelarc suspended by fish hooks inserted all over his body. Rosenthal's point was not to demonstrate publicly an unusual sexual preference but rather to confront members of the audience with their fear of and revulsion from violence toward a performer, at the same time reminding them that they play the role of the sadist—and "the sadist always gives up first." Rosenthal concluded that masochism is a psychophysiological structure that originates from a position of power. It is not an illness. Performance artists, in her view, seek pain in order to rise above society as shamans, magicians, sexologists, martyr-devils, and demonic saints. . . .

. . . Although performance art has never shied away from taboo subjects, Rosenthal's decision to ground this presentation in the subjects of sexuality and violence is significant. Rather than continuing the autobiographical direction of earlier work, she is now placing in perspective both her own performance art and the genre itself.

Rachel Rosenthal as the Bad Queen in an Instant Fairy Tale, c. 1963–66. Horseshoe Stage Theater, Los Angeles. Photo: unknown

Farghestan, stoneware, 1973. Photo: Rachel Rosenthal

Charm, Rachel Rosenthal *(left)* and members of the Instant Theatre Company, 1977. Mount St. Mary's Art Gallery, Los Angeles. Photo: Cynthia Upchurch. Permission by Rachel Rosenthal

The Head of Olga K., Rachel Rosenthal *(in chair)* and members of the Instant Theatre Company, 1977. Institute for Dance and Experimental Art, Santa Monica, California. Photo: David E. Moreno

The Arousing (Shock, Thunder), 1979. Institute for Dance and Experimental Art, Santa Monica, California. Photo: Lyn Smith. Permission by Rachel Rosenthal

My Brazil, Rachel Rosenthal with Anthony Canty, 1979. Institute for Dance and Experimental Art, Santa Monica, California. Photo: Kim Kaufman. Permission by Rachel Rosenthal

Rachel Rosenthal with Tatti Wattles in *Traps,* 1982. Espace DBD, Los Angeles. © Photo: Basia Kenton

Rachel Rosenthal as the Bag Lady in *Gaia, Mon Amour,* 1983. The House, Santa Monica, California. © Photo: Basia Kenton

KabbaLAmobile, 1984. Parking lot of Department of Water and Power, Los Angeles. © Photo: Basia Kenton

Rachel Rosenthal with human and canine members of the cast of
The Others, 1984. The Japan America Theater, Los Angeles.
© Photo: Basia Kenton

L.O.W. in Gaia, 1987. Laguna Art Museum, Laguna Beach, California. Photo: Jan Deen

Was Black, with Linda Sibio, Rachel Rosenthal, Curtis York, Shelley Cook, Cynthia King *(from left to right).* 1986. John Anson Ford Theater, Los Angeles. Photo: Jan Deen

Rachel Rosenthal as Marie Antoinette in *Rachel's Brain,* 1987. Los
Angeles Theater Center, Los Angeles. Photo: Jan Deen

Rachel Rosenthal as Homo Erectus in *Rachel's Brain,* 1987. Los Angeles Theater Center, Los Angeles. Photo: Gail Garretson. Permission by Rachel Rosenthal

Rachel Rosenthal with "cauliflower brain" in *Rachel's Brain*, 1987.
Los Angeles Theater Center, Los Angeles. Photo: Jan Deen

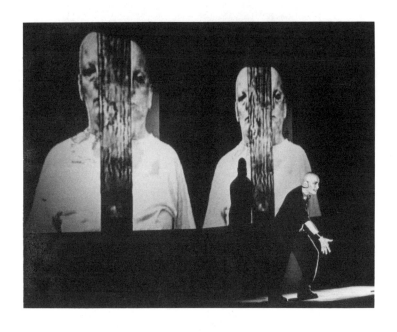

Pangaean Dreams (video image by Dain Olsen), 1990. Santa Monica Museum of Art, Santa Monica, California. Photo: Jan Deen

Rachel Rosenthal and Harvey Perr and members of the "Throng" in *Zone,* 1994. UCLA Center for the Performing Arts, Wadsworth Theater, Los Angeles. Photo: Jan Deen

Timepiece, The Rachel Rosenthal Company: Rachel Rosenthal, Imesol Moreno, C. Derrick Jones, Michael Morrissey, Rochelle Fabb, Tad Coughenour, 1996. State Playhouse, Cal State Los Angeles. Photo: Martin Cohen

Sally Banes

Excerpts from "Rachel Rosenthal:

As the Egg Turns"

. . . *Traps* is a global exorcism. Can performance art change the world? In the cultures where it can (or seems to), performance isn't an esoteric form for art world audiences. Given the context of her performance, Rosenthal comes as close to restoring some kind of faith in the power of consciousness as anyone. There's something she understands about the charismatic, healing force of the performer who can inhabit and then shed personae like so many masks that is worlds away from the mystical mumbo-jumbo so often served up in the marriage of feminism and religion or in the fashionable readings of performer as latter-day shaman. If Rosenthal is any kind of priestess, she is the Zen sort, who whacks the neophyte across the ass and cracks the most irreverent jokes, all integral to subtly pointing out the way. No accounts I've read of Rosenthal's "holistic" outlook and "ritualistic" performances prepared me for a presence so unpriggish, so ironic, so rough-hewn. On the other hand, her picture on the Franklin Furnace program—a woman with jutting jaw, shaved head, black gash of a mouth, pugnacious gestures, and camouflage pants—belied the moments of grace, coquetry, tenderness, and warmth.

The performance begins with the projection of a color slide of the ocean, out of focus. We hear the ocean's sounds as Rosenthal, in a white hooded cape and mask, scatters dried beans among the spectators. The ghostly figure stands still as Rosenthal's voice, on tape, recites the riddle of doctrine from Huang Po: "The fundamental doctrine of the Dharma is that there are no Dharmas, yet this doctrine of no-Dharma is in itself a Dharma." For Rosenthal, the mind's own traps

Originally published in *The Village Voice,* December 6, 1983, 125.

are fundamental, but there are also endless traps that are biological, social, political.

In a scene that seems straight from a Japanese Noh play, she sits at a table, lights a candle, and repeatedly twists bits of paper into puppet moths that fly into the flame and explode. Disrobing to become the guerrilla soldier of the program photo, Rosenthal mimes shooting and tossing grenades while she raves about insects in a virtuoso mad scene. Another change of character, and she is a simpering hostess. "I would like to tell you a little story in pictures." As she snaps her fingers to signal slide changes, she re-creates the events that led up to her in-advertently causing the fall of her blind dog, Zatoichi, from her studio balcony. Now Rosenthal becomes professorial. The anecdote was an object lesson in how we lay traps—"acts committed by one part of you to entrap the other part." She illustrates her analysis of traps with poster-paper titles. But after urging us to recall our own "recent and/ or spectacular traps," she exhorts us to broaden our vision, to see how minuscule our own traps are from the perspective of the biosphere.

She tells a fairy tale about two countries poised on the brink of war. Then her honeyed voice mimics the narration of an educational film as slide images show, through the interaction of hard-boiled eggs (halved and whole) and small colorful toy animals, trees, and geomet-ric forms, the story of viruses. The last slide shows the eggs destroyed by the invader toys. Rosenthal blows out the candle with a scream.

But there is a coda. "It can't end like this!" Rosenthal protests. She reminds us that we are not insects, programmed by our genes. She obsesses about scientific theories that point to hope for the future. Five times she picks up an egg from the white table. "Will it be all . . ." she throws the egg on the floor. It splatters—"Or nothing?" The sixth time she throws the egg at the audience. "Chicken!" she reviles us as some duck. The egg is hard-boiled.

Finally she urges us to look for the unexpected, untapped sources of affection in the world. Slides show her combing and caressing a pet rat, to the sound of Chopin. The final slide shows a whole egg. And somehow, that simple hope, utterly without sentimentality, makes you believe her.

Fidel Danieli

Excerpts from "Gaia, Mon Amour"

... The title refers to the acclaimed French film *Hiroshima Mon Amour,* first shown fifteen years after the bombing of that city. Forty years after the first use of atomic weaponry the danger of their ultimate use still persists. Our violence committed against one another continues to multiply as more contaminants ruin lives, as more species disappear, and as the world's stockpiles and ill-considered reliance on sophisticated armaments grows.

Some interesting comparisons can be made between Resnais' film and Rosenthal's performance. It is often overlooked that the film was scripted by Marguerite Duras, one of Europe's leading women writers, and the story's unnamed female lead is French and Jewish. Both works are antiwar statements and begin with an overwhelming sequence of images of destruction, suffering, and death. Both begin their story lines with a rising up of the leads from the horizontal—the "atomic" lovers from their bed, the comic Rosenthal from beneath her blanket of garbage. Next comes the flashback to the death of the actress's lover, just as Rosenthal's first move is to an earth-formed body of the symbolic "dying mother" figure. The movie's star Emmanuelle Riva proceeds to move into and out of her role as an actress making a film within a film, and is blocked by and works through memories of her personal tragedies. Rosenthal, too, moves from role to role in her dramatization. She pretends to have lost her place, supposedly steps out of character, and begins the piece over to take it in another direction. The film depends on the use of dissolving, interrupting cross-cut flashbacks to explore the damage of the heroine's past in the same way the performer utilizes slides, areas of action, and changing personae to

Originally published in *Visual Art* (Summer 1984), 29–32.

outline the "herstory" of the prepatriarchal world. Both works hold out the promise of the salving effect of recalling the past at either the level of private trauma or mythological reconstruction. Rosenthal proclaims she's laid to rest the ghosts of her past in one of the piece's most electrifying moments when she embraces the enormous, projected photo image of her mother. If we must allow ourselves to be terrorized by the past, the present, and the future, she has upped the ante. Rosenthal enlarges from personal experience and now takes on the global and the cosmic.

A long, ambitious, and demanding work, *Gaia, Mon Amour* is elaborately complex and filled with numerous marvelous meldings of image, text, movement, and sound that are well worth examining. The first slide is explained by a taped voice as the picture of a fungus killing an ant, with the moral that "its triumph will be short-lived: a successful parasite never kills its host." There immediately follows a long, astonishing speech by male voice-over in rhythmic and maddeningly hypnotic cadence outlining the prerogative of masculine authority to "rape and kill" the earth; that line of male supremacy of the devotees of Mars, the paradigm and nadir of machismo, that still believes in "the conquest of nature" without reasoning what people are to do, how they are to live, once the host is killed. Heavily loaded pictures of brightly packaged war toys alternate with distressing images of tortured, maimed, and dead animals, waste, and pollution. At the blackout the horrendous, long torrent of a bomb explosion fills and reverberates through the hall. It is all very obvious and equally offensive and disturbing. This is, however, no straw man she has set up, but the very real specter of total annihilation.

Rosenthal's first appearance is striking in an opposite mode. Onstage but hidden all this time, she rises from a pile of debris into contrasting red and green lights, to the sound of the mechanical tapping of a geiger counter and the buzzing of flies. She fends off this aerial plague, swats, and kills one. The long Master Race monologue blows out to the final eternity of a nuclear blast, and her first action is the killing of a fly. These similes define both ends of an enormously wide scope that extends from the microscopic to the omnipotent, from the mundane to the supernatural, from the life sustaining to the destruction of nature.

Slowly folding to the ground, the artist is resurrected in a magical about-face to the "glasses and false nose," cartoonish know-it-all. Tension is released as she undercuts Gaia's assertions and remarks sarcastically on the intolerableness of women: "Mothers are *the* worst! Too much tit, not enough tit. Mothers are always wrong." This is a reference to the damage wrought on her by her own mother, then a segue to Devouring Goddesses and processes of destruction that ends with the declaration, "Mothers demand the dissolution of the Self!" They create, then reabsorb. Continuing with her broad exaggeration, she outlines a feminist mythos crediting the invention of everything from sexual domination, medicine, the calendar, agriculture, and the industry of pottery to women. It is done with such keen humor so as to reassure the skeptical, or those in the audience who may not have been exposed to these theories of developments in prehistoric matriarchies.

Why did these historical matriarchies disappear? Rosenthal places the blame on the literal interpretation of the need for blood sacrifices to Goddesses of Destruction, unearthing skulls from the "dying mother" mound, terming this ritual demand the "Norman Rockwell of the Neolithic." Embracing the huge projection of her own mother at the time of Rosenthal's birth she buries, with a sense of due and moving finality, her autobiographical base: "It took me five decades to realize she was mortal . . . and to accept not loving her. And to weep no more." Here, as in the opening moments, the opposition of scale is crucial. The ant and the fungus, the war toys and the bomb, the bag lady and the fly. The mother is younger than the daughter; the daughter, now an adult, is tiny compared to her memory of the mother.

The loose draping of her costume suggests a ragged street person or a comical bag lady who, when she turns to face us, startles and reassures. With short-cropped hair and overdone jewelry, she is wearing heavy-rimmed glasses and a large fake nose and in her opening line declares the place a dump. She raises us up for the relief of fun with a burlesquing, cliché-ridden wise-acre. This character will be a fountain of practicality and folk wisdom. Clomping about and falling into grotesquely exaggerated poses, she moves to the foreground. She cavalierly treats a "dying mother," a shrouded, shaped mound of earth and proclaims ironically on the triumph of destiny, of death. Then in quick succession she is shocked, pleads, rages, and loses the story line. In sudden turn she metamorphizes from the clown to the clutching child to the angry adult to the performer whose personal problems have leaked into the make-believe and distract her from the business at hand. Okay, crew, let's take it again from the blackout.

What crawls out of the refuse pile of contemporary culture this time is a phantom from the dawn of society. Not Rosenthal as Mother

Earth; she *is* Gaia. Standing firmly planted on wide-spread legs she moves only from the waist up. Her stare is fixed, nearly demonic in its intensity. Her hands and arms gesture, meaning to convey animals, suggestive of free-flowing and ever-changing variations of tai chi, symbolizing contained energy, alternately expanding the size and range of her body, and framing and focusing attention to her face. Her costume no longer appears to be cast-offs but classic, even archaic. An open-necked, heavyweight dress, tight at the elbows and belted at the waist, falls into patterns of deeply shadowed folds as she moves. Her makeup recalls ancient Egypt; her oversized and mismatched bronzen earrings now hark back to the treasuries of Mycenae. The extreme illumination—blue from the side and bright white overhead—highlights her constant, slow motion throughout the monologue and produces an otherworldly, disembodied effect. Her speech is sharp and threatening as she describes her various female guises as the source of birth and nourishment, but also, as destroyer. The final ringing words are, "I am the Matrix. You are in and of my Body. I am the Mother. I am the Daughter. I am the Lover. But scorned, I am also Lilith, the Maid of Desolation. And I dance in the ruins of cities." At that moment Rosenthal literally and single-handedly could avenge the wrongs done to the earth.

As Rosenthal next constructs a cozy corner at the rear left, we come to realize and appreciate that she has composed the large, square performance space in the form of a symbolic mandala. The foreground, the front one-third, is the zone of the mythic, of living, of dying. The center is the arena for action, storytelling, and conflict. The rear one-third is modern life—on the left the false values we hold so dear and on the right the pile of commercial excrement of a package-wrap culture that won't go away. In two opposing corners are horizontal death mounds—one ancient, one modern. In the other two she sets up temporary constructions wherein the ego may be asserted—one modern, and as we shall see later, one ancient.

In voice-over the Gaia persona describes the earth as a hospitable place, intended to be protected from the unleashing of the power of the stars, thus returning to the antinuclear premise of the work. The blended slides take us from a lovely home interior in stages of distant and grander scale to end with views of galaxies. In seconds we travel from the hearth's comfort to the infinity of expanding outer space. "We have come of age. The Age of Chaos!"

For a second time Rosenthal deals with the question of what went wrong in a truly impressive monologue as a Year King or "Moon Bull." This concerns a tradition of killing or forcing suicide on a male leader when times were bad, or after an allotted reign (one or seven years), or as has been held, when the queen simply tired of his stud service. Rosenthal dons a long robe, erects an open framework construction, and stands in quiet dignity holding its vertical supports. The screen protects and it imprisons, it stands apart and it inhibits. Another lengthy speech is delivered in a declarative monotone, finding its rhythms in short sentences and strings of vivid phrases. It opens with, "When I was a young boy . . . ," and eerily enough—with her strong features barely lit, close-shaved head, and the ambiguity of the covering garment—she becomes a heroic male, he who will be the first king to refuse to die. "He" describes the self-destruction of a previous ruler and says he had wanted to call out the king's real name to acknowledge the victim's individuality as a way of expiating his guilt at watching this annual, imposed immolation. He asserts his masculine ego, unwilling to comply with the shedding of more male blood in ultimate and obsequious honor to the Queen/Mother/Goddess. The result is a cleverly reported offstage battle of the sexes and the triumph of the patriarchy with reason and logic, theorems and language, systems, geometry and grids used as weapons to subjugate women. The conclusion hinges on these two brilliant lines; with patriarchy, "The ME generation is born . . . but they had thrown the babies out with the bloodbath water."

There comes a plea for sanity and balance and a moving healing ceremony. Establishing a sacred spot front-center, she drums and chants as pictures of arid but voluptuous rock formations are projected behind her. Still seated, she shifts effortlessly to her final somber, even subdued Mother Earth speech: "To love me, Gaia, is to love yourselves. To observe nature is the same as introspection. To revere her works is the same as self-respect." And at the end, "Embrace me. It is the same as holding yourselves. It is all ONE. I am you. YOU ARE GAIA NOW."

Jacki Apple

Excerpts from "The Romance of Automobiles"

Carplays—a three-day, Labor Day weekend performance festival co-sponsored by the Mark Taper Forum and the Museum of Contemporary Art in conjunction with their exhibition *The Automobile and Culture*—was billed as "an unabashed celebration of our love affair with the car." . . .

. . . *KabbaLAmobile,* a brilliant tour de force by performance artist Rachel Rosenthal, exemplified not only what a Carplay could be, but what great art is all about. It was an exhilarating, "magical" experience—one of those brief and shining moments when we are transported beyond our ordinary lives and given a glimpse of another reality, another extraordinary realm in which we may also reside.

KabbaLAmobile was a perfect synthesis of form and content, a breathtakingly dramatic visual spectacle at the service of its subject matter. Rosenthal is in control of style and structure as her tools of communication, not as ends in themselves. The meaning of language itself came into a new perspective as previously unrelated concepts were juxtaposed, merged, and transformed in a spectacular evocation.

In the intense late afternoon light, Rosenthal made an unforgettably dramatic entrance. She was dressed in a billowing white costume with red and black quilted sections and yellow sash, her head shaved, her face made up in white with black and yellow lines, brilliant blue across the eyes, her fingernails gleaming white. Arms wide open, palms up, kimono-like sleeves flapping in the wind, she walked the full length of the Department of Water and Power parking lot and climbed a scaffolding platform facing the audience, like a sorcerer who had suddenly and mysteriously materialized from the Tarot.

Originally published in *Artweek,* September 29, 1984, 1.

The massive faceless institutional architecture of the Dorothy Chandler Music Center loomed behind her. A pale white moon hovered in the bright blue sky like a wispy cloud. She stood before us as a magician of the highest order, an alchemist who called forth all the powers of transmutation through the Word. Her voice thundered forth, "Remember the name YDVD, our God interpreted in my name . . . Porsche 962 Jaguar XJR5 Lola T616 . . . Datsun 280Z SSA . . . Seven divided three against three, with one balancing the others . . . one has merit, one is defective, and one balances the other two."

The cars appeared—six convertibles and one red Dodge Daytona—driven by three women and four men from Tom Anthony's Precision Driving Team. For the next twenty minutes, they performed elaborately choreographed, synchronized maneuvers across the vast parking lot and around Rosenthal. They moved in blocks of three, circled in lines, about-faced; serpentine Ss turned into braids. Their "dance," which was directly related to the cabalistic aspects of the text, culminated with the red car approaching and circling Rosenthal on its side, on two wheels.

Amazingly, the spectacle of the stunt cars did not overshadow Rosenthal's performance but was, instead, perfectly balanced with it. Her hands and arms moved continually as she spoke, as if they were a remote control device that manipulated the cars. Her presence was compelling, mesmerizing. She proclaimed "the great NAME, heroic and terrible, square and triangle, engraved as YDVD pointed it to me." She chanted as if possessed.

Her text was based on material from cabalistic literature, including the Book of Creation, interwoven with automotive information. The cabala is a mystical Jewish system of interpretation of the Scriptures based on the belief that every word, letter, number, and even accent of the Scriptures contain mysteries. These signs and writings are used as amulets and in magical practices. Rosenthal applied the cabalistic concept to our contemporary culture via the automobile.

She called forth the "two points—one under the other—serving the smallest golem-possessor of permutations, whose form is the shape of SAMEKH MEM . . . Bore and stroke Turbocharger; Waste gate; Valve gear; Compression ratio; Maximum boost pressure; Redline Torque; Power Power POWER . . . and the point is the dwelling of the living God breathing through us all."

The music, composed, performed, and produced by The Dark Bob especially for this piece, beautifully complemented the text and infused the visual spectacle with heightened drama, tension, and energy. This collaboration exemplifies what successful collaboration is all about. Well-acquainted with Rosenthal's previous work, Dark Bob spent a lot of time reading and thinking about her *KabbaLAmobile* text, the way she uses her voice and body and the meaning of what she was saying. The color, tone, and textures of the music, the changes of rhythm and mood from section to section, and the overall orchestration not only reflected Dark Bob's complete esthetic and spiritual rapport with Rosenthal's intention and vision, but also gave her new ways of working with her text, both vocally and through movement.

In *KabbaLAmobile* Rosenthal defined what differentiates quality performance art from the mundane theatrical exercises of most of the other *Carplays* pieces. Despite the extreme theatricality of the performance, Rosenthal wasn't "acting." She became the medium of expression for her material. She took us into her reality, allowing us to experience it with her. And for that brief and precious moment, she altered our vision of the world. This is what great art can and should do. It doesn't happen very often, but when it does I am deeply grateful. *KabbaLAmobile* was a masterpiece!

Sylvie Drake

Excerpts from "Rachel Rosenthal Puts on the Dog at Japan America"

. . .Tuesday at the Japan America Theater she [Rachel Rosenthal] shared the stage with about forty animals, a few ordinary people, and several children, but it was her show all the way.

. . . . Rosenthal, who has proclaimed that, in the past few years, she has "received a kind of injunction, like a calling, to do art that is healing to the Earth," took a huge risk with her latest performance piece—and won. *The Others* was a cry—outcry?—for animal rights and a valentine to all the animals who grace our planet.

With help from Don Preston's unobtrusive music, projected texts of Descartes, Milan Kundera, and Harry Beston (moral reinforcement), and with the magnifying live video of James Kent Arnold (a stealthy omnipresence), Rosenthal engaged in a variety of pointed monologues, alternatively pleading, entertaining, and informative.

Intermingled with the words and the video was a discreet, playful parade of stunning animals—a gorgeous Appaloosa mare, regal snakes, a pygmy goat, dogs, cats, rabbits, rats, hamsters, squirrels, doves, parrots, monkeys, macaws, and a turkey. . . .

. . . Rosenthal asked for our compassion, shocked us with accounts of appallingly commonplace violence done to animals, and proved over and over that we treat them no better than our own kind.

If the outrage was predictable, the facts were often unfamiliar and almost always startling. Was it preachy? Here and there.

Most savvy and skillful was Rosenthal's drunken barfly's account of a romantic misadventure. It dipped extensively into our lexicon of

Originally published in *Los Angeles Times,* December 21, 1984, Calendar, 1, 22.

animal imagery, stingingly revealing the extent to which we abuse animals in our verbal subconscious as well as physically.

On the whole *The Others* could have used more of that sort of indirection. A segment on hearts—including, inescapably, a baboon heart—came close to that same sort of accusation by allusion. But a good deal of the rest of the show was preachment as much as performance. Not art, exactly.

. . . . While the audience at *The Others* seemed largely to consist of enthusiastic anti-vivisectionists and other animal activists, the show was *not* a tract for the already persuaded. The success of any piece of work must be measured in part at least by the degree to which it draws us into the realm of its primary concerns. In that, Rosenthal amply succeeded. . . .

Donald Karwelis

"Speaking to the Enemy"

One of the most difficult and challenging things that an artist can do is take on subject matter that, in the instant-gratification 1980s, we prefer to avoid or have learned to deflect. Rachel Rosenthal, in a solo performance of *L.O.W. in Gaia,* took on the subjects of aging, death, pollution by toxic and nuclear wastes, and humankind's relationship to the earth and its creatures, resensitizing her audience with a near-demonic energy.

Performing in the Festival of Arts Theatre under the sponsorship of the Laguna Art Museum, Rosenthal, who began her career as a dancer and actress, brought all her acquired skills and experience to this piece. Her personae were embodied in three characters: the fortieth-century monster, not of woman born; Gaia—the Death Crone (the Greek earth goddess); and Rachel as Rachel-the-tourist.

The experience of time in *Gaia* was the experience of dislocation, transformation, and metamorphosis. One persona became another with a change in sound and background slides, or one time evolved into another with a change in lighting. To see each scene as a distinct event, however, was to be distracted, for Rosenthal's logic was not linear. It was more related to a dreamtime, where rapid leaps are possible. For example: the "monster," a lipless, fingerless, hairless creature making birdlike sounds, was innocently curious in its quest for flies to eat in the irradiated future Garden of Eden/Horrors, even while it was frustratingly occupied in a search for treasured bits and pieces that were actually shards of twentieth-century radioactive warning signs. A moment later, Rachel-the-tourist was onstage in battle fatigues, proclaiming in glibly comic tones her love of the earth and her determina-

Originally published in *Artweek,* September 5, 1987, 18.

tion to use this, her first vacation in years, to get her act together in the peace and quiet of the desert.

Rosenthal moved like a dancer while telling her audience to dispose of toilet tissue properly after peeing. The Death Crone deglamorized the heroic death of battle and presented us with the deaths of gout, cancer, Alzheimer's disease, and despair. We were dramatically reminded of the consequences of our casual attitudes in using the earth as a commodity for the disposal of technological wastes. The whole performance was an illustration of Rosenthal's analysis of Western culture: that we place our faith in technology rather than nature and are as a result on a course of ever-increasing alienation and distancing from nature. Ultimately our course, or curse, is to become fortieth-century monsters.

What I found more interesting than Rosenthal's portrayal of the various personae was the cumulative effect of her presentation. Her revelation of herself as both *Loner On Wheels in Gaia* and as *Lover On Wheels in Gaia* was slow, measured, and contained a hint of desperation, a desperation that revealed her as all too humanly bound to the ways of the world and her inability to break free in spite of heroic resolve.

The most evocative and unsettling of Rosenthal's personae was her portrayal of Gaia as, with little light on stage, she identified with the pain caused by our culture—the pain of laboratory rabbits, their eyes burned out with cosmetic testing. She showed us Gaia, filled with love and violence as we destroy the earth with toxic wastes, dropping to her knees, picking up a lighted candle, and pouring hot wax on her bald head. Rosenthal held her audience spellbound with this mesmerizing moment—she was Gaia!

The Sisyphean cycle was completed; Rosenthal's message had been executed with sledgehammer blows and pinpoint accuracy. This was a terrifying and powerfully moving performance that left me with an echo of a quote from the past: "We have found the enemy and it are us" *(Pogo)*.

Sasha Anawalt

Excerpts from "*Was Black* Overshadows

Other Visions"

When the nuclear reactor at Chernobyl melted down, the news seeped into our bones and our imaginations glowed with the horror. It did not take performance artist Rachel Rosenthal long to put the imaginary glow onstage and answer the terrifying questions of what happens to our bodies and our humanity after a blunder the size of Chernobyl.

Thursday at the John Anson Ford Theater, Rosenthal cut through the junk of other people's dances and presented *Was Black.*

The evening, "Visions at the Ford"—produced by Visions Interarts for the inauguration of Los Angeles's summer dance festival, Kaleidoscope—was not intended to be hers. But Chernobyl wasn't intentional either, and like it, Rosenthal has a way of making headlines that overshadow other newsworthy items. . . .

In *Was Black,* Rosenthal walks over to a white pedestal. Placing her hand on its edge, she—dressed in a long, black gown that emphasizes the white powder on her totally shaven head—begins to sing a Russian folk song that her mother sang to her as a child.

In the background three women and a man—Shelley Cook, Cynthia King, Linda Sibio, and Curtis York—lower the newspapers they are reading. They are naked, yet dusted thoroughly in white powder.

The news is apparently disastrous. Their mouths gape, their bodies writhe and send clouds of the white powder, reminiscent of nuclear mushrooms, into the air. Rosenthal continues to sing, but her voice cracks. We can almost hear the radiation coating her chords and eroding their otherwise smooth sweetness.

Originally published in the *Los Angeles Herald Examiner,* June 28, 1986, B1, B5.

131

On the screen behind, a negative film image of a black-and-white floral branch is increasingly blemished by a mustard-yellow growth. The poison is pervasive. It ruins us; it ruins our environment.

Choral music by Penderecki almost seems to mock Rosenthal's operatic stance, as her voice ascends to a harrowing scream. The dancers—including a pregnant woman—put on black clothing and toast each other with wine glasses into which they've poured table salt. It is a potent moment of black humor: we think of the SALT II treaty and watch the dancers' cocktail gestures, the polite kisses on the cheeks and false smiles, with appalled disbelief.

In the final image of *Was Black,* Rosenthal is wrapped in blinking Christmas tree lights that trace her body in the darkness. We can see through her. She no longer exists, except as a ghostly glow burnt into our imaginations—permanently.

Every move, every prop, every shading of color in *Was Black* had a need to be there. One cannot imagine Rosenthal presenting her feelings on the subject of Chernobyl in any other way. It is tight and, for once, not a pretentious or self-serving work. *Was Black* enlivens our vision. . . .

Alisa Solomon

"Worm's Eye View"

Rachel Rosenthal makes performances to mend the world. But knowing that her works center on ecology, the protection of animals, and the preservation of the earth can hardly prepare you for the brutal way they grab at you.

In this excerpt from *Soldier of Fortune,* she moves back and forth from storytelling, to autobiography, to polemical harangue, continually slapping one image or tone against its opposite. Her silk gown and elbow-length black gloves flow against the angular contours of her chiseled features and shaved head; her beautiful face is slashed with streaks of blue eyeliner and black lipstick. Standing in a diva pose—head erect, arms aloft—she narrates a roughing-it trip in the wilderness. In operatic recitative she describes how she "peed close to the car and froze my ass off." Without warning, this grotesque juxtaposition melts away; crouched and pinched, she howls like an animal.

Accompanied by Steve Nachmanovitch on souped-up violin, Rosenthal tells a simple story about seeing a wounded coyote on the road and wanting to help it, using the image to connect all living beings to each other, and everything to the cosmos—Zen content, Jewish form. "I hate this world," she growls in a voice that comes from her feet. "I hate what creatures do to creatures. I hate what people do to animals. I hate what people do to people in the name of science, art, love, patriotism." Her delivery is so ferocious, her presence so authoritative, so much is at stake, that I couldn't retreat by refusing to be taken on a guilt trip; Rosenthal's kaddish for humanity is a much more complicated emotional journey.

The piece crescendos into a duet of high-pitched chants, then quiets

Originally published in *The Village Voice,* August 18, 1987, 88.

down. Matter-of-fact, even friendly, Rosenthal talks about worms. Drowned in overwatered lawns, they come out onto the sidewalks to dry. But, she explains, the cement dehydrates them too quickly, and they soon die. "So," she concludes, "whenever I see an earthworm still alive, I pick it up and toss it into the grass." The gesture seems enormous, hopeful—almost as large as the gesture of Rosenthal's art.

Erika Munk

"Brainchildren of a Lesser God"

How fitting, to see Rachel Rosenthal's piece the day *Discovery* roared into what its crew still considers the heavens. Rosenthal stands on a tall ladder, peering up, to shout her last lines: "Hey! Deus ex machina! I'm here, the willing sacrifice! Hey up there! Can you hear me? . . . No one up there." She's shivering in panic. "Put me down!" Humanity, says *Rachel's Brain,* should get down, should reverse its attempt to escape the body and the earth, an attempt Rosenthal finds wasteful, cruel, and destructive. A *Times* head rhapsodizes, "5 Astronauts Roar Back into Space, Renewing Hope." For Rosenthal, this roar *is* hopelessness, and god from a machine worse than no god. She herself isn't hopeless at all; despite the discrepancy in worldly power between her art and their craft, she shows a ferocious will toward change.

Performance art is famously resistant to dealing with the outside world; its politics, when present at all, not only spring from autobiographical impulses but remain limited by them. Constricted themes, narrow skills, and inflated, needy egos plague this kind of theater. (Not so badly as they plague psychological "realism," of course.) Rosenthal controls and has ironic fun with the egoism of the genre, she expands its field, she's playfully virtuosic. The ecological-feminist ideas shaping the work are so deeply rooted in the idea of the personal as the political that a one-woman show directly addressing the audience is the most natural fusion of medium and message. *Rachel's Brain* would be agitprop for the 1980s, if there were a Green Party in this country. Perhaps it will be an agitprop of the 1990s.

Rosenthal appears first as Marie Antoinette. Her pearly gray dress,

Originally published in *The Village Voice,* October 11, 1988, 103, 106.

135

all furbelowed and frilled, is rigid over a visible scaffolding of stays and hoops, an absurd foot-high wig with a three-masted frigate set on top—the ship of state, of exploration, trade, conquest. The queen says she's "the flower of the Enlightenment." "I am a higher animal, head severed from body. . . . I am a thought machine, 'je pense donc je suis.'" She'd rather forget "bloody wombs, smelly placentas, disgusting semen." Her duality makes her suffer, but she won't let go of it; she won't abandon ship. Nevertheless, of course, she's beheaded.

In soft tunic and pants, somewhere between tie-dye and camouflage, Rosenthal reappears masked as an early hominid. A word is projected: slides—sometimes related, sometimes incongruent—flash by: the evolving creature painstakingly enacts the word. The sentence shapes itself at last: "A thought fights its way into consciousness." Against a circle of burning light, Rosenthal is framed like Leonardo's perfect man, shouting "Fire on the lake! The image of revolution." Downstage, she berates herself: "I am ugly guilty stupid fat a fraud nothing," the tedious litany of psychotherapeuticized blame, a failure of human insight she wryly asks us to acknowledge. "500 million years of brain evolution for *this?*"

Rosenthal, unmasked, is now her stage self. Her shaved head and black lipstick turn her into a sacred monster, prowling, androgynous, somewhere between the sensual and grotesque. "Who has the guts to look the gorgon in the face?" she asks later. *She* has the guts to be a Medusa stripped even of her snakes. Her movements give no hint that she's sixty-one, only her face shows it: goddess, demon, and the lady next door.

Standing at the table with bowls, knives, and blender, she demonstrates the nature of the brain, using a cauliflower. Behind, a slide of a screaming research monkey with an electrode in its head. "Did you know that there are about 100 billion neurons in a single human brain, and that the number of their possible interconnections exceeds the number of atoms in the universe?" She hacks at the cauliflower. "The earth is overlaid with a layer in the image of our image of the cortex: dry, smart, ingenious, and deadly."

Downstage again, she plays with variations on "To be or not to be" and "I think, therefore I am." Then, at the table—"Food for thought!"—she does a series of comic routines about meat-eating greed as cauliflowers descend from on high and her stomach talks back to her, accompanied by a long series of famous atrocity photos from the past twenty years. "I eat when I'm not hungry, to fill the empty spaces." The humor falls away.

It comes back when Rosenthal turns into both Koko, a gorilla learning to speak in sign language, and Koko's chirpy teacher. Koko finds it hard to be serious about Shakespeare or Descartes: "Therefore not I be not am be be am therefore I to to." Her private gorilla thoughts are different: "I abandon myself and drift, tenderly rocked as I navigate among the branches, feeling the tug of the Mother in my gut." The capital-M Mother, deified, is then invoked—"Marvel and apotheosis!"—in a ritual (cauliflower, dirt, watering-can) right before Rosenthal, reversing these impulses, starts up that ladder.

The piece is compelling and splendid to watch. (It's accompanied throughout by Leslie Lashinsky's amazing bassoon score, which in its range of style and emotion becomes the second actor, with as many personae as Rosenthal.) But I was provoked to running disagreement, a muttered, quibbling yes-but. Take the opening scene. Such a strange, paradoxical image: Marie Antoinette as the Enlightenment? The Enlightenment severed her head from her body—and "let them eat brioches" was the last cry of an old order, not the warning signal of a new consumerism. Would Rosenthal really want to live in a West shaped by absolute monarchy and the most repressive aspects of Catholicism?

Okay, maybe I'm being obtusely literal. To argue with this piece on such grounds sounds like a denial not only of its metaphorical flights but its philosophical premises, invoking rationality and history when Rosenthal believes the world is dying from "left-brain" primacy, from the dominance of the abstract and technological. I don't for a moment, however, disagree with either Rosenthal's vision of the world's waste or her multivalent images. That Great Mother worship is just another damned appeal to religious authority seems less important than the intensely mobilizing effect of her artful didacticism, which works for left brains, too. Still, I wonder what she thinks of the German Greens. . . .

Martin Bernheimer

Excerpts from "Rachel Rosenthal Guides E.A.R. Unit on an Amazon Safari"

Rachel Rosenthal . . . bills herself simply as a performance artist.

That's about as accurate as calling the Taj Majal a house.

The woman is a monument and a marvel. She is a force of nature. She materializes upon a stage, just sits in an ornate chair, and defies the observer not to be magnetized.

Her eyes glare with intense zeal. Her shaven skull gleams with defiant pride. Her mouth curls in passion mitigated, perhaps, by a trace of self-mockery.

When she moves, she really moves. Her arms rise in arcs of formidable defiance, whisking away invisible demons. Her fingers flick profoundly mysterious messages into the air, along with prosaic scraps of paper.

She insinuates the semblance of a samba. She flails into a mock arabesque. With ritualistic abandon, she swivels hips in transit. With crazed grace, she hurls her body at unseen enemies.

She recites a text that is sometimes intelligible despite primitive microphonic distortion. She keens. She croons. She roars.

She flits from mature *Sprechgesang* to the sing-song of an itty-bitty child's voice. She takes off in fragmented flights of coloratura dementia, then dives bravely to basso profundo grunts.

Rosenthal has been around. She knows the secrets of melody. She savors the force of rhythm. She observes the limitations of form. She exults in the dynamic fascination of theater.

She is timeless, ageless, gutsy, quirky, exotic, potentially poignant. She is also very clever.

Originally published in the *Los Angeles Times,* May 18, 1990, F18.

She deserves a great showpiece. Unfortunately, *Amazonia,* which she has concocted in collaboration with the resident E.A.R. virtuosos, does not seem to be it. Not yet, anyway.

The elaborate four-part piece surrounds the diva with a lot of exotic trappings. Slide shows depict jungle paintings by Henri Rousseau and, at the other extreme of innocence, fanciful drawings by children aged six to nine.

Four accompanying performers—Arthur Jarvinen, Amy Knoles, Robin Lorentz, and Dorothy Stone—stalk the boards. They chant, play with nonsense syllables, toy with homemade percussion instruments, pour water from bowl to amplified bowl, crinkle cellophane, manipulate folk symbols, and strike picturesque poses.

All this is done in support of a Message—yes, capital *M.* The Brazilian rainforest must be saved.

Fervently protesting ecological waste, Rosenthal champions a noble, multilayered cause. In the convoluted process, she invokes geological and biological history, recounts myths, and stacks metaphors.

Amazonia meanders too much to muster a profound artistic statement, much less a profound sociopolitical argument. It does, however, serve to focus the talent of a fascinating creative artist. In this day of delirious dilettantism, one must be grateful.

Ross Wetzsteon

"Stand-up Shaman"

When Rachel Rosenthal, at the beginning of *Pangaean Dreams,* slowly rises up out of her wheelchair, majestically discards her wrist pads and knee braces and crutches, and luxuriously stretches as if her muscles and bones were tectonic plates shifting into a new configuration, she's revealing that her vision is precisely the opposite of anthropomorphic—rather than endowing the natural world with human characteristics, she attributes planetary faculties, functions, and even feelings to human beings. A kind of stand-up shaman, she treats geologic eras as anecdotes, deals with continental drift as autobiography, and performs her vigorously meditative one hundred-minute monologue as if the Earth itself were using her as a Delphic voice to express a solipsistic reverie.

In one of her rare New York appearances, the sixty-four-year-old grande dame of performance art—a title, she says, she dislikes, but prefers to *grandmother* of performance art—demonstrated her thesis that "All of Gaia dances in harmony and we humans are the only ones out of step." Even gurus have gurus, of course, and Rosenthal pays particular homage to the German astronomer and meteorologist Alfred Wegener, who several decades ago first proposed the concept of a primordial supercontinent that gradually separated into several land masses. The Earth, devotees of Gaia deduced, is a living being—breathing, pulsing, constantly evolving—and humankind can't survive if it insists on remaining severed from nature.

To attempt to embody this ecoterrestrial vision in a solo performance would seem the ultimate oxymoron—after all, Gaia isn't a metaphor, or, for that matter, even a sacrament—but paradoxically Rosen-

Originally published in *The Village Voice,* August 6, 1991, 83.

thal's piece works best when she enacts her convictions, least when she merely declaims them. Through the use of trance, dance, vocal ejaculation, videotape, live and recorded music, and most of all her striking stage presence itself—tall, multivoiced, forcefully agile, with her legendary shaved head—Rosenthal evokes an immersion in rather than an adversarial relationship to "the laws of chaos" she sees governing the universe. Her aphorisms are often provocative ("I am a gay man in a woman's body," "I want a permanent out-of-body experience," "The fabric of our society is composed of strands of synthetic desire"), but less so than the segments in which she has incantatory dialogues with herself (in her incarnations as angel and dinosaur, for instance), or when she stands in a huge, white, billowing shroud and chants as fuzzy films of the Earth are projected onto her body. Throughout the piece, she gradually constructs a human skeleton out of an archaeological dig and at the end elevates it halfway into the flies—as if to suggest that humankind has the choice between hanging and ascension?

Unfortunately, Rosenthal doesn't seem to trust her performance to convey her complex meaning and frequently lapses into simplistic exhortation. When impersonating that angel and that dinosaur, for instance—utilizing a comically revelatory irony—she's utterly convincing, as if she's released long-submerged and conflicting aspects of the natural order. But as soon as she begins to preach—solemnly forsaking that irony—her vision starts to seem predictable, as if rhetoric were part of the severance from nature against which she's inveighing. As so often happens, the self-conscious attempt at universality quickly comes to seem parochial, the self-conscious attempt at timelessness quickly comes to seem dated—we're no longer in Gaia, but in California in 1991.

Still, for most of the evening Rosenthal demonstrates—with Whitmanesque vigor, stunning theatricality, and a cave-painter's mastery of prehistoric imagery—that the more we immerse ourselves in the natural world, the stronger our sense of self becomes.

Alisa Solomon

Excerpts from "Rosenthal Performs *FUTURFAX* for Whitney in New York"

New York—it's Rachel Rosenthal's eighty-sixth birthday in *filename: FUTURFAX.*

Alone in a room, she lights a stub of a tiny candle and sings "Happy Birthday" to herself. As a celebratory treat, she has bought three long, limp carrots. Gingerly, she removes them from her cloth shopping bag, pats and kisses them, and lays them on the table. "Six hours in line for these," she exclaims. "It's worth it."

The year is 2012 and the Earth is collapsing toward virtual destruction. Armed hooligans could break in at any moment and make off with her rare vegetables.

In her terrifying yet hilarious solo performance, premiered here at the Whitney Museum, Rosenthal inhabits this dystopia, bringing to life a vision of the future that she suggests most certainly awaits us if we don't change our ways.

As in earlier pieces, such as *Pangaean Dreams* and *Rachel's Brain,* Rosenthal combines text, movement, and sound score into a compelling—if discomfiting—examination of human hubris. More shaman than performance artist, Rosenthal is a contemporary Cassandra, an Earth prophet, sent to dramatize our doom.

Much of Rosenthal's seventy-five-minute monologue ("You think I ramble on? That's what happens when there's no more TV") centers on our concepts of the progression of time, and, especially, of eternity.

Purgatory, she reasons, is "time bought out of eternity—what a scam!" If Rosenthal hints, on the one hand, that we're living in the waiting room of Purgatory now, as we use up the Earth's resources

Originally published in *Los Angeles Times,* April 25, 1992, F16.

without regard for the future, on the other, she dissents from the very assumption of eternity, at least as it applies to human beings.

Word from the future reaches her via fax, telling of a world where, after the calamity, humans live on in self-sustainable communities— sterile, domed biospheres where implants keep their behavior within moral bounds, and "no art has been manufactured since a long time ago when our lawmakers deemed it superfluous and subversive, and we have trouble conceptualizing what it might have amounted to in the past."

Before long, a "computer-generated clarification" (a recorded male voice) explains, these last remaining humans (all of them female) will die out, "and the species will be extinct."

But Rosenthal doesn't survive to read this addendum to the futur- fax. She's been shot by the hooligans who have come for her carrots. She lies motionless on the stage, as the fax slides onto her body, and the machine whirs on and on and on.

Amelia Jones

"Rachel Rosenthal: UCLA Center for the

Performing Arts"

Living in fin-de-millennium California, I, like Rachel Rosenthal, have felt threatened by the seemingly random, vicious violence of contemporary life and have found myself obsessing about chaos, death, and human evil. A substantial orator and actress who moves like a dancer or a queen, Rosenthal—who plays the last Russian tsarina, Alexandra—intones throughout the chiliastic spectacle *Zone,* 1994, about the evils of human voracity and cruelty, epitomized by the Romanov family ("assholes in brocade," as Rosenthal puts it in her typically blunt fashion). At the same time, her nihilism is tempered by an anxious nostalgia. The Romanov family, all clad in diaphanous white, is attacked by the multicolored "Throngs" (a roiling crowd of anonymous people of color dressed in deep blues, blacks, grays, and purples); the Romanovs are finally murdered because they represent, as Rosenthal writes in the program notes, a "metaphor for patriarchal Western civilization and its demise."

Rosenthal's vision is driven by an ingenuous idealism; she repeatedly recalls the 1960s or early 1970s as a golden, less barbaric time. (Was it really?) Contaminating her own bracing cynicism with an artless and sometimes almost cloying expression of hope, Rosenthal implies that the chaotic rise of the colored masses will ultimately restore a peaceful and ecologically sound "order" to the world. But this begs the question of whose order it will be. Doesn't order imply regulating and hierarchizing boundaries? Is there order beyond patriarchy?

Rosenthal's compelling oratory, self-presentation, brilliant staging, and choreography comprise a disappointingly uncritical view of history in which the murder of the Romanovs (and Rasputin, who is

Originally published in *Artforum,* April 1994, 103.

thrown in peripherally as a Hitler-esque seducer of the masses) signifies the rise of materialism and the loss of spiritual values in modern life. By staging this moment as an origin of negativity, Rosenthal implies that what came before it was free of such venality and cruelty; she also conflates environmental disaster with colonialism, the Cold War, patriarchy, and a generalized notion of human depravity. This conflation reduces each specific instance of oppression and destruction to a vague category of "human evil," defusing the potential for resistance.

Rosenthal's choice of the family of Nicholas II to epitomize Western patriarchy fails in a way that I found powerful. While she seems to view history as a downward spiral of increasing turpitude, with Western patriarchy blamed (perhaps rightly) for every crisis from the destruction of the environment to the murder of the human spirit, her Romanovs are a many-sided, sometimes likable bunch. They are both pathetic and noble in their suffering, hatefully imperious and sympathetic (especially Alexandra, whom we associate with the overall critique, since she is played by Rosenthal), rapacious and generous, bumbling and graceful. They come across as misguided rather than simply bad, complicating Rosenthal's otherwise unswerving excoriation of "patriarchy" as a monolithic entity. People of color and women aren't simply free of greed, lust for power, or ecological sin, but are participants within a system—admittedly asymmetrical—of social contracts.

I found myself wishing that Rosenthal had deployed her poetic and passionate monologues and fabulous imagery—the "Throngs" writhing in dark heaps around the luminous family; the crowd welded into a knot of humanity by two beams of overhead light, green-covered hands slowly reaching up like buds extending toward the sun; bodies splitting off in twos from the crowd, then slamming and rolling against one another—within a narrative more closely attuned to the seductive vicissitudes of power and less generalized in its attack. Rosenthal's outrageous and outraged presentation, which pointed to what she calls the "spiritual ozone hole" in contemporary Western life, outlined a system of power that is far more complex than she allows.

III Writings and Scripts by Rachel Rosenthal

Rachel Rosenthal

Excerpts from "Rachel Rosenthal"

Dearest Eleanor,

You asked me to give you my "best recollection" of émigré days in southern California. As a professional émigré (World War II refugee from France via Portugal, Brazil, and New York City), daughter of émigrés (Father, then age fourteen, from the Caucasus to Paris in 1888, and Mother from the Bolsheviks to Paris in 1920), and with an atavistic hunch that there were roaming Scythians and perhaps Amazons in the remote past of my genes, I am ready to recount my very personal colonization of early Los Angeles. . . .

Ah, the stories I could tell! But I learned my lesson where personal anecdotes are concerned, in 1964, at the dinner party honoring Jasper Johns before the opening of his Pasadena Museum retrospective. I was sitting at Irving Blum's right at the black-tie affair, having a couple of my Johns in the show. My husband, King Moody, and I were stone broke at the time, and we had scrounged some $$s together to—he, rent-a-tux, and me, get a do, which looked like a feather duster on top of my head. Anyway, during dinner, I was engaged in banter with my right-hand table companion, a collector, and I was about to regale him (he leaning eagerly forward) with some juicy tidbit of early Johnsiana, at which point I received a stinging kick in the left shin under the table from Irving. In a flash—of pain!—I realized the whole mechanism of legend building in the art world, and developed an instant case of massive and lingering amnesia. . . . I shall try and resurrect my mem-

Originally published in *Journal: The Los Angeles Institute of Contemporary Art,* February 5, 1974, 11–15. In the 1974 publication of this text several paragraphs were out of sequence; they have been put in the correct order here.

ory for you now, in what I hope is a balanced blend of discretion and exhibitionism!

I trekked over on the three days/nights New York–Los Angeles Super Chief with Dibidi and Tioutick, my two Manhattan cats, in September 1955, after my father died earlier that summer in Beverly Hills. I was "starting-a-new-life," leaving my loft near the Lower Manhattan fish market to Bob Rauschenberg, Jasper Johns already inhabiting the floor below mine. I was ostensibly going to "earn-a-living" after a very Bohemian number of years in Paris and New York, and had a job offer at the Pasadena Playhouse to prove it. I was to teach acting and dance, fresh as I was from dancing in Merce Cunningham's troupe, and from assisting Erwin Piscator in his Dramatic Workshop "regies." On a subaction level, however, I was fleeing from a vortex of supercharged energy made up of Jap [Jasper Johns], Bob [Rauschenberg], John Cage, Merce Cunningham, Ray Johnson, Cy Twombly, M. C. Richards, and others, that was threatening to engulf and destroy my still-immature soft center.

Greater Los Angeles, in those days, was quite practicable. There was visibility and room to roam, and innocent palm trees that were not yet "Ed Ruschas." A tall house had two stories and the Sunset Strip still had Ciro's. I learned to drive a box MG, and my cats and I ensconced ourselves in Pasadena, where I proceeded to write my death warrant with the old fart guard at the Playhouse: I brought a much-watered-down version of N.Y. avant-garde to the academic curriculum, while wearing a red-headed natural, denim shirts, and culottes. These aberrations didn't much bother the kids (among whom was the very talented youngster Ruth Buzzi), but I was nonetheless booted out because of my hubris as much as for my black tights (Panty-Hose not having been invented yet). So much for "earning-a-living." I, with my MG, and Dibidi and her first litter then immigrated to Hollywood (poor Tioutick having been killed by a car), leaving Pasadena Playhouse, which sank of its own dead weight not too long afterwards.

After floating around for a couple of weeks, I chanced upon the unlikely "Salon" of Vanessa Brown, ex-quiz kid, now actress and Kultur Kween. Vanessa officiated in curlers and dirty dressing gown and slippers every Wednesday in her $150,000 mansion north of Sunset, for a livingroomful of Hollywood characters, hopefuls, starlets, and (we were always told) Famous Producers. She talked into a tape recorder in the middle of the glass livingroom filled with inside-outside trees and free-flying parakeets, while starlets ducked and protected their bouffants. Vanessa wanted to "Form A Company and Tour Israel," and we heard this often. It was a kind of ritual mantra that sustained us through the excruciating Wednesdays, until we started looking for a place in which to workshop.

My friend, the poet Natalie Tolin, and I discovered the little proscenium workshop stage of the Circle Theatre on El Centro—a perfect space. But Vanessa flatly refused because some actors in the Circle had been blacklisted, and chose instead the banquet room at the now-defunct Gotham Delicatessen on Hollywood Boulevard, where we tried to rehearse scenes among the clanking of dishes and shouted orders of lox.

I decided to lease the little Circle Workshop, and "Qui m'aime me suive!" Vanessa's groupies then included such budding stars as Vic Morrow, fresh from *Blackboard Jungle,* and Beverly Michaels, a very talented actress totally misused by the film industry because she happened to be beautiful and a blonde, and many forgettable and forgotten luminaries. About one-half came with me at the time of the Great Schism, and we began what was at first supposed to be an Actor's Lab where scenes were rehearsed. The group included Tab Hunter, Susan Harrison of *The Sweet Smell of Success* fame, Paul Gaer (now a producer), Jud Taylor (now a director), Vic Morrow, and Barbara Turner, then his wife (who became a screenwriter), Tony Perkins, Rod McKuen, Bill McKinney (who's just making stardom now), and many others, like Mark Damon and Frank Wolff, who both made careers in Italy in spaghetti westerns and Hercules epics, and still others who eventually made TV careers or dropped out.

It soon became obvious that nobody was going to study scenes. I was conducting the workshops as experiments for my own ideas that had their genesis in the fertile loam of the early 1950s in Paris and N.Y. underground aesthetics, and the attraction was irresistible, even for people whose training and penchant lay with Hollywood celluloid.

To better situate what follows, let me give you a brief sketch of that period, as seen through my experience. We are now speaking of 1956–57. Rauschenberg and Johns (who was "discovered" by Castelli soon after I left New York), were not yet seen in these parts, and West Coast Abstract-Expressionism still thrived. John and Merce were too poor to tour as far west as Los Angeles and were not well enough known yet to be brought out by educational institutions, as UCLA was to do a couple of years later. Antonin Artaud's *Le Théâtre et son Double* (my

theater Bible since Paris 1949) was to be translated by M. C.
Richards and published by Grove Press in 1958, after which time I was
able to use it as a "textbook" in my workshops. The *Evergreen Review*
came out in 1957 with the first translated fragments of French absurd-
ists Beckett, Ionesco, Adamoff, Genet, etc. No one had seen performances of their plays in English, and mighty few had read them. Zen,
which had become familiar to New York circles mainly through Cage's
involvement, was very new here. Alan Watts was not too widely read
nor was D. T. Suzuki a household name. Gary Snyder was in Kyoto,
Kerouac and others came later, the word *beatnik* had been "à peine"
coined, and there were vague rumors of "mushrooms" wafting in from
the desert. . . . La Cienega was for restaurants, Ed Kienholz lived in a
shack on the east side of the street, on the west side a guy named
Chico [nickname for Walter Hopps, the curator and historian] by his
friends had opened a modest gallery called the Ferus, to show Bay
[Area] people and a few southerners whose work was really way out,
and Jim Baker made sandals when he wasn't totaling irate husbands
with karate chops.

It was in this Pre-Cambrian atmosphere that flowered the beginning
of what was later to become my INSTANT THEATRE.

INSTANT THEATRE, or I.T., as we called it, evolved in that first workshop in 1956. Through certain exercises, some inspired by the Jean-
Louis Barrault techniques (J. L. B.'s school being my theater alma
mater in Paris), some influenced by early Bay Area precursors of sensi-
tivity training, and with a liberal sprinkling of Zen and Cage philosophy and ubiquitous Artaud, we achieved an incredible liberation of
inhibitions and released extraordinary potentials of individual and collective creativity. The energy level was so high, the achievements of
unsuspected feats (both physical and psychological) were so overwhelming, that we existed on a real high from session to session.

The ingredients of I.T. evolved gradually. At first, for instance, the
lights were all hand-held and a part of the action, with the spot-people
emphasizing or toning down the stage action by the manipulation of
the lights and large fans, weaving in and out among the performers.
When it became too dangerous to have all that live spaghetti onstage,
we rigged up stationary lights but still used two offstage hand-held
spots for that liquid, flowing effect. Our gels were never straw or "bas-
tard" amber, but orange, cerise, emerald, purple, cobalt. . . . We there-

fore anticipated in a small artisanship way what was later to be called "light shows" and "psychedelic" shows. At first our sound was from records. I had brought Cage records from New York, and Lou Harrison, Varèse, Musique Concrète, etc. Pierre Schaeffer had made the first record of Musique Concrète from American sound effects records (the sounds of the sea, the jungle, etc.) that I sent him. I would put a few long-playing sides on the turntable, and we would just go until they were played out. Later, we began doing our own sound. We used any noise-makers for percussion, from toy pianos to Kabuki drums, bells, flutes, pots and pans, Chinese gongs, washboards, car horns, and radios. Slowly, we accumulated props and sets and costumes. At first, we raided our own detritus, or side alleys on garbage nights. Then, people began bringing us *their* garbage. I bought a lot of things at the 5 and 10, and we used brooms, old dolls, discarded windows and doors, soap bubbles, cards, ladders, tree cuttings, Coca-Cola bottles, palm fronds, beach balls, coat hangers, old telephones, bird cages, etc., etc. . . . These were assembled into object trouvé environments, or handled and used, almost never as their original purpose dictated, and became abstract symbols in a highly surreal ambience, with light and sound complements. Costumes, likewise, were added in layers, with safety pins and clothes pins. There were thrift shop treasures (now priced out of sight, then expensive at $2.00!), as well as rags. Visually, we achieved a Neo-Dada collision of gas masks, Japanese umbrellas, chains, tutus, periscopes, army boots, and strings of fake salami, or on the other hand, could piece together from bits and pieces the most authentic eighteenth-century French silhouette. We made masks, and we and the stage were giant, living Assemblages!

At the beginning, the stage action would start, after a lot of relaxation exercises, as in a dream, by one person, joined presently by others, each one enriching the initial action either by enhancement or shocking contrast, like the slow buildup of a painting. It was a very amorphous form, very permissive, and almost always yielded, when allowed to last an hour or more, some grandiose friezes and frescoes of Boschian and Jungian imagery, as well as a great deal of very individual psychological residue. Indeed, in the early days, those long sessions of movement, light, sound, color, poetry, surrealistic humor, and breathtaking acrobatics were so overwhelming (and totally unseen by any spectators except myself) that I used to sit there transfixed, almost afraid to breathe, thinking that I was so privileged to witness the performance of some extraordinary primeval mystery and sacred rite, never to be repeated, never to be recorded, gone forever as I sat there, ephemeral, infinitely beautiful . . . and totally lost.

The big mistake I made at the time and in subsequent years, I can now see, was to have aligned us with theater, thus eliciting a whole complex of responses that did not fit, and evoking in the spectators' minds certain habitual expectations that were not fulfilled. But, and unlike subsequent art forms involving people, such as Happenings, Performance Art, Video, etc., we were still very much geared toward performance. We trained to be aware of the stage as a whole, and to become, each one of us, our own director. Thus our deepest affiliation was still with theater and we never envisaged the possibility of audience boredom as an acceptable aesthetic ingredient.

We gave, beginning in early 1957, a series of weekend performances, each of them one of a kind and never repeated, to packed audiences, and enjoyed a limited but quite brilliant "succès d' éstime."

The Ferus people would come, usually en masse. Walter Hopps, Billy Al [Bengston], who had just returned from Europe with a set of beautifully sensitive works on paper: little tears and holes with daubs of pigment pushing through . . ., [John] Altoon, dear Wally Berman and Shirley, who were there faithfully every weekend, also the poets: Bob Alexander—called Baza—who had a small press and would bring us little gems of "programs" to hand out every week, printed on Braille paper, popsicle sticks, poems, telephone directory pages, or whatever . . . David Melzer, John Reid . . . George Herms was a regular, and to this day he generously tells me how important our performances were to his developr̄ent as an artist. Ed Teske, Ed Kienholz and Mary, Oliver Andrews and his then wife, excellent actress Betty Hartford, Dorothy and Michael Blankford, Charles Eastman and his sister, Carol Eastman (who later wrote *Five Easy Pieces*), etc., etc. . . . After the shows, everybody walked around the corner to my place behind the theater, where I lived without furniture but with my Linus collection of early Rauschenbergs, Johns and Twomblys, with Dibidi and her four litters (eighteen cats by then), and black walls and ceilings. We had cookies and coffee, talked, made new relationships and undid old ones, and after that, some of us would go to Samson's, a few blocks up the street.

Samson de Brier, the undisputed grand seigneur of Hollywood weltanschauung, held perpetual open house at night in his "opium den" of a house. He would receive with the hauteur of a Roman emperor, had standing room only into the wee hours throughout the week, and never offered anybody so much as a glass of water. He didn't have to. The secret of his success lay in his style, and his uncanny matchmaking abilities. If you were new in town, or if you needed contacts in any field, and were lucky enough to be brought to Samson's by a friend, you were bound to strike gold. Samson knew how to bring the right people together. A young filmmaker could see the films of and meet Kenneth Anger, Stan Brakhage, or early Curtis Harrington, or talk to Tony Richardson if he was in town. A would-be guru fresh from India could meet artistic matrons to enlist in his spiritual gang-bang experiments, actors met producers, and girl met boy, and boy met boy, and girl met girl. Cameron the Witch was there in her improbable body, as well as in Kenneth Anger's masterpiece, *The Inauguration of the Pleasure Dome,* which featured Samson himself in a kitschy bacchanalia. Anaïs Nin (seemingly swathed in gossamer mists) was there often, having also been a star of *Pleasure Dome.* People read poems, swapped mates, got high, committed suicide, it seemed at an accelerated pace, while Samson the Warlock remained as still and centered as an icon and just as ageless.

That phase of my life that I file under the archeological name of I.T. One came abruptly to an end during the summer of 1957. I was flat broke since no one kicked into the theater and my money sense was a total zero in those days. There were incredibly convoluted and passion-racked internecine complications within the group, and the fleas had taken over my living quarters. So things came to a screeching halt and I took my cats and retired to Laurel Canyon to pursue a hermit's life and forget theater forever . . . or at least until 1958.

During my hiatus, I met King Moody, my future husband, a professional actor who fell in love with my stories of INSTANT THEATRE and made me go back to workshopping in 1959, and henceforth became my partner in I.T. until 1966. In the meantime, the undifferentiated cultural blob began to split up and multiply like an amoeba. The poets and some music people went the coffeehouse route, and places like Dutton's "Positano's" in Malibu thrived by catering to an in-crowd of knowledgeable culture vultures and "Concerned Intellectuals." KPFK attracted a lot of good people whose ideas were thus disseminated over the incestuous ether. Irving Blum came (unlike Bodhidharma) from the East, and took over the now very important Ferus, when Hopps went to Pasadena. I.T., in its subsequent eras of I.T. 2, 3, 4, etc., became more and more of an "in" thing, playing in dance studios, pocket theaters, storefronts, private homes, and introducing the original Commedia Del Arte to the young Renaissance Faire, whose creators, the Pattersons, were part of our troupe. Improvisational musicians such as Emil Richards and Ali Akbar Khan dropped in unannounced at the theater to "blow" with us. "Light shows" that had cut their baby teeth with us gave visual and audio concerts on the Strip and elsewhere.

We lived and worked marginally, too engrossed in our artistic and physical survival to worry about posterity. Thus we committed the unforgivable sin of innocent negligence. We neglected *our* legend, while helping build up so many others. People stole ideas from us right and left, adapting them to their needs. Even gag writers from TV shows plagiarized our satire! But, with characteristic munificence, we would say, "Let 'em! There's plenty more where that came from!" And indeed, our inventiveness seemed boundless at that time. Nevertheless, our pride and snobbish genius backfired and it really hurts us today to read all the heroic accounts of similar enterprises without a single nod in our direction, or to know that so many celebrated art performances were based on concepts similar to those we had used as technique exercises. I know my present retroactive regrets are absurd. My total lack of fastidiousness where documentation was concerned was due to a personal quirk of character that was part of my makeup, for better or worse: I hated the past, I never thought of the future, the only reality I dealt with was the present, and my lack of reverence for yesterday or prescience of tomorrow was positively animal-like. When I see the care with which every art performance today is documented, recorded, disseminated, and catalogued, I marvel. Of course, there was also the matter of money. We were continually and determinedly broke, and that eliminated a number of possibilities such as film, video, or even slides and stills.

A lot was happening underground, just beneath the big movie industry tree whose roots reached wide and deep. This baobab spread its shadow over all of us. Most of our friends were either partially or wholly dependent on the industry for their livelihood, and most resented and hated this. Art patronage was so minimal as not to count at all. But people were always attracted by the zany—the bizarre—and the underground people were already becoming polarized or torn asunder between the demon pull of drugs on the one hand, and the big sell-out on the other. The hallucinogens were all around us. For some, they were catastrophic. For others, they brought renewal and re-creation. Drugs also had a side effect in the new self-consciousness. For people under their influence, simple, everyday things seemed meaningful in a totally new and unexpected way—and therefore worthy of notice, attention, and recording. Everyone began *noticing*. I feel that, in its benign aspect, the drug demon created an attentive generation, and this attention to humble things spawned the strong movement toward the Earth, the simple life, and ecology, leading later on to the more baroque flowering of the folk movement exploding in the hand-made houses, crafts, eccentric dress and lifestyles. A healthy by-product.

Thank you, dear Eleanor, for asking me to remember "things past"—it turned out more sweet than bitter an activity! I hope you find it of some interest.

Love,
Rachel

Rachel Rosenthal

Letters to Barbara T. Smith June 19, 1975 and

July 17, 1976

June 19, 1975

Dear Barbara,

I am writing the first of our contractual epistles. I thought long about what I would like to tell you. I figured that as one of the things uppermost in my mind right now is the problem of losing weight, it would be soothing and soul-filling to talk about food.

My weight problem is, of course, made up of a small number of mishugas. But I believe it all began when I was a child because we had one of the great gastronomical households in Paris. Our cook, Julie, was a "Cordon Bleu," and was with my mother for about eighteen years. I say with my mother because she and my father didn't live together until he built her a beautiful little *hôtel particulier,* or townhouse, in a lovely *quartier* of Paris near the Bois de Boulogne. Then he moved in with her on a sporadic basis at first, since he was lavishing himself on two households. At the time, my mother was what was pejoratively called a "kept woman," and they didn't get married until I was seven, when his first wife finally relented for an astronomical settlement!

In those days, however, astronomical didn't even make a dent in my father's fortune, and Mother's household thrived on more than half a

This is the first of three letters that Rosenthal wrote to Barbara T. Smith, the Los Angeles performance artist, in the context of Smith's *A Week in the Life of.* . . . I am deeply grateful to Smith as well as Rosenthal for permission to reprint two (this and the last letter of July 17, 1976) of the three letters. A few minor, mechanical corrections have been made in the texts. For further discussion concerning the circumstances of these letters in the context of Smith's performance, see my Introduction.—Ed.

dozen servants, and extra help when the need arose. And the need did arise often enough because my parents' social life was intense and festive; therefore Julie was kept busy, which was the way she liked it best.

Julie came from a tiny village in Haute-Savoie where she still lives, carrying on a correspondence with me in spite of her arthritis and old age. I haven't seen her since right after the war, when we met again briefly, after a five-year separation that felt like a century. One of the last memories I kept of her from the time just before we became war refugees was when we heard the fall of France announced on the radio and I saw my father weep for the first time: Julie held him in her arms and rocked him like a baby. . . . She remained in the South, from where we had made our escape into Spain, and soon returned to her village where she owns a house, purchased on Mother's advice with her earnings in our service. Every letter of hers is an elegy to the beautiful days when she cooked in our house!

The day started with Julie coming up to the second floor where my parents had their bedrooms. Mother would still be in her Marie-Antoinette bed with the gilded baldachin, the cherubs holding white satin drapes in rococo folds, and the crêpe-de-chine sheets with satin appliqué and silk embroidery. Julie always came in with suggestions for the menus of the day, and Mother always went along because Julie suggested what she felt like eating that day, and Mother knew that her cooking was at its best when it matched her appetite. After the morning ritual Julie went out to buy the ingredients for her oeuvre, and then retired to the kitchen for the magical preparations.

The kitchen was below street level as in most Parisian "hotels," with barred slits for windows close to the ceiling and level with the sidewalk. The basement was a place of delights and mysteries for me when I was a child. I was seldom allowed downstairs, so when I went, it was as to a foreign land, enticing and forbidding, made quasi-mythological by the extremes of fire and ice, and the alchemical transmutations performed therein.

Julie reigned supreme in the kitchen. There were huge coal ovens whose flames she controlled, her happy face flushed and perspiring, by adding or removing concentric iron rings from the burners with an iron poker. It clanged a lot and sparks flew like in a forge. The kitchen was large, with ceramic tiles and plaster walls. There was a big marble-top table in the middle and the walls were resplendent with copper pots of every dimension. The table was laden with "works in progress": eggs in a wire basket waiting to be beaten, vegetables in various stages of cuttings, meats being trimmed, pastries in batters or rising under linen towels. Sometimes semolla gnocchi were hardening on the marble, icecreams turning inside their wooden cylinder, and always, the smell of freshly ground coffee greeted you at the door. As you came down the stairs, you first found yourself in the servants' little dining and sitting room. Then came the kitchen, and at the far end was the pantry where Alexandre, our butler, held the fort. He had belonged to a top-drawer Russian grand duke, and he was an incredible character. He had a shiny moon face, never learned French, and service was his whole life. He was like Firs in *The Cherry Orchard*. He feuded continually with the other servants, adored our family, and had a real reverence for the house and all its furnishings. He would polish silver, shine up the Baccarat cut-crystal glasses, painstakingly change the water of the two large aquariums, dust all the precious knickknacks with a huge feather duster, and never left the house for the holidays, preferring to stay home and use it as its temporary master for the two months of sweltering Paris summer. His only outings were to the "Bourse," or stock exchange, where he went to gamble, wearing a black bowler hat and carrying a cane. He remained in the house during the Nazi occupation, working for the Germans in order to take care of our things. As the tenants helped themselves to our belongings, he became emotionally ill. After the war, I found him in a nursing home, totally senile and mute, and eating his feces. But he recognized me and I visited him every week. We just sat. After several months, I skipped a week. When I returned within a fortnight, he was dead.

But to go back to my story: behind the kitchen and the pantry were the slightly frightening freezers and wine cellars, rooms that were dark and cold. The temperature was kept low by blocks of ice, delivered every week by workers who carried them over little pieces of carpeting on their backs, held by large hooks. At the very end of this suite of rooms was the "monte-charge" or dumb-waiter, that serviced all three floors.

So this was the layout of the realm from whose depths the monte-charge dredged up the daily miracles and wonders concocted by Julie.

It started out at breakfast, with its repertoire of brioches, croissants (homemade, of course), and more elaborately, wondrous coffee-cakes and—my father's all-time favorite—the gâteau de savoie (sponge cake) that only Julie could make crispy on the outside, paved with a brittle and sugary crust, and almost guiltily hiding a holy of holies of barely cooked batter in its center. This lovely meal was eaten in my father's room, with its art deco "moderne" furniture, and with a slew of people sitting all around while Father ate in bed like a king, on a bed-table cantilevered over the sheets on its fashionably curved tubular armature, reminiscent of Lichtenstein's "modern sculptures."

Lunch and dinner were served in the dining room, on a circular pink Carrara marble table, with Sèvres and Wedgwood sets over placemats of old lace, every setting boasting a dozen silver utensils and tiny individual silver and crystal dishes for salt and pepper. Alexandre (whom I had nicknamed Babka) served everyone on their left side and cleared from the right. There were always at least a dozen people at the table: family, friends, business associates, or important guests. The meals, at their most informal, were never less than five courses: soup; an entrée that could consist of cheese soufflé, or gnocchi Parisienne, or croque-monsieurs, or croûtes au fromage, or quenelles de brochet, or stuffed artichoke hearts, etc. . . . Then there was meat or fish, with several exquisite vegetables. Julie used to prepare things that I never ate since: rognons (kidneys) cooked in wine, riz de veau (sweetbreads), beignets de cervelle (brain fritters). Although I didn't like carrots then, I always loved spinach. My favorite dish (but one that was served only when I ate upstairs with my nurse) was what I called "pâtée de chien." It was a slice of delicious Parisian ham with boiled potatoes and creamed spinach à la Julie. Perversely, I would cut the ham in tiny pieces, mash the potatoes, and mix everything up in the spinach—a slop that I ate slowly and delectably, and that looked just like what the dogs ate down below.

Back to the dining room meal. After the main course was a lovely green salad served with the most delicate and delicious herb, oil, and vinegar dressing, and then was the moment I really waited for: Julie's dessert! She was famous as a pastry cook throughout Paris. When we had parties that sometimes counted guests in the hundreds, Julie would cater everything herself: there were incredible layer cakes, pound cakes, fruitcakes, chestnut cakes, tarts, St. Honorés, icecreams, chaussons fourrés, chocolate and vanilla soufflés, petit fours, croquembouches, profitrolles, éclairs, mille-feuilles, and truffles. . . . She became a poet, a sculptor, an architect, an acrobat, an inventor, a dancer, a landscape artist! I remember the tea parties I gave as a little girl, for my school chums. We sat in the garden around the round iron table covered with a bright tablecloth, little flowers in our liberty dresses, organdy and dotted swiss frocks, around veritable little vegetable gardens arranged with the severe frivolity of a Louis XIV parc: plates of tiny cucumber open sandwiches, tomato slices bull's-eyed with egg, radish blossoms, sardines swimming in swirls of homemade mayonnaise, crab mimosa, all in mandala formation on their serving trays, a beautiful baroque geometry. And the taste! Everything fresh, organic, straight from the "marchandes de quat' saisons," those little ambulatory carts that superimposed on the map of Paris a daily tracery of edible bouquets.

Sometimes, Julie departed from the strict cuisine classique to dash off a Russian dish to please our Slavic souls—and also her palate, which grew quite fond of cotelettes Pojarsky, beet borscht with piroshki, or calves' foot stoodin. I remember getting wild over her tarte frangipane with the thin glassy coat of caramel, her pommes de terre surprise, the mysterious baked potatoes that yielded, when opened, a cache of egg cooked in cream, her incredibly complicated stuffed salmons or just as incredibly simple sole meunière. And the eggs! En gelée, en omelette, brouillés, mollets, hachés, flambés, you name it! One had never tasted eggs before biting into one of Julie's! . . .

The beauty of each dish was enhanced by the beauty of the utensils—dishes, plates, bowls, and compotiers having been chosen for their subtle affinity in color, design, or spirit, with the course they presented to us. And after fromages et fruits, finger bowls of Japanese lacquer, no two alike in design, would delicately refresh your extremities with lemon water, fresh blossoms floating above the gold and red cranes, plum blossoms, and pine trees.

I wasn't always allowed to eat downstairs with the grownups. But when I was, I don't think I was much aware of convivial conversation or anything past Babka's route. I listened eagerly for the sound of the "monte-charge" and secretly cursed Babka for his stately and excruciatingly slow rhythm. From the pantry, he would emerge with a dish, in a silver server, held with white gloves and an immaculate white towel. He appeared from behind the Jean Dunand lacquer screens where pink flamingoes stood around preening and catching fish against a dull gold background. He walked to the center of the brass stairs, came down the three steps carefully, glided silently with a fiercely devout expression on the Chinese rug, and deposited his precious cargo on the console against the wall. There it remained, under the Claude Monet, for an exasperatingly long time. When at last all plates were changed and every stray crumb had been brushed off the tablecloth, Alexandre would begin his rounds. When I was little, I was served first. It had definite advantages: first of all, I wouldn't have to wait, and Babka would tip me off discreetely as to which slice the prize in the Galette des Rois was most likely to be found in, or how to pick out the hearts in the lettuce salad. But then it was an awful drag because I had to wait for Mother's signal to start eating, and of course she didn't start until the important guests had been served. I was also terribly put out because people talked and ate slowly and there was what seemed like hours of waiting between courses.

Sometimes the meals were hilarious because my father was a practical joker and loved to buy cheap tricks at the magic store and play jokes on his friends. I remember, for instance, how he rigged up the soup plate of his friend Marius Moutet, then Minister of Colonies, to jump up and down. It was a big luncheon and Marius was expounding on some topic when his plate began to wiggle. He didn't notice but others did. As he continued talking, the plate began twitching, reeling, lurching, bouncing, and finally leaping, spilling soup all over the table. The guests snickered, giggled, and ended up hysterical, and still Moutet didn't notice. At last, he bent down to look at his fly, thinking that it was open and causing the general hilarity. That was the last straw. We broke out in uncontrollable glee and I almost pissed in my panties! There must be an allegory on colonialism here somewhere . . . !

I wanted to share these memories with you, for the sheer joy of it, and the nostalgia of outrageous, naive, and unselfconscious times. I've spent my life in vain pursuit of the palate glories of my childhood, always frustrated and yet not giving up. I have seen your ham and your fish, and I have a feeling that, of all people, you will understand!

> All my love
> Rachel

July 17, 1976

Dearest Barbara,

I started this, my last "official" letter, a ½ dozen times. Each time I tore it up because it seemed confused, downbeat, and depressing. Not that I actually felt so low, but I really had nothing to say, and was floating around aimlessly.

A week ago, I made a big decision. In reality, *something* decided for me. King and I were going to Hollywood to see a movie. On the freeway, apropos of something or other, he said something like: "Boy, if we were doing Instant Theatre now . . ." and before I knew what happened, I popped up with "Let's do it!" He nearly swerved off the freeway! Then he waited twenty-four hours to see if I would change my mind. I didn't. Needless to say, he's come back to life: huge plans, possibilities, goals. As for me, I'm still in a daze trying to figure out what happened. . . .

I feel this has been brewing for a long time. I did a couple of Art Performances in the winter of 1975, and they were very well received—which at least took away what would have been a tremendous amount of doubt about still being able to perform. But in addition, I've been reviewing my life and the various tensions that developed at different stages, as a result of the pull of conflicting energies that always quartered me between theater and visual arts.

As far back as I can remember, I've been gifted in all aspects of theater. This talent is probably inherited. As it happens, my family on Mother's side is thoroughly steeped in it. Mother's youngest brother, Batya, was a set designer. She herself had always dreamed of going "on the boards," but was thwarted by prejudiced parents. The children of her mother's sister, her first cousins, turned out, one and all, to be theater beasts. The older brother, Alexis Granowsky, was a very famous theater and film director in Germany and France between the two World Wars, somewhat of Piscator's stature. He is documented in theater history texts. The second brother, Leonide Azar, became an award-winning and much prized film editor in Paris. The younger brother, Boris Ingster, began his career at the Moscow Art Theater, was an early assistant of Eisenstein, and emigrated to Hollywood in the 1930s, where he became a movie producer, director, and script writer. The young sister, Beatrice, started out as a very gifted actress on the Moscow stage against her parents' wishes, before her career was cut short by an illness that caused the left side of her face to be paralyzed. My mother, although she never pursued a real career, possessed an incredible contralto, and in her Moscow days, had picked up the knack of singing songs just like the gypsies—the gay blades of the period would prolong their white nights well into the dawn in gypsy camps on the outskirts of town. My father loved the theater, and the two of them counted some well-known Parisian theater personalities among their acquaintances and friends. But, as was to be expected, having a daughter who was talented in performance and encouraging her in a professional career in theater were two very different things.

So, as it turned out, I was actively pushed into being a visual artist, since I displayed the usual child's interest in drawing and painting. For some reason, that was thought to be more decorous. And my dancing and acting were considered charming hobbies, not to be taken seriously. As for ballet, it was good for the health and made you graceful.

I can remember all throughout my young years, hearing Father make derogatory remarks about the theater "milieu." The quality and extent of the unhealthy ambience that permeated it, according to him, remained a mystery to me. But his influence was so great that I remember myself mouthing these same pronouncements as rationalizations when, in my early twenties, I was faced once again with my overwhelming penchant for the stage and, again, turned my back on it and went "orthodox" with art.

I was always happier and more comfortable with theater: acting, dancing, and/or directing. I enjoyed it most. I got results. It's weird to think that the indoctrination against it was so strong that I never really noticed I was making a mistake, and was a mediocre artist. I was bored doing art, my temperament went counter to working alone in a studio, and I flourished in every situation involving a group of people doing things for an audience! And the funny part is that my father never had to say "no." I took lessons, I went to acting school, but I never committed myself *really*. I just never asked. . . .

When I did Instant Theatre, and was working at it full-time, I somehow still felt that I was slumming; I wasn't doing what I should be doing, which was art. There is a lot here to say about the reinforcements in the direction of an art career that I got all through the years from people I was close to: the Rauschenbergs, the Johnses, etc. But to make a long story short, from 1956 to 1966, the I.T. years, I tried returning to art two or three times. Every time, I was tempted back into workshopping "just once a week," and ending up full-time again, kicking and guilty because I had "abandoned" art, yet feeling alive and in my element once more!

When I had to quit in 1966 because of my knees, I was almost relieved: now I *had* to stick to art; there was no alternative. I had visions of myself at last becoming a painter, stuck before an easel in a wheelchair. . . . Well, it's been ten years. I did a few things but did not ignite the world of art. Worse yet, I am bored! I have used every excuse in the book not to work. I've avoided being alone in my studio, and when I did work, I didn't get any high. I have "good taste," and so the objects I put out there were acceptable. They did not blaze trails and they did not satisfy me. My nostalgia for "an artist's life" is pure nineteenth-century Romanticism. It's absurd. It was absurd to live almost a ½ century with delusions of thinking myself other than what I am.

My father had been dead a year when I created I.T. Mother never quite understood or approved of it. She liked the fairy tales but I knew I wasn't satisfying her. And satisfying my parents while, on the surface, seeming to rebel against them, was the name of the game. Now that Mother is dead, many things are beginning to emerge from the fog. Things about myself I wasn't at all aware of. And the trip back to Paris after twenty-two years was an eye-opener also: you really can't go home again.

I had a dream some weeks past, in which I told my mother that she never was any good at art, and was much more talented in theater!

All of this was brewing just below the surface but I still wasn't entertaining reconversion plans. It sort of shot up of itself on the Ventura Freeway eastbound!

Barbara, needless to say, I am petrified. Here I am, almost fifty, having to have my knees operated on, overweight, ten years older, out of shape and training, trying to resume one of the most difficult and demanding forms art can take. It was ahead of its time then. But a lot has happened since. Will it be, in its new incarnation, revolutionary or quaint? How will it differ from before? How will I teach it now, how will I perform, with no knees and a bad back, but ten extra years of life and experience? Am I jacking myself off? Will I be accepted by my peers in the art world, or will I lose whatever respect for me they might have? Do I still have it? The quick wit, the stamina and endurance, the enthusiasm, the inspiration? Will it develop, regenerated by the momentum of the activity itself? Will it crash in a humiliating way? I never had so many doubts and fears. Will they disappear when we begin workshopping? Or IS IT TOO LATE? . . .

When we did it last, King and I hocked all we had. We were always broke. We paid ourselves Equity minimum and lived on that, and everything else went into the shows. We never had extra money for publicity, documentation, salaries. Today, we can afford all that. How much will technical facilities take the place of invention and youthful energy?

Excepting a few isolated cases such as the New York-based dance groups, the Living Theater, Grotowsky, a few others scattered around in holes in the wall (and, of course, Art Performance, but that's something else), is theater today that much more advanced than before? Yes and no. There is permissiveness, a different emphasis in content and form, but as far as I know, nobody pulled off what we pulled off in the 1950s and 1960s. If we can cause the right people to surface, form a good company, and train them well, we still have a unique form that no one else had the guts to even try.

We saw many improvisation groups (I hate the word for its tacky connotations) and haven't seen but have read about "Grand Union" and other experiments. But it seems that no one has attempted to create a collective performance the way we did, with all the arts and artisanships of spectacle converging together onstage at the instant of creation: lights, sets, action, music, costumes, etc., all working spontaneously and in total unison for the life of the stage event that would never be repeated. It was quixotic, absurd, and grandiose. We did it, we achieved it, and it went unnoticed by the media but had an odd, insistent, and lasting effect, in an underground way, on mores, clothes, expressions, and forms. What will happen to it above ground?

So many question marks theoretically thrown at you! And no answer expected except from the living of it. Funny. I am still on a quest, still haven't zeroed in on my center, still am an overage adolescent trying to "find myself." But suddenly, my future is taking a physiognomy, sketchy but real. Before that, I had a vision of months and years trailing faceless and dull into eventual dotage, and I got scared.

We may be doing something extravagantly crazy, but at least we'll try. And as we're trying, there will be such fun! And fun is something I prize highly. It's also something I've never fully felt otherwise than standing on a stage, under the lights, laying it out there for the people.

Wish me luck!

All my love,
Rachel

Rachel Rosenthal

Excerpts from "The DbD Experience"

For a year and a half I have been conducting a very unusual weekend workshop called "The DbD Experience." It's an intensive weekend that produces growth and transformation through the medium of performance.

In 1956, I used my talents as an artist to create what was then a revolutionary form of total and spontaneous theater. I called it Instant Theatre, which was a play on pop culture and Zen teachings of the primacy of the moment. Over a period of years, I developed training techniques that enabled members of my company to present a total piece of theatrical art without rehearsal, direction, and almost no collective point of departure or communication between them.

After Instant Theatre closed in 1977, several former members advised me to convert my theatrical training methods into experiential workshops for artists and laypersons alike, in order to make available its benefits to larger numbers of people. This is how "The DbD Experience" came to be.

"DbD" takes place in a professional studio equipped with theatrical lighting, dimmer board, and a sound system. The walls and floors are white and reflective: a floating space of air, color, and light. The work is a nonverbal succession of processes—relaxation, awareness, guided imagery, paired-off techniques, body work, and voice work—culminating in full performance. The participants take turns (as in Instant Theatre) operating the light board, building sets, performing, or making music. The energy rises and ebbs, the group bonds and shapes itself into a unique physiognomy, each workshop emerging with its individual dynamic. And the participant encounters who she or he is.

Originally published in the *Light Bearer,* January 1983, 3, 12–13.

Through this signature of the body, the timbre and expression of the voice, the way in which an assignment is approached and carried out, the image is clear and the feedback evident. Imbalances are corrected within the timeframe of the workshop. There is spectacular movement in two and a half days.

Metaphors in action are taken literally: a man fetters himself with an imprisoning costume and blames others for not setting him free; a woman literally swallows back the tears with her voice, which is not allowed to fully emerge; one who fancies herself open and loving sees the extent of her manipulations in a piece. The man, made aware of his self-blocking, forces himself to costume in ways that leave him free. He realizes that he, not others, is his jailer. The first woman vomits out her voice and with it her pain, her tears. The channel is open. She smiles. Her voice emerges clear as a bell. The last woman sees how she misuses her power with "power trips," unmasks her controlling ploys, and begins to change.

Unlike psychodrama, the work is nonspecific and symbolic. The clues are not autobiographical. They are the tension of certain parts of the body, attention to detail, the way a person focuses on others and lets others rule their actions, or the persistence of rigidity: nonacceptance of interplay, blindness to opportunity, ignoring the environment. These and other behaviors are quickly spotted and become the turning point for the new. There is a shock of recognition, sometimes a complete surprise: "Is *that* what I do?" Awareness is reinforced by feedback from the group; change is encouraged and applauded.

Only one ingredient is missing: the consequences of risk taking are not dire, nor are they irreversible.

After all, this is theater. Therefore, you can take risks. It is safe to push your limits. You become the least integrated facet of your personality. You act out your worst fears. You clown, you play. You are a buffoon, a murderer, or death. You trot out myriad personae like a puppet show. All the while, deeply, you breathe in the reality of your life . . . choice availability, disclosure or the veiling of emotion, the tension between radiating power and social appropriateness. You go beyond ego positions; ploys fall away. No one competes. Competing for what? Against whom? The paradigm shifts; only organic cooperation will do. If you pull the blanket, the fabric unravels.

The work emphasizes esthetic issues. Thus, the participant quickly stops focusing on himself or herself in a self-conscious and critical way. First and foremost is the production of art. It is through that effort and discipline that the self is revealed and healed. The work is beautiful, and in some cases, it is the very fact of participation in the creation of an art piece that raises consciousness ecstatically.

People report varied results from the workshop. For some, it is merely a release, an interlude in which a whole area of playfulness is allowed expression. For others, it may range from specific benefits (i.e., the dissolution of writer's block) to a universal overhaul. Changes may be spectacular, complete about-faces, or they may be gradual, the workshop acting as an initiating catalyst toward a new direction. It can become a rite of passage. Whatever the person is ready for happens. And what happens sticks. For the metamorphosis is not only intellectual, but total. You are the gains. You are change. You are *Do*ing *by Do*ing.

Rachel Rosenthal

Rachel's Brain

Stage-Right: *A 25-ft-high airlift, a small wooden bench-box.*
Stage-Center: *An 8-ft-long platform, one ft high, parallel to the stage. A large screen hangs* up-center.
Stage-Left: *A kitchen table with a bowl of water containing a cauliflower head, covered with a large pink napkin; a blender, a measuring cup, assorted knives and kitchen utensils (choppers, graters, etc.).*
A pink scarf is laid alongside the center platform, downstage of it. A bowl containing earth sits onstage behind a black box, center, *under the screen. A cauliflower head and a watering can filled with water are placed at the base of the airlift. A bag with toys is hidden in an opening behind the small box* stage-right.

Blackout

MUSICIAN *enters. She is wearing black. She plays for about one minute an eighteenth-century-sounding minuet.*

Slide: "The evolution of the brain not only overshot the needs of prehistoric man; it is also the only example of evolution providing a species with an organ that it does not know how to use: a luxury organ, which will take its owner thousands of years to put to good use—if he or she ever does. The history of science, philosophy, and art is the slow process of the mind learning by experience to actualize the brain's potentials. The new frontiers to be conquered are the convolutions of the cortex."
—Arthur Koestler

Unpublished text, 1987.

Slide: A baroque stage set.

Enter ROSENTHAL *as "Marie Antoinette," wearing a gray crinoline gown, a high wig on top of which is a three-master frigate, in typical Louis XVI fashion style. She is singing to the minuet-like music. She delivers the following speech in a half-operatic, half-sprechtstimme style.*

I am the flower of the Enlightenment!
The Head of State! The crowning glory!
The apogee of all that is reasonable, rationalism
radiantly redeemed.
I am a rose on a wire stem, my precious bud high up
there in the frigate's crow's nest, floating on spun
sugar.
My head, hovering over a cloud of talcum powder, is
neatly severed from the beast.
I am a higher human!
My control center dispenses enlightened commands.
There is illumination in all the nooks and crannies:
a neuron plant a-buzzing, synapses a-hopping, no
shadow, no lazy cell anywhere!
I am a thought machine!
Je pense donc je suis.
La tête c'est moi.
My head is me.
I am to be.
I have no doubts.
The others are below.
The others, foraging in the dirt for grubs, are
beasts. But they have their place. They are the
walkway of flesh over which my slipper lightly
treads. Only my head has weight.
My body is inexistent, but I hate it nonetheless.
Remnant of a filthy past, of connections I'd rather
forget, of organic fallibilities I choose to ignore.
Reminder of bloody wombs, smelly placentas,
disgusting semen, tampons, cramps, solitary
pleasures, taped fingers, the rod . . .
Ecstasy and agony . . .
Shame and longing . . .

The beasties under the pillow creeping down, down
along the sheet . . .
NO!
Get up! Get dressed!
There is no consciousness but cortical consciousness!
The animals don't feel a thing. Their agonized
bellows and blood-curdling screams when, with four
paws nailed to a board, you cut them open to observe
the slow uncoiling of their guts, no! NO! they have
nothing to do with pain, with consciousness! RUN!
with your hands over your ears! They feel nothing.
The sounds are mechanized, like the tinkly bells of
the dancing music box. Only worse, worse, abominable
approximations of agony, unbearable mimicry of
suffering, just to frighten us . . . NO! You cannot
shake the fact of my supremacy, my separateness, my
severance from the natural order of things.
Ah, silence.
At last. Their vocal cords have been severed.
Relief.
My cup runneth over.
My head is a vessel, the Grail of the Age of
Culture. I am the recipient and the bearer of gifts.
Let them eat cake!
It's all there: the Astrolabe and the Cotton Gin;
Newtonian Physics and the Iron Maiden; the Strait
of Magellan and the genetically engineered Toy
Poodle.
My Ship of State is rocking. Rats scurry down the
ropes.
Within my Three-Master is all of Culture. My left
sail is Locke and Bacon. My right sail harbors
bacterial cultures and I ignore their alarming
proliferation.
I am infected.
Enlightenment undernourishes me.
The cord is cut. No nutrients can reach me from the
Mother's blood.
Viruses and bacteria multiply in the dark folds, far
away from curious, probing eyes.

Pockets of infection suppurate.
There is no renewal, no access to the scandalously
visceral rejuvenations of Nature.
It's a closed system, groping for oxygen and the
relief of decay.
The viruses ooze down the cording of the Three-
Master, down through the floury curls, down, down
through the three brains: the Cerebellum, the
Amygdala, the Reptilian Stem, and OUT, through the
mouth, as WORDS!
I'm choking. My throat is on fire. Flames to
starboard! The sails are burning! All hands on deck!
Abandon ship!
Sauve qui peut!
The scrambled bytes of knowledge spew out. The
system fails!
My head melts.
My neck beckons.
Off with her head. OFF WITH HER HEAD!
I am blinded by the light!

MARIE ANTOINETTE *comes* down-right *to the box, kneels behind it, and
inclines her head over it with her arms outstretched to the sides.*

Où est le bourreau?
Oh, please, let him hold a rose between his teeth!

She is beheaded.
ROSENTHAL *takes off the costume and the wig.*

Slides: A very fast succession of images from R's life.

Music: A collage of sounds, voices, and music out of R's life ("Rachel's Brain Static"), interrupted seven times by the following:

Slides: A/THOUGHT/FIGHTS/ITS/WAY/INTO/CONSCIOUSNESS

Sound: Voice-overs by ROSENTHAL saying these *words* with great
effort, as though they were coming from the depths of being and
prehistory.

With each word, ROSENTHAL *is discovered in a light, wearing a gray ensemble and a mask of* Homo Erectus, *our ancestor, and miming the slow evolution from Primate, through Hominid, to modern Homo Sapiens.*

At the end of the sequence, ROSENTHAL *goes* up-center, *takes off the mask to the end of the* sound *tape, and shouts the words:*

A THOUGHT FIGHTS ITS WAY INTO
CONSCIOUSNESS!
Fire on the lake! The image of Revolution.
Thus the superior person
Sets the calendar in order
And makes the seasons clear.

Sound tape ends.

Live music: Violin.

Slides: A sequence of seven slides of drawings depicting ROSENTHAL's shaved head schematically, with a succession of dotted lines coming down her forehead.

ROSENTHAL *moves her finger down her forehead in rhythm with the slides and the music, indicating the dotted line. She continues to indicate a dotted line coming down the front of her body, and down on the floor before her. She walks in rhythm following the imaginary line until she steps up on the* down *platform. As she does, she recites:*

I am ugly
I am stupid
I'm an idiot
I am guilty
I'm a phony
I am nothing
I'm a failure
I'm a fraud

She repeats the above, beating herself on the head and over the body, slapping herself, until she suddenly stops, freezes, and says:

Five hundred million years of brain evolution . . . for this?

Blackout

Slide: "The failure to develop the right brain with the left results in both psychic and intellectual imbalance. Behavioral and learning disorders in abundance are the product. The high premium placed on technology and rationality is now seen to be taking an equally high toll in human fulfillment."

—Stuart Litvak and A. Wayne Sanzee

Lights on the left *table area.*

ROSENTHAL *goes to the table, lifts the napkin over the bowl, takes the cauliflower head out of the water, and lifts it high for the audience to see it.*

Slides: A series depicting the brain.

Dazzling object!
Precious!
Extravagant!
The only organ we cannot transplant and still be
ourselves.
We used to eat it, you know . . .
Long ago. We knew, even then, its importance—that
the self and the entire universe were enfolded
within.
Carefully, slowly, with effort, we used to bore a
small hole at the base and then scooped out . . .
(mimes tasting) all of it! The Power . . . The
Memories . . . The Identity . . . The Spirit!
Magic! The cosmos! Knowledge inherits the Earth. Let
them eat cake!

She begins to cut the cauliflower with knives.

We don't do that anymore, of course. We're way
beyond this barbarism.

Now we're simply curious: we wish to know when,
where, how . . .

Slide: A monkey in a restraining apparatus with electrodes im-
planted in his brain.

We implant electrodes, dye the tissue, separate the
folds . . . of live animals, of course.
Did you know that there are about 100
billion neurons in a single human brain, and that,
in a single human brain, the number of their
possible interconnections exceeds the number of
atoms in the universe?

Slides: Neurons and stars in the cosmos.

When first we got it—and where did it come from?—
it was pristine, blank, empty. For the most part.
We're only now beginning to inhabit it.
Why did we buy this huge, myriad-room, unfurnished
mansion when all we needed was a hut?
And now that this piece of real estate is mine, and
mine to interior-design, what style do I furnish it
in? Retro? Futuristic? Revolutionary, or Safe?
Make no mistake: the decorator is me. I can't hire a
pro to do the decorating for me.
Do you think it's easy to be your own brain surgeon?

When I was little, I understood it all.
Where is this ecstasy? Here? Here?

In this sequence, ROSENTHAL *cuts, breaks, gouges, and otherwise manipu-*
lates the cauliflower.

The memory of true oneness, of the excruciating love
for the Earth . . .
Where?
The knowledge of aloneness, of being seduced and
abandoned, where?
She loves me . . . She loves me not . . .

The first inkling of sex. Here? It didn't smell like
this . . .
How can I ferret out the structures, the wiring, the
programs, the communicative chemicals that will
explain as plain as two plus two why I am the
difficult person I am?

ROSENTHAL *leaves the cauliflower, and works her way around the table
during the next speech. She ends up* downstage *of it.*

I am a primate.
Timid. I hide in branches, in caves, behind rocks.
I'm naked. I can't defend myself. I am scared.
Many of my people die of a crunched skull—the
leopards . . .
But hey, the brain is the way to go: from hand to
mouth to eyes to runaway feedback!
A ziggurat! A Tower of Babel!
EXTENSION!
Reach! Reach!
Control radiates!

She reaches and loses her balance.

We are out of control . . .
Our brain extensions are coating the crust of the
Planet.
Like a lichen.
Like a fungus.
The Earth is overlaid with a layer in the image of our image of
the cortex: dry, smart, ingenious, and
deadly.

ROSENTHAL *pants rhythmically, turns* up-stage *looking at the screen, and
lets out a piercing, drawn-out scream.*

Slide: "If you put god outside and set him vis-à-vis his creation,
and if you have the idea that you are created in his image, you
will logically and naturally see yourself as outside and against the
things around you. And as you arrogate all mind to yourself, you

will see the world around you as mindless and therefore not entitled to moral or ethical considerations. . . . If this is your estimate of your relation to nature *and you have an advanced technology,* your likelihood of survival will be that of a snowball in hell."

—Gregory Bateson

ROSENTHAL *pours some water on her skull, walks slowly* down *toward the platform* down-center.

To be I
To be not
I therefore am not to be
Or am I?
Am I one of evolution's countless mistakes?

ROSENTHAL *sits on the platform and takes the pose of Rodin's thinker. She then sits casually.*

I think therefore I am.
I think who I am.
I think I think . . .
I am me thinking.
I sit up there and see me thinking.
Yes. My thought is thinking me sitting up there
watching me thinking.

ROSENTHAL *freezes in midgesture. Bassoon* music *for a few seconds. When the* music *stops,* ROSENTHAL *unfreezes and begins to speak again.*

But my thought wonders how it arises to think of me
thinking and having thoughts that identify with
themselves, so who is this other one sitting up
there watching this me-identified thought, and who
brought it up in the first place?

Same business as above.

As for me, I identify with me.
So who am I watching?
Are there two of me?

And if there are, who is watching whom?
And how do I know who it is that I am when I think
of me thinking, wondering who's watching, and
knowing I can't be in two places at once, but unable
to decide which place I'm in since the thinking does
the watching and the watching is a thinking too, and
anyway, there's no place up there, it's a metaphor.

Same business as above.

To be or not to be.
I am me, that's a fact.
I know I am and am not not, because to be I need to
think of being, and thinking, I know that not to be
can't be since I think to be.
But there again, I can't tell who is who is me,
being . . .

Same business.

When I think I am, my thinking is catching up with
me being because, in retrospect, it seems I've been
being all along, and that the thinking of being is
the thought of a me that's been doing the being all
along.
But perhaps that's an illusion . . .

Same business.

Because it's only when I think of me being that it
seems I've been being all along. But how do I know
that's true, since I don't know I'm being until I
think of me being and perhaps there's no being at
all unless there is the thinking.
So where am I when there's no thinking if there's no
being?

Same business.

To be or not to be . . .
That's a damn good question!

Let me see.
I think therefore I am.
I know: I'll stop thinking and I'll see where I go
when I'm not busy being.

ROSENTHAL *is trying to stop thinking and having trouble doing it.*

It's hard not to think . . .
I mustn't be afraid of not being because all I have
to do to be is to think. Right?
Right. Hmmm . . . But what if I am not when I think
not?
And if I'm not, I can't very well start thinking,
can I? So who will do the thinking for me to come
back and be?
Aye, *there's* the rub!

Same business, freeze and music, *unfreeze.* ROSENTHAL *rises.*

If I stop thinking and there's no me to be, then no
one can do the thought that will make me be again.
Well, by golly, better not stop thinking!

Music, *ending with a bump and grind.*

ROSENTHAL *lies down* upstage *of and perpendicular to the platform with
her head resting on it. In the next sequence, she moves slowly beside and
over the platform.*

Slides: Images of ROSENTHAL in *Rachel's Brain* up to this moment.

The Past . . .
Almost . . . almost . . .
NOW!
Gone! . . .

My past is the brain-building protein that creates
my now and future mind.

Everywhere I turn, I see my own reflection. What is
out there? I process and interpret the signals with
available structures. I create a universe
constituted of my brain's limitations and of the
unlimited inventiveness of my mind.

Everywhere I turn, a self-portrait!

I yearn to shatter the mirror, to touch and feel the
reality beyond, to burst my cocoon, to go through
the crack in the Cosmic Egg!

I yearn to be a rocket, to pierce the unknowability
of the cosmos, to tear me from myself!

Perhaps only in death . . .

The last lines are spoken by ROSENTHAL *on her back, perpendicular to
the audience, with her head upside down, dangling off the* downstage *side
of the platform. After the last line, her arms and legs slowly lift off the
platform and seem to float up.*

Blackout

Slide: "At the time when vertebrates first appeared, the direction
and progress of variation in the Arthropoda was leading, owing
to the manner in which the brain was pierced by the esophagus,
to a terrible dilemma—either the capacity for taking in food without sufficient intelligence to capture it, or intelligence sufficient
to capture food and no power to consume it."
                    —"The Origin of Vertebrates," W. H. Gaskell

Slides: In the next sequence, there are twenty-eight slides of the
clichés of recent historical atrocities toward humans and animals.

I think I'm hungry.
Hmmm. Yes, I can feel a cramp *(touching her head)*.
It's telling me something.
I must be hungry.
Yum yum.

She goes to the table stage-left. *Ties the pink napkin around her neck like a bib.*

Food for thought!

Calls offstage left.

Hey! Kill me that and bring it nice and rare to the
table!

A shot is heard. A cauliflower on a nylon thread falls down from the rafters and stops in midair before ROSENTHAL. *She cuts off the string, cuts the cauliflower, and places some pieces in the blender.*

I like that! Saignant!

She punctuates the following speech with bursts of blending.

More, more . . . Mmmm . . . MORE!
Hey, some of this too. And some of that. Hey, that's
delicious!
Gimme that. A little bit more . . .

She indicates that the next voice is her STOMACH. *Gravelly voice.*

STOMACH: I've had enough.

ROSENTHAL: Shut up! Tastes good! . . .

STOMACH: Hey, I'm full!

ROSENTHAL: Shut up! Mind your own business.
(*Off*) Kill me another! (*Another cauliflower falls
from the rafters.* ROSENTHAL *cuts the string and
proceeds to maim it and to feed it to the blender.*)

STOMACH: Oooooo! Too much!

ROSENTHAL: You keep out of this! I know what I want! I know what
I need!

(Off) Kill me two more! *(Two cauliflowers fall.* ROSENTHAL *makes them attack each other. She barks.)*
Dog eat dog!
(Blending) Mmmmm . . . Yeah! Mmmmm . . . Yum! Mmmmm . . . Slurp!

STOMACH: Ouch! I'm going to burst!

ROSENTHAL: What? What? I didn't hear that!
My brain is hungry! I must fill the empty spaces . . .
(She presses cauliflower pieces to her head.)

STOMACH: I'm passing out! I'm in a coma! I'll shut up.

ROSENTHAL: Good riddance!
(Off) Okay. Kill me a whole field, a herd, a forest! I must have it or I'll die! HORROR VACUI!

STOMACH: What goes in must come out. Where go the wastes?

ROSENTHAL: Who cares? It's too delicious. EAT OR BE EATEN!

STOMACH: Where goes the garbage?

ROSENTHAL: I don't give a shit. I'll think of something.
Tomorrow is another day!
What, no more oil? Steal it from the Indians, the caribou.
What, run out of uranium? Toss in the Third World!
Let them eat cake . . . or opium!
I'm hungry!
I know I'm hungry because my head tells me I'm starved! Fill 'er up! *(She grabs the blender cup and pours the cauliflower mixture on her head over the bowl.)*
FILL 'ER UP! *(Same business.)*
It never fills up . . .
DON'T STOP, MOTHER! DON'T TURN OFF THE TIT!
What, nothing left?

I can't stop cold turkey, make sacrifices,
conserve . . .
MOTHER!
(She turns on the blender to blend on steadily. Noise. She moves to
center.)
GIVE ME MORE OR I'LL KILL YOU!
Whaddayamean not rational? Rational is where it came
from in the first place, asshole! *(She steps up on the* down *platform.)*
I eat therefore I am!
I'll eat you and you and you! *(indicating people in the audience. She*
steps down downstage *of the platform.)*
I'm hanging on the Mother's tit like a bulldog. When
the tit is bitten off, I'll start on the pancreas,
the liver, the calf!
ALL!
I want it all. NOW! Before it's too late! *(She goes back to the table and*
turns off the blender.)
I won't let *you* devour *me,* Mother. We'll see who
eats who first.
Le boudin! Le boudin! BLOOD SAUSAGE! *(Turns the blender on*
again. Goes center *again.)*
The bloated goose-liver, force fed—the bloated
Biafra bellies of starvation.
Hunger strikes—and Balanchine boulimia.
The parsimonious elegance of a hyperexpensive plate
of "Nouvelle"—and the near-empty bowl of prison
slop. *(She steps up on the platform again.)*
Let them ALL eat cake!
The appestat is in the brain. *(She steps off the*
platform and walks backward upstage. *Indicates her*
head.) Eating disorders. Appetite suppressants.
Hunger pangs. Epigastric cramps. Aie! Aie! Aie!
Acquired Immune Deficiency Syndrome attacks the
brain cells *(She takes a step forward with each word.)*
We are all AIDS viruses in the Mother's brain!
(Walks back to the table and turns off the blender.)
I've earned the Earth.
I made my brain.
I get the prize.

I deserve to die . . .
I can't think straight!
(Collapses in sobs.)
MOTHER! WHY HAST THOU FORSAKEN ME?

Slide: "Do you not see how logical thinking, in order to even function, must limit to a specific, and that this specific is then the only apparent reality—and how this fragmented form of thinking then orients quite naturally around the notion of *scarcity,* the idea that in order to have we must take from and deprive others since only a limited amount can be seen?"

—Joseph Chilton Pierce

ROSENTHAL *walks forward during the* slide, *eats a piece of cauliflower slowly, then spits it out into the bowl.*

Sour taste.

She walks around the table, mimes entering her skull with her finger and trying to pull something out. She looks at her finger. There is obviously nothing there.

I've never seen my brain. What is it anyway, a
gland?

She walks forward to sit on the downstage *platform, facing the audience.*

Slide: "At present, the world of brain science is in the middle of a revolution. Scientists now regard the brain as a hormonally driven gland, not an electrically driven computer. Holism replaces reductionism in a new paradigm that gives human thought qualities that are warm, soft, wet, colorful, qualitative, timeless, communal, and united."

—"The Fabric of Mind," Richard Bergland, M.D.

ROSENTHAL *takes the scarf with both hands, holding it taut and moving it horizontally up her legs and torso until it rests under her chin.*

There's nothing below.
NOTHING! BELOW! (She crumbles, doubled up.)

Ooooh! I have to go to the bathroom! It's
disgusting!
And I'm hungry too . . . I have to pee, I have to shit,
my knees hurt . . . *(Places the scarf suddenly under her chin again.)*
NO! *(She slowly lifts her arms up as the scarf makes a* V *under her face.
She screws up her features in a grimace.)*
Oooooh! I did it in my pants! It's disgusting! I'm
sorry . . . *(Suddenly, she lies down, parallel to the audience, her head
protruding from the side of the platform, her legs and arms flailing the
air. Then she holds the scarf like a guillotine above her neck.)*
NO! Not now! Not yet!

The music *gives three strong blasts. On the third, the "guillotine" falls.*
ROSENTHAL *"dies."*

Blackout

Slide: An image of the Rousseau painting representing the "Sleep-
ing Gypsy," but instead of a lion, a gorilla sits next to her.

Slide: "You can always trust an eating gorilla. Having found his
food, he has put aside all effort and concern for survival. . . . He
is simply eating. . . The eating gorilla perceives in any other one
who is eating a similar surrender to ordinary life, to the natural
state and order of existence."   —Bubba Free John

The following sequence is played on or around the small stage-right *box
and the* downstage *platform.* ROSENTHAL *alternates between playing*
KOKO, *the gorilla, and her* TRAINER, *the scientist who has been teaching
her American Sign Language.*

TRAINER: Hi. Thank you for coming here tonight. We're going to
    try to demonstrate what we've been teaching Koko.
    *(She sits on the box, takes toys out of a bag, and
    places them in front of her on the floor.)* Of
    course, she might be a little shy in front of all
    you people. But we've been practicing a lot and
    hopefully she'll be able to perform.

KOKO *(Looks around.)*

TRAINER: Oh, I mustn't forget to warn you about gorilla
  etiquette: You mustn't look Koko straight in the
  eye. That's very threatening to a gorilla. It's the
  same as if I did this to a human *(obscene,
  aggressive gesture)*. So please avert your eyes when
  you look at Koko.

KOKO *(Looks around, gets up, snorts.)*

TRAINER: Koko, let's see if you can remember what we did yesterday.
  (Signs) What . . . is . . . this . . . ? *(Indicates one of the toys.)*

KOKO *(Picks up the toy, cradles it, looks around.)*

TRAINER: Now, Koko, pay attention! Come back here. Yesterday
  we decided that this was a . . . ?

KOKO *(Signs, looks at the toy, and eats it.)*

TRAINER: Now, Koko, you know this means "This is a banana."
  But this is a "pin"! *(Bowling pin.)*

KOKO *(Signs and cradles the pin.)*

TRAINER: Now, Koko, you know this means "baby." Sometimes she
  can be so stubborn . . .

KOKO *(Lies down on the box, scratches her underarm.)*

TRAINER: I'm not going to tickle you now, in front of all
  these people! Later. Now we'll do something else.
  (Picks up doll.) You signed "baby." Does Koko love
  baby?

KOKO *(Takes the doll. Makes ho ho ho sounds, taps the doll on the behind,
  signs, cradles it, more sounds, and then smashes the doll on the platform.)*

TRAINER: *(Retrieves the doll rapidly and scans the audience
  worriedly.)* I hope no one's been looking at her too

closely . . . Now, Koko, go over there and sit. *(Picks up the ball.)* Koko want to play?

KOKO *(Throws the ball to the audience and laughs. Some interplay.)*

TRAINER: Koko has a great sense of humor. She tells jokes, she lies, and she's very contrary.

KOKO: *(Sits propped against the* stage-right *box, signs and talks.)* Koko fine animal . . . Koko fine gorilla. So hard to make people understand. Koko knows what she wants. Ho ho . . . Koko *(grabs her toe)* . . . How to tell her? *(Lies on her back with her feet up.)* Koko loves . . . *(Stands and leans on the box on her knuckles in gorilla stance.)* Koko loves to play in trees . . . Koko always feels love for the Big Mother . . . Nipples of the Big Mother everywhere. Koko loves Big Mother's food. She abandons herself to the ecstatic trance of feeding. Koko makes nest anywhere when sleepy.
(She moves up on the box, lies down, does many moves in gorilla fashion.) Koko wants to tell about the sky, the food, the playing, and the breaking of branches. She wants people to know about the feelings of fine animal who loves life. Everything is serious and important. This frees me to play, to laugh, and to clown. *(She puts the toy bag on her head.)* I am a good clown. *(The bag falls off.).* I know the Mother likes me when I clown because the glee I feel is her glee, barking through my giggles. Koko is a fine gorilla. Koko loves to break things. Hard to remember to say things in small pieces . . . When Koko speaks *(up on the platform)* it all comes out in one big gorilla piece, one big gorilla feeling, one big gorilla love!

TRAINER: *(Off the platform, sits on it.)* Koko, come sit down. We're going to learn something new today. Pay attention. *(Signs.)* To be or not to be, I think therefore I am.

KOKO: *(Signs.)* Therefore not I be not am be be am
Therefore I to to *(very pleased with herself)*.

TRAINER: Now watch carefully, Koko. Again: To be or not to
be, I think therefore I am.

KOKO: *(Starts lying on her back, gets up during the speech
and stands on the platform.)* What I love best is the
feeling I get when I am both me and the Big Mother,
when She is both herself and the shoot I eat, the
screeching bird, the boy gorilla, the overhanging
cliff, and the attentive Moon. And I, being Her, am
too the Moon, the leaf, the gorilla brother. I live
in an enchanted world.
(Sits on the platform, signs.) To think be think or I
think therefore
am to therefore or not therefore.

TRAINER: One last time, Koko, this is the good one.
To be or not to be, I think therefore I am.

KOKO: *(Chuckling and scratching herself.)* I am my beard's
friend, my nipples' friend, my big belly's friend.
And I like all these parts tickled, fondled, and
hugged. Moments ever new, surprising, nurturing,
dependable. I know and trust they'll be there. So I
abandon myself and drift, tenderly rocked as I
navigate among the branches, feeling the tug of the
Mother in my gut.
*(She mimes hanging and swinging gently from a
branch, her eyes closed, ecstatic. She comes to,
sits on the platform, signs correctly.)* To be or not
to be, I think therefore I am.

TRAINER: You got it, Koko! Good girl! Smart gorilla!

KOKO: *(Yawns.)* Gorilla sleepy. *(She begins to lie down in
Trainer's lap.)*

TRAINER: *(Mimes receiving Koko who lies down in her lap. She
strokes her as she speaks to the audience.)* Well,

that was a bit rocky but you saw a little of what
she can do. *(Koko is getting up and going* upstage *as
Trainer follows her with her eyes.)* She now has more
then a thousand words . . . We must process all the
data that we've gathered so far to prove that what
Koko is doing is indeed speaking. There is still a
lot of resistance to that. *(She picks up Koko's toys
and places them in the bag as she speaks.)* We feel
confident that in two, three years, when all the
information is in, these doubts will be dispelled.
Koko . . . ? *(She looks around for her.)* Oh. She went to
bed.
Thank you very much for coming.

ROSENTHAL *puts away the bag and picks up the bowl with the earth. She
stands* upstage *during the* slide.

Slide: "Do no dishonor to the Earth lest you dishonor the spirit
of man. Hold your hand out over the Earth as over a flame. To
all who love her, who open to her the doors of their veins, she
gives of her strength, sustaining them with her own measureless
tremor of dark life."   —Henry Beston

ROSENTHAL *begins a chant with the* MUSICIAN. *She comes forward with
the bowl and pours the earth down in a heap. Then, still chanting, she
gets a cauliflower head from beside the airlift, brings it down, and "plants"
it in the earth. She then picks up a watering can and waters the cauliflower.*

Slides: A series depicting a cauliflower head in nature: on the
earth, in a stream, in trees, among flowers, etc., ending with one
against the blue sky. The last slide coincides with the end of the
chanting and planting.

Music: Violin.

Old Mother Earth, sacred Gaia!
My brain, just like my heart, is hollow at the core.
A mind-womb secreting liquid consciousness diffused
throughout the body,

thought-rivers flowing from the brain to the body,
from the body to the brain,
thought-rivers overflowing the banks of the self and
creating vast cross-currents of mind in the multi-
dimensional Universe.
Marvel and apotheosis!
It took five hundred million years for the Mother to
create a consciousness of herself.
I am Her brainchild.

Slide: "If we could look at ourselves from anything approaching
cosmic time, if we had any sense of cosmic power, cosmic deli-
cacy, then every indicator would point the same way: down.
Down, down, down, we do not need this new direction, which
is up."   —Martin Amis, "Einstein's Monsters"

ROSENTHAL *chants again. The chant ends in a discordant note.*

Music: Discordant synthesizer sounds.

But I'm scared.
Getting down . . . Accepting gravity, centering low,
coming to my senses . . .
Going below. To the violence within . . .
Burning with it!
The rite, the ordalie. Gaia, Persephone, Ereshkigal!
Mothers of blood, rot, and fermentation!
Testing the mettle.
Where is the courage?
Who has the guts to look the Gorgon in the face?
Tough love, Mother . . .

ROSENTHAL *begins to back off toward the airlift. She takes on a new persona, that of a person who avoids "getting down."*

Besides, the call of duty is over and above, isn't
it?
Why mud pies when Higher Consciousness beckons?
Think up!
Pull up by the bootstraps, climb the highest

mountain, grow wings! *(She begins to climb up on the airlift.)*
Fly high, and away from the viscera! *(On the platform.)*
More cortical thinking, more knowledge, more
artificial intelligence!
I know it all!
All I've ever wanted to know and was afraid of
knowing!

The airlift takes off, with a big blast of fog machine.

Sound: Blast-off on the synthesizer.

Lights: As the platform climbs higher and higher, the airlift is lit in
all the colors of the rainbow. It also looks like going up the chakras.

I am the biped with the Big Brain! Born fully armed
from the head of Zeus!
That's it! The Mother is a Father!
The brain is the womb. There *is* no Mother! *(Another climb on the
airlift.)*
Look at all us orphans!
Floating up like farts in a bathtub! Up up and away!
(Another climb.) Hey up there! I'm coming after you!
We put you up there, way out of reach, out of touch.
I don't know you. Must I look up in supplication? Is
that the attitude? *(Another climb.)*
Hey, Deus ex Machina!
I'm here!
I take on the sacrifice. I am the burnt offering,
skewered on a paradox, for us all!
Take me! Accept me!
I want to be one of the chosen, whisked up,
tremulous and grateful, as the holocaust roars
below! . . .
(Another climb. She is nearly out of sight.) Hey up
there! Can you hear me?
What, no one up there? *(Looks around in a panic.)*
The waters are rising . . .
The air is thinning . . .
The deserts are growing . . .

The missiles are coming . . .
So where are you?

Slide: The Earth from space.

Hey, now you see it, now you don't . . .

Slide: Off.

Lights: Off, except for a small, wan light on ROSENTHAL, which
grows dimmer and disappears during the following sequence.

What the hell am I doing here?
Put me down!
Put me down!
Put me down!

(The sound is like a hollow echo, getting more distant and dying off.)

Blackout

Silence

THE END

Rachel Rosenthal

"Statement"

I am becoming less and less inclined to think of myself as making "art." I put out ideas in a certain form. I play them out with the help of various media. There is an audience. I get paid to put out this product. I try to get bookings. I am looking for a wider base, more popular venues. I am eager to expand my public, to be heard by those who know nothing about "art" and who are not the already converted. I do nothing else with my life but produce this product and then attempt to market it. I believe in my work and have no sense of how others perceive it. I am always amazed when I get feedback, either when it reaches and touches, or when it draws a blank. But to me, the propagation of ideas, beliefs, and worldviews is the most important and significant thing I can do with the time allotted. A superstructure of the art world has been created. I don't feel that I belong to it in any way. Nor do I belong to the theater world. I, and others like me, are square pegs. We don't fit in the round holes, but neither do we fall through the cracks. I believe in expressing things with vigor and passion. I want to perform in a way that will make people uneasy with the easy way out. We can't afford to go easy on ourselves in these times. Culture, art, they are in the fashion business, on Wall Street, on Madison Avenue. I am not interested in any of that. Yet, to gain a wider audience, these elements will perhaps come into play: paradox, irony, exasperation. Our times. . . . Ideas as marketable goods. You can't escape that if you want to have access. Still, I don't worry so much about purity as I worry about time running out. I want to do film, video, CDs, books, I want to direct. . . . All these things must go to market if they are to exist and make a dent. Communicate!

Originally published in *High Performance* (Spring–Summer 1988), 65–66.

Communicate! My deep preference is always to chuck it all and go live with animals in the bosom of the Earth! I keep putting it off in order to perform pieces that bring the Earth into conscious focus. That's rather funny. I don't know about the "function of the arts" today. But I know that the above is the function of my art, and when you consider the real and present danger to our life and to life as we know it on the planet, I wish it were indeed the "function of the arts" generally.

Rachel Rosenthal

"Letter from the Future"

It's been a very long time after the birth of one Jesus the Christ. Who is that, anyway? I don't know. No one knows. There is no one to tell us but we still count years that way.

There are very few people. All animals are pests but they are growing bigger. And they seem to be getting all the food. We've dug out all the dumps, which covered most of the available land, for pieces of things to use. The ones before really were extravagant. They threw good things away. That's great for us because we can't make anything. The machines don't run. We've forgotten the rules. We are very stupid. Our brains can't hold onto things for too long. They have shrunk, too, and the rats' brains are now almost as big as ours.

We can't bathe or sail. The water is too dangerous for the health. We've learned to process rain and our stomachs have developed a tolerance to its acidity. There are so few of us left that we can share the rain. But it's getting scarcer. It's so hot, the rain seems to evaporate before it reaches us. There are expeditions to rain places, high up in the mountains, etc. to bring some back. It's back-breaking work.

We are scavengers. The land doesn't nourish us because the deserts are everywhere. We outwit the insects and sometimes the rodents and the birds. Some plants are plentiful. They are very tough and we need strong teeth. We make metal dentures with the parts from the dumps.

There is a lot of activity below us, and we have come to believe in a subterranean deity who is very angry at us. We see her as a frightening being who is out to get us for what the old people had done. But it's not our fault. They did it, not us. So we try to be meek and serve her. Sometimes we send one of us down a caldera as a gift. The Earth

Unpublished manuscript, 1990.

shakes under our feet and the wind tosses great dust storms up in the air.

Life is hard. We are constantly afraid that it will disappear. When we hear a bird we are overjoyed. Song birds, like in the old days, are gone, of course. But other birds do still make croaking sounds. Our ears are sharp. We sense the coming of earthquakes. Our noses too. We can smell the riftings in the Earth that send up the poison gas put there by the old people. We flee.

Our worry is that the great deity under our feet will refuse to go on. We have so botched up her works. What if the great sounds of life under there stopped? If the floor beneath the sea stopped moving? If the lands stood still? Oh yes. We know all about that . . . that is the knowledge that was not allowed to die. You see, that knowledge is what keeps us going. It says that yes, our kind have killed the surface, but underneath she is still strong, still moving, still capable of starting over . . . but we worry. What if she stopped? What if the dance of the lands ground to a halt? The existing mountains would slowly erode, all would be calm, even, flat, boring. The changes in animals and plants would stop. No incentive because the climate would even out and remain unchanging. There would be no challenges, no surprises to spur us on to great leaps of faith. All would become gray, easy, and dead. We fear that the most. Everything on our planet is due to everything else. That's basic knowledge, isn't it? So since life, and everything, is dependent on the motion of the great being underneath, couldn't she be influenced also by what is going on on the surface? Why not, we furtively think when we are depressed. That's our big worry. When we are in the throes of this anxiety, more people are dispatched down the caldera.

We hope to hell that works.

Rachel Rosenthal

Excerpts from "The Indecency of the NEA's Decency Clause"

Restrictions on art making are abhorrent. All right, I can already hear the objection: "We aren't putting restrictions on art making, only on grant giving." But, were this a country where there is cultural honor and pride in the artists we harbor, if those artists were truly sustained by an economic structure that regards art making as integral and indispensable to the health of the people, then yes, we could speak of the separation between restrictions on art making and restrictions on grant giving. We all know that this is not the case. . . .

. . . All the restrictions that the NEA is asked to adopt deal with the human body. Nothing new here. The body has frightened people out of their wits for millennia. The body can make us feel. It can also arouse feelings in others. *Homo Sapiens* is a highly sexed species. Fear of the body is peculiar to the Christian world. The Christian Church has demonized the body and its functions as well as women and homosexuals, whose otherness scared the pants off the Church Fathers. The history of the Western world is that of Christianity fighting Paganism, and the present fight over the NEA is the same battle in a new guise.

Our critics in the legislature are afraid of genitalia and excreta. I have reverence for shit and pee. What an invention! How amazing that we ingest nourishment, which is absorbed by the extremely complex function of digestion, enabling us to continue to create our bodies and to stay alive. What the body cannot use, it expels. How can this be

Originally published in *International Friends of Transformative Art Newsletter*, Fall 1991, 7–8. The statement regarding repressive language in the granting guidelines of the National Endowment for the Arts was delivered for the Congressional Record before a House subcommittee briefing held at the Museum of Contemporary Art in Los Angeles, September 30, 1991.

seen as obscene? How can it be considered indecent? Only when the mind of the self-styled moralist is filled with fear, shame, guilt, frustrated longing, and self-hate.

Decency standards are the most slippery of all social covenants. What is indecent today will be household tomorrow. We laugh at the squeamishness of the past. In our time of ultrarapid change, social conventions and acceptability shift constantly before our very eyes. Only yesterday did the Hayes Office forbid filming a married couple in a double bed. Courbet's nudes, Manet's *Olympia,* were the Mapplethorpe of their day. Now they are tasteful calendar art.

The body remains a taboo, and contemporary artists have used the body in shocking ways. Artists break taboos. The body is the ultimate signifier. How can it *not* be used as an instrument to shock those who are shocked by nudity and human functions? Today's art-loving audience can discern the difference between strong art statements that break taboos and pornography. And if it can't, then it should have the opportunity to learn. . . .

. . . The so-called Decency Requirements are indecent. They are far-reaching in their toxic effect. Not only are artists who use body iconography automatically shut out from grant applications (as is Karen Finley, a performance artist of stature and depth), but other artists whose output is not as clearly defined find themselves self-censoring in order to apply. Even more insidious is the effect the Decency Clause has on artists' presenters. Here we can see censorship flourishing. Galleries and art spaces begin eliminating "dangerous" or "difficult" artists, effectively erasing a vast spectrum of American art. The richness and diversity of our art output, which had placed us on the world map as the leading art nation, will dwindle to "safe" and "popular" art, thereby eliminating itself from world competition. We will lose the edge in the history of art.

The American public, alone in a world of repressive societies, has been able to select what it needs and wants on an individual basis. This remarkable ability, and its legislative support and endorsement, are our heirloom and birthright through the instrument of the great Constitution of our unique government. The fabric of democracy is strong yet fragile. It can be frayed by those who seek power at the expense of our political structure and guarantees.

The Conservative Right has an agenda, and it is sinister. The attacks on gays, women, and artists, typical actions of a dying patriarchal caste, is still vigorous enough to maim us as a democratic and free society. These people, following in the footsteps of Bolsheviks, Nazis, and dictators everywhere, know that it is easy to glean popular support or passive acquiescence by curtailing the freedoms of those with little public support or sympathy: minorities, women, gays, artists. Those who are bent on dismantling civil rights and freedoms begin by curtailing them from these groups. If the majority will accept this, they have established their claim, their foot is in the door, and they are free to continue the destruction of our political and civil rights achievements. This is where we must be ever vigilant, and refuse with all our might this pernicious first step toward totalitarian rule.

The NEA is a small government agency. Many people in this country have never even heard of it. Its funding is minimal, compared to the other agencies. But its importance today, now, in the history of our nation, is vast. If artists' freedom of expression is curtailed here, if unpopular or offensive artworks (to some) are successfully snuffed out, as they were in Nazi Germany, we have begun a dangerous plunge into a bottomless pit.

Let not the last decade of our century, of our millennium, be marred by the triumph of repression and fascism in our midst. Let us refuse to accept the erosion of America's shining freedoms and restore to our artists, to their public, and to the international community, the openness and generosity of spirit that characterize us and for which we are envied and admired by the entire world.

POSTSCRIPT: Well, hallelujah! Jesse was defeated! But wait a minute . . . Oh NO! his defeat was obtained as a swap for our waiving higher grazing fees on western government lands! The so-called porn for corn deal! You just can't win. Environmentalists have been pushing for higher fees for years because cattle are killing the land and native habitat. For an artist like myself, who also happens to be an ecofeminist and vegetarian, the victory comes at a very high price indeed.

Rachel Rosenthal

"Rachel Rosenthal"

I was in my early thirties when my knees started to go bad. It was around 1957. The nurse looked at the X-rays and exclaimed that she had never seen such old knees on such a young woman. It was degenerative arthritis. I was told to go to bed and not move. I continued to perform, first in my company Instant Theatre, then as a solo performer, until now. I was a great mover and I loved to move. I danced and I studied martial arts (karate, kung fu, tai chi). My stage work was very movement-oriented. Little by little, I had to abandon it all, one thing at a time. It was like a long, drawn-out punishment.

In 1976, I had an operation on the right knee, my worst. It was helped for a couple of years and then deteriorated again. By the end of the 1980s, my right leg was bowed; I couldn't extend it or bend it beyond a short arc. I couldn't put weight on it, thus stressing my left knee (not so hot either) and distorting my spine. I was in pain in bed, walking my dogs, carrying groceries, negotiating the stairs, sitting, and standing in place. The latter caused me to stop going to art exhibits. I didn't take any pain-killers because I wanted to know what went on in there. When I performed, I felt nothing. Euphoria masked the pain. Endorphins, I guess. I developed a way of moving onstage that camouflaged my problem pretty well. People noted that only at the curtain calls would they notice the limp. But I damaged myself further with each performance because I pushed too far.

I became very tough to pain. I watched my pain like a thing, objectively. When it was too excruciating I would tell myself: "It's only pain . . . !" I was dichotomized. I also became vain about my toughness and gave myself unnecessary ordeals.

Originally published in *Performing Arts Journal* 46 (January 1994), 27–29.

Perhaps this constant state of pain pickled me because I wasn't aging at all. Since my suffering had been uniform for upward of thirty years, I didn't feel the flow of time that triggers decade crises in many people. In 1986, however, the year I was to turn sixty, it suddenly hit me. SIXTY! I became aware for the first time that I was no longer young. This realization made me old. As with Dorian Gray, my face changed extremely rapidly. That year, I did my piece *L.O.W. in Gaia,* and the Crone emerged for the first time in my work.

1990, the year I premiered *Pangaean Dreams* (a piece about the breakup of the supercontinent Pangaea 200 million years ago), was the year I suffered a series of bone breaks, the worst of which were two compression fractures of the vertebrae. I thought I knew all about pain. Nothing compared with that agony. It was the knee to the 100th degree! I literally howled into the night trying to turn from side to side in bed. Every tiny move was torture. I incorporated that experience in the performance. I healed after about six months. At the end of the year, a terrific surgeon performed a knee-replacement operation on my right knee. At the same time, he straightened my leg, and after crushingly hard physical therapy, pushing through the pain, I recovered almost my entire flexibility. It was a Lazarus thing. I was reborn! Last year, the same surgeon took out a bone that was floating around my left knee, causing inflammation and pain, and in my late sixties now, I feel whole, painless, and agile.

This saga distorted my sense of aging. What I feel now is a strange mix: I have never performed so well. I feel that every time I am on-stage, I learn something new and I hone my performing skills. I have ambitions of doing more and more difficult things and I feel confident that I can handle them. On the other hand, I have lost my range of movement, especially in the spine, and my balance is poor. My legs and knees need a lot of retraining and I don't know if my older brain is ready to undertake that. In general, I tire more easily. I have huge reserves of energy during performances. Everybody remarks on that. But my endurance isn't what it was. I catch myself longing to quit the racket, chuck it all, and go somewhere in nature and take it easy! Then another performance comes along and I am like a race horse at the gate.

The real sense of aging that I have, and it is wonderful, is that of perspective. I was born in the 1920s, 1926 to be exact, in Paris, France. I have seen and personally experienced the bulk of the century's astounding and catastrophic changes in my lifetime. I look over the decades as over a chain of peaks after climbing a tall mountain. This gives me a sense of immense richness. I perceive the passage of time like a long panorama of extreme contrasts unfolding in a stately procession before or within me. I use this breadth in my work, trying always to access "The Big Picture," and give an audience a feeling for the multifariousness and layering of life and its extensions into deep past and future.

I have transformed myself over the years to the point of nonrecognition. Yet one part of me never matured: I am emotionally and sentimentally stuck in my early years. For this reason, I try not to involve myself in relationships that call for emotional maturity! I can only fake it up to a point!

This distance helps me focus on my work exclusively. I have my animals to take care of the rest!

Thus will I continue until I die, I believe. Still learning, trying to put order into chaos, expressing ideas in art terms. I don't know if I feel young or old. It really doesn't matter. I can walk my dogs without pain and move about the stage without looking too ridiculous. Isn't that a miracle?

Chronology

Moira Roth, with Elise Griffin, Lorraine Lupo, and Annika Marie

1926   Rachel Rosenthal is born in Paris, France, into an assimilated Russian Jewish family. Her parents are Leonard Rosenthal, a merchant of Oriental pearls and precious stones, and Mara Jacoubovitch Rosenthal, a socialite. Is close to her half brother, Pierre Rosenthal, and to her first cousin, Nicole Habib (Landau), who after the war becomes a lifelong friend. In *Charm* Rosenthal describes this early Parisian childhood; and *The Head of Olga K.* is based on her relationship with her half sister, Olga Klein. Studies ballet with Olga Preobrajenskaya.

1940   In June, the Rosenthal family flees from the Nazis, first to Portugal and then to Rio de Janeiro. Later this experience inspires the creation of *My Brazil.*

1941   In April, the family sails from Brazil to the United States and settles in New York, where Rosenthal attends the High School of Music and Art (from age three onward is always interested in an artistic career); artist Allan Kaprow and composer Morton Feldman are among her fellow students. Her family is part of New York's Russian colony; close to children of the famous bass baritone Fyodor Chaliapin and to Hollywood actor Akim Tamiroff and his wife, Tamara. The Rosenthal family is also friends with painter Marc Chagall, singer Jenny Tourel, and the young Leonard Bernstein. Impresario Sol Hurok, a family friend, helps Rosenthal, then a rabid balletomane, see the great ballets of the 1940s, including *Fancy Free* (the precursor of *On the Town*).

1943   Pierre Rosenthal, Rachel's beloved half brother, is killed in Algeria during the Sahara campaign of 1943. He dies a hero's death and is posthumously decorated.

1945   Becomes a citizen of the United States. Graduates with honors from the High School of Music and Art in New York, and studies with

205

Hans Hofmann (1945–46). The Rosenthal family is friends with Vladimir Horowitz and wife, Wanda Toscanini.

1945–47 Attends the New School for Social Research; takes classes with Meyer Schapiro and Rudolf Arnheim. Also studies engraving with William Stanley Hayter.

1946–54 Commutes for eight years between New York and Paris. After the war, wants to go back to France but encounters legal limits on her stays as she is now a U.S. citizen.

1947–48 Studies at the Jean-Louis Barrault School (Education par le Jeu Dramatique) and at the Sorbonne in Paris; attends lectures by Maurice Merleau-Ponty. Reads Antonin Artaud's *Le Théâtre et son Double* (not available in the United States until 1958).

1948 Meets John Cage and Merce Cunningham in Paris. Also reads and sees many other theater of the absurd plays in Paris at this time. Studies with Roger Blin, who directs the premier performance of *Waiting for Godot* in 1953 (where he also plays the role of Pozzo).

1949–51 Attends Dramatic Workshop after it leaves the New School for Social Research and studies with Erwin Piscator (Rosenthal is also his assistant); she directs Anthony Franciosa and Ben Gazzara in their first play. Also is assistant to Heinz Condell, set designer for the Metropolitan Opera. In addition, studies with Cunningham in New York along with Remy Charlip, with whom she strikes up a lifelong friendship. Dances in Cunningham's junior company.

circa
1949–55 During her New York visits, she becomes an intermittent member of the circle of John Cage and Merce Cunningham; this includes composer Lou Harrison, pianist David Tudor, sculptor Richard Lippold, writer and ceramist M. C. Richards, artist Cy Twombly, and collagist Ray Johnson (who gives Rosenthal her first cat). A period of intense exchanges between Rosenthal and Robert Rauschenberg, who joins the group, as does Jasper Johns. She is visited by Parisian friends whom she introduces to this New York circle. Among them is Bénédicte Pesle, later to become the booking agent in Paris for Cage and Cunningham. Rosenthal lives in Lower Manhattan in the same building on Pearl Street as Johns. Rauschenberg lives nearby on Fulton Street and later moves into Rosenthal's loft after she leaves. In 1954, exhibits in group show with Johns at Tanager Gallery, New York. At this time Rosenthal is making black, metal and tar sculpture. In this year, acquires her cat, Dibidi, from Cunningham dancer Carolyn Brown and her composer husband, Earle Brown; the cat, a constant companion for Rosenthal until her death in 1972, is among the many animals in Rosenthal's life.

1953   Exhibits engravings in group show, Salon de Mai, Paris.

1955   Rosenthal's father dies in Beverly Hills. Moves to California and settles in Los Angeles. In 1955–56, teaches at the Pasadena Playhouse; seen as too avant-garde, she is asked to resign.

1956   Creates Instant Theatre in Los Angeles, at what is now the Cast Theater; this first version of the company lasts until 1966. Works with improvisation and attracts many artists (John Altoon, Wallace Berman, Ed Kienholz, etc. as audience) and Hollywood actors, including Anthony Perkins and Tab Hunter, as workshop participants. Also time of "Hollywood Underground," hosted by Samson de Brier; meets Kenneth Anger and Curtis Harrington, the filmmakers. Is part of early coffeehouse scene. During this time, becomes friends with Anaïs Nin, the writer. It is the period of a new California art style, centering around the Ferus Gallery (directed by Ed Kienholz and Walter Hopps); its artists respond to Rosenthal, who is a major conduit for ideas coming from the Cage-Johns-Rauschenberg-Twombly New York experiments.

1957   Buys a small house in Laurel Canyon in the Hollywood Hills; moves there with her seventeen cats.

1960   Marries actor King Moody. In 1962–63, they convert house into theater. They become partners in Instant Theatre. In the late 1960s, Moody is contracted to play the role of the Ronald McDonald clown in television commercials.

1963–66   Instant Theatre moves into a professional theater, the Horseshoe Stage Theater (now called the Zephyr) on Melrose Avenue in West Hollywood.

1967–68   Studies with John Mason and makes series of clay sculpture pieces. Begins to exhibit frequently as a visual artist until 1975. Also in late 1960s acts in several television shows: "Combat," "It Takes a Thief," "The Virginian," etc.

1970   Visits Japan.

1971–72   In 1971, moves to Tarzana, located in the San Fernando Valley, a suburb of Los Angeles, because now has five dogs and six cats and needs more space. In January 1972, attends Cal Arts West Coast Conference on Women Artists; this begins her involvement in the southern California feminist art movement. Also influenced by being brought into the circle of Miriam Schapiro and Judy Chicago, who create the Feminist Art Workshop at Cal Arts. Begins to read feminist literature by authors such as Betty Friedan, Adrienne Rich, and Mary Daly. Attends June Wayne's "Joan of Art" seminars and later teaches them with Gilah Yelin Hirsch and Bruria Finkel.

Rosenthal's Dibidi, her much-loved eighteen-year-old cat who had been paraplegic for twelve years, dies.

1973 Is founding board member and co-chairperson of Womanspace in Los Angeles. Its group shows include "Female Sexuality—Female Identity" and "You Art What You Eat." Also is involved in Grandview, an early women's collective gallery, which is located in the newly formed Woman's Building in Los Angeles, and Double X, a feminist art collective.

1975 Rosenthal's mother dies in Beverly Hills. Creates her first two performances: *Replays* and *Thanks*. In this year Barbara T. Smith, the Los Angeles performance artist, auctions off "interactive time-based events" in a piece called *A Week in the Life of . . . ;* Rosenthal buys three "times," among which are an exchange of three letters, together with walks, accompanied by their respective dogs, with Smith; a friendship develops between the two artists.

1976–77 Reopens Instant Theatre, but it lasts only a few months. Among the company members are performance artists Cheri Gaulke and David Moreno. Performs *Charm* (in 1968, re-creates this as a radio play). Uses improvised music for a performance for first time (although earlier had accompanied Instant Theatre pieces with music); in future will include a variety of live music on occasion. First performs *The Head of Olga K.* Both shows are performed with members of the Instant Theatre (revival) Company.

1978 In January, travels to the Grand Canyon; this experience inspires her performance *Grand Canyon* (in July creates radio version of *Grand Canyon*). Visits the Soviet Union. Divorces King Moody. Moves back to Los Angeles. Performs *The Death Show;* this is Rosenthal's first scripted (as opposed to improvised) performance, and is created in the context of an exhibition, "Thanatopsis," at Space Gallery, Los Angeles.

1979 First performs *The Arousing (Shock, Thunder)* and *My Brazil.* Begins The DbD Experience workshops in performance and theater, intensive thirty-five-hour weekends, which take place at various Los Angeles sites. Named DbD after her cat, and also stands for "Doing by Doing." Since then has taught regularly—both DbD workshops and weekly classes in her studio as well as residencies in art and theater departments of major institutions, locally and nationally.

1980 Performs *Bonsoir, Dr. Schön!;* this is created partly in response to Rosenthal's new "power," through DbD. Is evicted from soon-to-be destroyed West Los Angeles apartment; stays for five months in Barbara T. Smith's studio in downtown Los Angeles in the same building as Astro Artz/High Performance and LACE Gallery. At this time Rosenthal adopts Tatti Wattles, the rat, from Kim Jones, the performance artist. Buys storefront at 2847 South Robertson, where she has lived ever since; Paul McCarthy, the performance artist, helps her renovate and expand the space.

1980–83 Opens Espace DBD, also named after her cat, in her new building. This space houses Rosenthal's The DbD Experience workshop and presents performance art by established and emerging artists every weekend; also puts on exhibitions of performance documentation.

1981 In January, loses all her savings, having entrusted her money to a financial manager who turns out to be a crook. Goes through period of deep depression, feels suicidal, cancels performance at LAICA as feels unable to work. Decides to go to Death Valley with Tatti Wattles; a transformational experience. In February, performs *Leave Her in Naxos* in which she has her head shaved for the first time. First performs *Soldier of Fortune;* its theme revolves around Rosenthal's relationship to money, a response to her recent financial loss. (She and Daniel J. Martinez also make an artist's book *Soldier of Fortune.*) From here on begins shift away from autobiographical subject matter to more global focus. First performs *Performance and the Masochist Tradition,* part of *Taboo Subjects,* a trilogy with Susanna Dakin and Giuditta Tornetta. Adopts Zatoichi, a ten-year-old blind poodle, who is featured in *Traps* (1982), *The Others* (1984), and *Zatoichi* (1989).

1982 First performs *Traps;* tours Canada with *Traps* and *Taboo Subjects.* This is the first of Rosenthal's intensive yearly national touring with several pieces in repertory. In August, Tatti Wattles, Rosenthal's much-loved rat, dies; he was featured in *Bonsoir, Dr. Schön!* (1980), the artist's book *Soldier of Fortune* (1981), and *Traps* (1982).

1983 Stops public performances at Espace DBD due to city requirement of parking spaces. Receives Annual Vesta Award at the Woman's Building in Los Angeles. Is awarded NEA Fellowship, and from here on increasingly receives grants and awards (Tides Foundation 1988, J. Paul Getty Fellowship 1990, etc.). Performs *Gaia, 1st Version;* first performs *Gaia, Mon Amour,* which tours the United States.

1984 Performs *KabbaLAmobile* with Tom Anthony's Precision Driving Team of seven cars at the parking lot of the Department of Water and Power in Los Angeles. In December, first performs *The Others.* Show includes forty animals and thirty-five human companions; employs a lighting designer for the first time. In Los Angeles meets Tom Regan, author of *The Case for Animal Rights* (a little later he arranges for her to perform *The Others* in North Carolina). Already concerned with that issue, but only now does Rosenthal read literature on subject; becomes active in writing campaigns, fundraising, demonstrations, rescues, and placements. In 1984, totally stops eating poultry (she had not eaten red meat for the previous twenty years).

1985   Performs *Foodchain* and *Shamanic Ritual.*

1986   Stops eating fish and seafood. Travels to the Mojave Desert alone for three weeks in a rented van; this experience inspires *L.O.W. in Gaia;* begins to perform this in 1986, and has continued to tour it extensively until the present. Performs *Was Black* (later makes video of piece).

1987   First performs *Rachel's Brain* in Canada and then Europe (documenta 8, Kassel, Germany). U.S. premiere of *Rachel's Brain* is for Los Angeles Festival. From here on tours Europe regularly. Also performs *Death Valley* for the first time. Receives the first of a series of NEA/USIA touring grants.

1988   Performs early version of *Pangaean Dreams.*

1989   Performs *Zatoichi* in memory of her dog who had just died. Receives Obie award for *Rachel's Brain.*

1990   Suffers two compression fractures of the vertebrae. First performs *Amazonia* (with four members of the California E.A.R. Unit) and performs complete version of *Pangaean Dreams* for Los Angeles Festival. Awarded NEA Solo Performers Fellowship but refuses to sign contract because of censorship clause until nine months later when this clause is judged unconstitutional. Rosenthal is active in protest speakouts and makes TV appearances, including on the "McNeil/ Lehrer News Hour." Is involved in "hook-up" with Moscow through Electronic Cafe technology. In February, receives award from the College Art Association for Distinguished Body of Work. In December, has successful knee replacement operation after many decades of increasing deterioration.

1991   Teaches "Spectrum," an ethnically diverse workshop under the auspices of Los Angeles Cultural Affairs Department; workshop gives performances at the Taper Too.

1992   First performs *filename: FUTURFAX* and begins to tour it in Australia and the United Kingdom. Lectures at Carnegie-Mellon University on "Who Needs Artists," one of her many public lectures. Photograph of her by Annie Leibovitz is printed in *Vanity Fair.*

1993   Featured in film *The New Age* by Michael Tolkin. Teaches workshop for people with HIV/AIDS.

1994   Performs *Zone* with five company members and sixty extras. First performs *Five Uneasy Pieces.* Receives a Women's Caucus for Art

Honor Award and is included in WCA 15th Annual Exhibition, Queens Museum of Art, New York. Creates installation for "Connections: Exploration in the Getty Center Collections," Los Angeles; her theme is animal-human hybrids. Receives award from the Fresno Museum. Represents "Theater" in Rauschenberg's "Tribute 21" limited edition. Appears on cover of *Ms.* magazine in special issue, "50 Ways to Be a Feminist" (July–August 1994). Receives Rockefeller Grant. Forms new company of sixteen performers; they perform *DbDbDb—D, An Evening* at Espace DBD in December. Teaches a workshop for battered women.

1995   Receives Ninth Annual Dolly Green Special Achievement Genesis Award from The Ark Trust for her work in support of animals. Performs at Spoleto Festival, South Carolina. Tours in Austria. Becomes a vegan vegetarian. Receives Los Angeles Cultural Affairs Department certificate of commendation. Creates an ensemble with her best students and premieres *5 Uneasy Pieces and Then Some,* a work with the new company at the California Center for the Arts in Escondido; The Rachel Rosenthal Company begins to present in-studio performances of *Tohubohu!* (Each *Tohubohu!* performance, as it is improvised, is always a different and discrete show.)

1996   Continues *Tohubohu!* performances in her studio and at various local venues, including California State Los Angeles and University of California, Los Angeles. First performs *Timepiece* in Los Angeles, and excerpts from it at the Association of Performing Arts Presenters, New York. Publishes her book, *Tatti Wattles, A Love Story.* Attends conferences on "Women and Aging" (Milwaukee) and "Performance Art, Culture, Pedagogy" (Pennsylvania State University) as a performer and speaker. Receives Los Angeles Cultural Affairs Award.

Select Bibliography

Articles, Statements, and Books by the Artist

"Animal-Human Hybrid Images in the Western World." *American Writing: A Magazine,* no. 10, 1994–95, 28–32.

"The Arousing (Shock, Thunder)." *High Performance* (September 1979), 22–23.

"Bonsoir, Dr. Schön!" *High Performance* (Fall–Winter 1980), 90–91.

"The DBD Experience." *The Lightbearer,* January 1982, 3, 12–13.

"The Death Show." *High Performance* (March 1979), 44–45.

"Genesis." *Heresies* 23, 6:3 (1988), 78.

"The Head of Olga K." *High Performance* (June 1978), 14–15.

"The Indecency of the NEA's Decency Clause." *International Friends of Transformative Art Newsletter,* Fall 1991, 6–7.

"KabbaLAmobile." *Spectacle* (1986), 46–47.

"Leave Her in Naxos." *High Performance* (Summer 1981), 64, 92.

"Lee, That's Just Not Cool!" *NoMag,* September 1981.

"Rachel Rosenthal." *Journal: The Los Angeles Institute of Contemporary Art,* February 1975, 11–15.

"Rachel Rosenthal." *Performing Arts Journal* (January 1994), 27–29.

Soldier of Fortune. A limited-edition artist's book by Rachel Rosenthal and Daniel J. Martinez. Self-published by Rosenthal & Martinez, 1981.

"Speakeasy." *New Art Examiner,* December 1990, 15–16.

"Statement." *City Lights Review* (1988), 47.

"Statement for the Congressional Record." *NAAO Bulletin,* July 1990, 5.

"Stelarc, Performance and Masochism." In *Obsolete Body/Suspensions/Stelarc.* Compiled by James D. Paffrath with Stelarc. Davis, Calif.: JP Publications, 1984, 69–71.

Tatti Wattles, A Love Story. Santa Monica, Calif.: Smart Art Press, 1996.

Published and Unpublished Scripts

In the artist's archives in Los Angeles are a number of unpublished performance scripts, including "Amazonia," "The Arousing (Shock, Thunder)," "Charm," "filename: FUTURFAX," "Grand Canyon," "The Head of O.K.," "Leave Her in Naxos," "The Others," "Replays," "Soldier of Fortune," "Traps," and "Zone."

"The Death Show." *Scenarios: Scripts to Perform.* Ed. Richard Kostelanetz. New York: Assembling Press, 1980, 573–80.

Gaia, Mon Amour: A Performance by Rachel Rosenthal. Buffalo: Hallwalls, 1983.

"In Search of the New *Pataphysical* Order." *City Lights Review* 5 (1992), 259–67.

"L.O.W. in Gaia." *Performing Arts Journal* (October 1987), 76–94.

"My Brazil." *Out from Under: Texts by Women Performance Artists.* Ed. Lenora Champagne. New York: Theatre Communications Group, Inc., 1990, 71–87.

"Pangaean Dreams, A Shamanic Journey" (excerpt). *Performance Journal* (Fall–Winter 1992), 10.

"Pangaean Dreams." *Wordplays 6: New American Drama.* Ed. Bonnie Marranca. Baltimore, Md.: Johns Hopkins University Press, 1995.

"Performance and the Masochist Tradition." *High Performance* (Winter 1981–82), 22–25.

Audio- and Videotapes

"Changing Worlds." Videotape produced by Lynn Hershman, 1991 and distributed by her, 1935 Filbert Street, San Francisco, CA 94123. Contains footage of Rosenthal.

"Sphinxes without Secrets." Videotape produced by Lenora Champagne, 1990. Contains excerpt from *Amazonia.*

The following tapes are distributed by The Rachel Rosenthal Company, 2847 South Robertson Boulevard, Los Angeles, CA 90034.

"Charm." Audiocassette produced by Jacki Apple with Los Angeles radio station KPFK and *High Performance,* 1986.

"filename: FUTURFAX." Audiocassette of radio show commissioned by New American Radio, 120 Tysen Street, Staten Island, NY 10301, 1990.

"Grand Canyon." Audiocassette of performance and interview with Bill Hunt for Los Angeles radio station KPFK, 1978.

"In Search of the New *Pataphysical* Order." Audiocassette of radio show commissioned by New American Radio, 120 Tysen Street, Staten Island, NY 10301, 1991.

"KabbaLAmobile." Audiocassette produced by The Dark Bob and Rosenthal, manufactured by MITB Records, P.O. Box 6461, Beverly Hills, CA 90912, 1985.

"L.O.W. in Gaia." Videocassette, 1987.

"Pangaean Dreams: A Shamanic Journey." Videocassette edited by Joe Leonardi, 1991.

"The Performance World of Rachel Rosenthal." Videocassette directed and edited by Rachel Rosenthal and Joe Leonardi. Commissioned by PBS for the Los Angeles Festival of 1987.

"Rachel on Stage in Gaia." Videodocumentary produced by Dawn Wiedemann, 1993.

"Was Black." Videocassette edited by Joe Leonardi, 1989.

Interviews with Rachel Rosenthal

Askey, Ruth. "A Catalyst for Change." *Reflex,* March–April 1989, 13–15.

Barkin, Elaine. "Conversation in Two Parts with Rachel Rosenthal." *Perspectives of New Music* (Fall–Winter 1982/Spring–Summer 1983), 567–81.

Boffi, T. Adam. "Rachel Rosenthal." *Venice, The Magazine,* June 1990, 38–40.

Borger, Irene. "Rachel Rosenthal: Performance Artist." *Dance Flash,* March–April, May–June 1983.

Chapline, Claudia. "Interview with Rachel Rosenthal." *Artists' News,* Winter 1981, 12–15.

Ginsberg, Elaine. "Rachel Rosenthal, An Interview." *Wordsworks,* June 1980, unpaginated.

Grilikhes, Alexandra. "Taboo Subjects: An Interview with Rachel Rosenthal." *American Writing, A Magazine,* no. 10, 1994–95, 10–26.

Josephson, Janna W., and Lowell Downey. "Rachel Rosenthal, Real Time and Real Living: Artist as Healer." *Vox,* Winter 1991, 8–10.

Lacy, Suzanne, and Rachel Rosenthal. "Saving the World: A Dialogue between Suzanne Lacy and Rachel Rosenthal." *Artweek,* September 12, 1991, 1, 14–16.

Leabhart, Thomas. "Rachel Rosenthal." *Mime Journal* (1991–92), 176–200.

Marranca, Bonnie, and Gautam Dasgupta. "Rachel Rosenthal." *Performance Art* 2 (1979), 26–31.

Meola, Denise. "Interview, Rachel Rosenthal." *Omni,* August 1992, 57–60, 74–75.

Moisan, Jim. "Rachel Rosenthal." *LAICA Journal* (January–February 1979), 51–55.

Muchnic, Suzanne. "Push-Pull of Feminist Art ." [Discussion between Judy Fiskin, Amelia Jones, Libby Lumpkin, and Rachel Rosenthal.] *Los Angeles Times,* Calendar, April 21, 1996, 8–9, 78, 80.

Neri, Barbara. "An Interview with Rachel Rosenthal." *Pform: a journal of interdisciplinary and performance art* (Summer 1995), 9–12.

Quinn, Joan. "Rachel Rosenthal." *Interview,* April 1985, 174.

Rico, Diana. "Artist's 'Opera' Brings Out the Animal in California." *Daily News,* December 16, 1984, 21.

Roth, Moira. "Interview with Rachel Rosenthal." September 2 and 3, 1989, in Los Angeles, Calif. Transcriptions of entire eight–hour interview available at the Archives of American Art, West Coast Regional Center, Huntington Library, 1151 Oxford Road, San Marino, CA 91108.

Zurbrugg, Nicholas. "Private Thoughts of a Public Performer: An Interview." *Art & Design,* no. 38 (1994), 36–47.

General Studies

Brentano, Robyn, and Olivia Georgia. *Outside the Frame: Performance and the Object, A Survey History of Performance Art in the USA since 1950.* Cleveland, Ohio: Cleveland Center for Contemporary Art, 1994, 204, 235.

Brown, Betty Ann, ed. *Expanding Circles: Women, Art and Community.* New York: Midmarch Arts Press, 1996.

Brown, Betty Ann, and Arlene Raven. *Exposures, Women and Their Art.* Photographs by Kenna Love. Pasadena, Calif.: New Sage Press, 1989, 112–13.

Gablik, Suzi. *The Reenchantment of Art.* New York: Thames and Hudson, 1991, 94–95.

Gadon, Elinor W. *The Once and Future Goddess.* San Francisco: Harper & Row, 1989, 295, 361–63.

Jones, Amelia, ed. *Sexual Politics: Judy Chicago's* Dinner Party in *Feminist Art History.* Los Angeles/Berkeley: Armand Hammer Museum of Art and Cultural Center/University of California Press, 1996.

Levy, Mark. *Technicians of Ecstasy: Shamanism and the Modern Artist.* Norfolk, Conn.: Bramble Books, 1993.

Loeffler, Carl E., and Darlene Tong, eds. *Performance Anthology: Source Book of California Performance Art.* San Francisco: Last Gasp Press and Contemporary Arts Press, 1989, see index for page numbers.

Marranca, Bonnie. *Ecologies of Theater.* Baltimore, Md.: Johns Hopkins University Press, 1996.

Peterson, William Dwight. *A History of Instant Theatre.* [Ph.D. diss., University of Texas, Austin, 1991] Ann Arbor, Mich.: UMI Research Press, 1991.

Raven, Arlene. *At Home.* Long Beach, Calif.: Long Beach Museum of Art, 1983. Reprinted in Raven, *Crossing Over: Feminism and Art of Social Concerns.* Ann Arbor, Mich.: UMI Research Press, 1988, 83–153.

Rosen, Randy, and Catherine C. Brawer, curators. *Making Their Mark: Women Artists Move into the Mainstream, 1970–85.* Ed. Nancy Grubb. New York: Abbeville Press, 1989.

Roth, Moira, ed. *The Amazing Decade: Women and Performance Art in*

America, A Source Book. Los Angeles: Astro Artz, 1983, 21, 23, 126–27. Text on Rosenthal by Mary Jane Jacob.

Rubinstein, Charlotte Streifer. *American Women Sculptors.* Boston: G. K. Hall, 1990.

Solomon, Alisa. "Rachel Rosenthal." *National Women's Caucus for Art Conference, WCA Honor Awards Brochure.* New York: Women's Caucus for Art and The Queens Museum of Art, 1994.

Tomkins, Calvin. *Off the Wall.* New York: Penguin Books, 1980, vii, 112–13, 116, 117, 118, 138n.

Withers, Josephine. "Feminist Performance Art: Performing, Discovering, Transforming Ourselves." In *The Power of Feminist Art: The American Movement of the 1970s, History and Impact.* Ed. Norma Broude and Mary D. Garrard. New York: Harry N. Abrams, 1994, 158–74.

Wilding, Faith. *By Our Own Hands: The Women Artist's Movement, Southern California 1970–1976.* Santa Monica, Calif.: Double X, 1977.

Articles, Reviews, and Theses on the Artist

Albright, Thomas. "A Look at Stoneware Sculpture." *San Francisco Chronicle,* June 30, 1969, 44.

Anawalt, Sasha. " 'Was Black' Overshadows Other Visions." *Los Angeles Herald Examiner,* June 28, 1986, B1, B5.

Apple, Jacki. "Mental Breakdown." *L.A. Weekly,* August 28–September 3, 1987, 36.

———. "Performance: The State of the Art." *Cal Arts,* November 1983, 13.

——— "Rachel Rosenthal." *The Art of Spectacle* (1984), 28–29.

———. "Reviving the Horror." *Artweek,* September 6, 1986, 9.

———. "The Romance of Automobiles." *Artweek,* September 29, 1984, 1.

———. "TRAPS by Rachel Rosenthal at Espace DBD." *Images and Issues,* November–December 1982, 2.

Askey, Ruth. "Exoticism and Fear in Rio." *Artweek,* November 17, 1979, 5–6.

———. "Rachel Rosenthal Exorcises Death." *Artweek,* November 18, 1978, 6.

Banes, Sally. "As the Egg Turns." *The Village Voice,* November 29, 1983, 125.

Barker, James Michael. "Rachel Rosenthal." Master's thesis, San Diego State University, 1991.

Bebb, Bruce. "The Many Trappings of Rachel Rosenthal." *The Los Angeles Reader,* July 16, 1982.

Bernheimer, Martin. "Rachel Rosenthal Guides E.A.R. Unit on an Amazon Safari." *Los Angeles Times,* May 18, 1990, F18.

Bettendorf, M. Virginia B. "Rachel Rosenthal: Performance Artist in Search of Transformation." *Women's Art Journal* (Fall 1987–Winter 1988), 33–38.

Breslauer, Jan. "Earth Mother." *Los Angeles Times,* September 14, 1990, F4, F14.

———. "Inside the Rosenthal Zone." *Los Angeles Times,* February 6, 1994, Calendar, 8–9, 72–73.

Burnham, Linda Frye. "The D.B.D. Experience." *High Performance* 26 (1984), 48–51, 90–91.

———. "Rachel Rosenthal, 'Leave Her in Naxos.' " *Artforum,* Summer 1981, 100.

———. "Rachel Rosenthal, *Rachel's Brain.*" *Artforum,* November 1987, 145–46.

———. "Images That Go Bump in the Night: Dreams as Tools in the Works of Two California Performance Artists." *Dreamworks,* Fall 1980, 248–53.

Carr, C. "On Edge." *The Village Voice,* December 16, 1986, 122.

Cyrrano, Maxwell. "Instant Fairy Tales." *FM & Fine Arts* (October 1964), 4–11.

Danieli, Edie. "Rachel Rosenthal: A Life History." *Artweek,* December 13, 1975, 13.

Danieli, Fidel. "Gaia, Mon Amour." *Visual Art* (Summer 1984), 29–32.

Darriau, J. P. "To Laugh and Cry at the Same Time: The Performance Art of Rachel Rosenthal." *The Ryder Magazine,* March 19–April 2, 1993, 16–19.

Drake, Sylvie. "Rachel Rosenthal Puts on the Dog at Japan America." *Los Angeles Times,* December 21, 1984, Calendar, 1, 22.

Forte, Jeanie. "Rachel Rosenthal: Feminism and Performance Art." *Women & Performance: A Journal of Feminist Theory* 42 (1985), 27–37.

———. "Women's Performance Art: Feminism and Postmodernism." *Theatre Journal* (May 1988), 217–35.

Frueh, Joanna. "Rachel Rosenthal." *High Performance* (Spring–Summer 1988), 116.

———. "Visible Difference: Women Artists and Aging." In *New Feminist Criticism: Art/Identity/Action.* Ed. Joanna Frueh, Cassandra L. Langer, and Arlene Raven. New York: HarperCollins 1994, 278–79.

Gehman, Pleasant. "Rachel's World." *Los Angeles Reader,* February 4, 1994, 8–11, 20.

Hayden-Guest, Anthony. "Women Who Shock." Photograph by Annie Leibovitz. *Vanity Fair,* April 1992, 204–13.

Hicks, Emily. "Examining the Taboo." *Artweek,* November 14, 1981, 16.

Hirschman, Jack. "Instant Theatre." *FM & Fine Arts* (May 1963), 7–9.

Howell, John. "Rachel Rosenthal." *Artforum,* March 1984, 97.

Hugo, Joan. "Gaia's Soliloquy." *Artweek,* November 12, 1983, 24.

———. "The Big Setup." *Artweek,* July 31, 1982, 24.

Jones, Amelia. "Rachel Rosenthal, UCLA Center for the Performing Arts." *Artforum,* April 1994, 103.

Jowitt, Deborah. "Taking the Plunge." *The Village Voice,* August 15, 1989, 91.

Karwelis, Donald. "Speaking to the Enemy." *Artweek,* September 5, 1987, 18.

Lampe, Eelka. "Rachel Rosenthal Creating Her Selves." *TDR* (Spring 1988), 170–90.

———. "Theatricality in Performance Art: The Work of Rachel Rosenthal." M.A. thesis, Department of Performance Studies, New York University, 1985.

Marranca, Bonnie. Introductory note to "L.O.W. in Gaia: Chronicle of and Meditation on a 3–Week Vacation in the Mojave Desert, January 1986. Written and performed by Rachel Rosenthal." *Performing Arts Journal* (October 1987), 76.

———. "A Cosmography of Herself: The Autobiology of Rachel Rosenthal." *Kenyon Review* (Spring 1993), 59–67. A revised version of this essay is included in Bonnie Marranca. *Ecologies of Theater.* Baltimore, Md.: Johns Hopkins University Press, 1996, 59–70.

Marowitz, Charles. "Call of the Wild: Alarms and Excusions." *Los Angeles View,* May 31–June 6, 1996, 45.

Muchnic, Suzanne. "Push and Pull of Feminist Art." *Los Angeles Times,* April 21, 1996, 8–10, 80.

Munk, Erika. "Brainchildren of a Lesser God." *The Village Voice,* October 11, 1988, 103, 106.

Roth, Moira. "The Passion of Rachel Rosenthal." *Parachute,* January–March 1994, 22–28.

———. "Toward a History of California Performance: Part Two." *Arts Magazine,* June 1978, 114–23.

Shirley, Don. "Clocking Life's Passages in 'Timepiece.' " *Los Angeles Times,* October 21, 1996.

Smith, Barbara T. "The Female Sexuality/Female Identity Exhibition." *Womanspace Journal* (April–May 1973), 23, 25–26.

———. "Rachel Rosenthal Performs 'Charm.' " *Artweek,* February 19, 1977, 6.

Solomon, Alisa. "Rosenthal Performs 'Futurfax' for Whitney in New York." *Los Angeles Times,* April 25, 1992, F16.

———. "Signaling through the Dioxin." *The Village Voice,* October 4, 1988, 39.

———. "Worm's Eye View." *The Village Voice,* August 18, 1987, 88.

Stayton, Richard J. "Rachel Rosenthal Confronts Her Beasts." *L.A. Weekly,* July 3–9, 1981, 6–9, 66.

"The Many Faces of Feminism." *Ms.,* July–August 1994, 57.

Weisberg, Ruth. "Autobiographical Journey." *Artweek,* November 22, 1980, 3.

———. "Reaching for Revelations." *Artweek,* March 14, 1981, 6.

Wetzsteon, Ross. "Stand–up Shaman." *The Village Voice,* August 6, 1991, 83.

Wiscombe, Janet. "Voice in the Wilderness." *Press-Telegram,* February 5, 1994, C1–C2.

Wortz, Melinda. "Los Angeles." *Art News,* October 1981, 189.

Performances

1975   November 14, *Replays* at the Orlando Gallery, Encino, Calif.

November 25, *Thanks* at the Wilshire Plaza West, Westwood, Los Angeles.

1977   January 28, *Charm* at Mount St. Mary's Art Gallery, Los Angeles.

April, first performs *The Head of Olga K.* at IDEA (the Institute for Dance and Experimental Art), Santa Monica, Calif.

1978   February 21, performs *Grand Canyon* at Cal State Dominguez Hills Art Gallery, Calif.

October 21, *The Death Show* at Space Gallery, Los Angeles.

1979   January 28, first performs *The Arousing (Shock, Thunder)* at LAICA, Los Angeles.

October 14, first performs *My Brazil* at IDEA, Santa Monica, Calif.

1980   October 30, *Bonsoir, Dr. Schön!* at the LACE (Los Angeles Contemporary Exhibition) Gallery, Los Angeles.

1981   February 13, first performs *Leave Her in Naxos* at the Art Museum of the University of California–Santa Barbara.

April 26, *Soldier of Fortune* performed under the title *Cancelled* at the Art Institute, Chicago, Ill.

July 10, performs *Soldier of Fortune* as titled at Newport Harbor Art Gallery, Calif., and at Tortue Gallery, Santa Monica, Calif., on July 18.

October–November, performs first run of *Performance and the Masochist Tradition* (part of *Taboo Subjects,* a trilogy with Susanna Dakin and Giuditta Tornetta) at Espace DBD, Los Angeles.

1982   May 4, first performs *Traps* at Women in Focus, Vancouver.

1983   May 18, *Gaia, 1st Version* at the University of California–Los Angeles, Caught in the Act Series.

September 22–25, 29–October 2, first performs *Gaia, Mon Amour* at The House, Santa Monica, Calif.

1984 September 1–3, *KabbaLAmobile,* for the Los Angeles Museum of Contemporary Art, and the Mark Taper Forum, Los Angeles, Carplays Series.

December 18, first performs *The Others* at The Japan America Theater, Los Angeles, Art of Spectacle Series.

1985 May 10, *Foodchain* at The Japan America Theater, Los Angeles. November 9, *Shamanic Ritual* at Espace DBD as a benefit for the Woman's Building.

1986 April, first performs *L.O.W. in Gaia* at the Marquette University, Milwaukee, Wis.

June 26, *Was Black* at John Anson Ford Theater, Los Angeles.

Creates radio piece, *Charm,* produced by Jacki Apple with Los Angeles radio station KPFK and *High Performance.*

1987 June 3–6, first performs *Rachel's Brain* at the Festival de Théâtre des Amériques, Montreal, Canada.

July 31, first performs *Death Valley* at Central Park Summer Stage Band Shell, New York.

1988 October, performs first version of *Pangaean Dreams* at the University of Arizona Museum of Art, Tucson.

1989 July 14, first performs *Zatoichi* at Beyond Baroque, Los Angeles.

1990 May 16, first performs *Amazonia* at Bing Theater, Los Angeles County Museum of Art, Los Angeles. September 17, first performs complete version of *Pangaean Dreams* at Santa Monica Museum of Art; part of Los Angeles Festival.

1991 Creates radio piece *filename: FUTURFAX,* commissioned by New America Radio.

1992 March 6, first performs *filename: FUTURFAX* at Cleveland Performance Art Festival, Cleveland, commissioned by the Whitney Museum of American Art, New York. Creates radio piece *In Search of the New Pataphysical Order,* commissioned by New America Radio.

1994 February 11–12, performs *Zone* at the Wadsworth Theater, University of California–Los Angeles.

July 25, first performs *Five Uneasy Pieces* at Snowmass Village, Aspen, Colo., Public Art Week Series.

December, first performs *DbDbDb—D, An Evening* at Espace DBD.

1995   The Rachel Rosenthal Company ensemble performs *Five Uneasy Pieces and Then Some* at The California Center for Performing Arts, Escondido. Begins run of *Tohubohu!* at Espace DBD.

1996   Creates *Meditation on the Life and Death of Ken Sarowiwa* and performs with Company at Schoenberg Hall, UCLA. Performs *Timepiece* with Company at Cal State Los Angeles.

Credits

Grateful acknowledgment is made for permission to reprint from the following writers and publishers: to Sasha Anawalt for "*Was Black,* Overshadows Other Visions," © 1986 by Sasha Anawalt; to Jacki Apple for "The Romance of Automobiles," and to *Artweek,* © 1984 *Artweek;* to Ruth Askey for "Exoticism and Fear in Rio," and to *Artweek,* © 1979 *Artweek,* and for "Rachel Rosenthal Exorcises Death," and to *Artweek,* © 1978 *Artweek;* to Sally Banes for "Rachel Rosenthal: As the Egg Turns," and to *The Village Voice,* © 1983 Sally Banes; to Elaine Barkin for "Conversation in Two Parts with Rachel Rosenthal," and to *Perspectives of New Music,* © 1982–83 *Perspectives of New Music;* to Martin Bernheimer for "Rachel Rosenthal Guides E.A.R. Unit on an Amazon Safari," and to the *Los Angeles Times,* © 1990 Los Angeles Times Syndicate; to Linda Burnham for "The DBD Experience, Rachel Rosenthal's Mind/Body Spa: A Bath for the Soul," and to *High Performance,* © 1984 *High Performance;* to *Artweek* for "Rachel Rosenthal: A Life History," © 1975 *Artweek;* to Sylvie Drake for "Rachel Rosenthal Puts on the Dog at Japan America," and to the *Los Angeles Times;* © 1984 Los Angeles Times Syndicate; to Alexandra Grilikhes for "Taboo Subjects: An Interview with Rachel Rosenthal," © 1994–95 Alexandra Grilikhes; to *Artweek* for "Examining the Taboo," © 1981 *Artweek;* to Jack Hirschman for "Instant Theatre," © 1963 Jack Hirschman; to Amelia Jones for "Rachel Rosenthal: UCLA Center for the Performing Arts," and to *Artforum,* © 1994 *Artforum;* to Donald Karwelis for "Speaking to the Enemy," and to *Artweek,* © 1987 *Artweek;* to Suzanne Lacy and Rachel Rosenthal for "Saving the World: A Dialogue between Suzanne Lacy and Rachel Rosenthal," and to *Artweek,* © 1991 *Artweek;* to Bonnie Marranca for "A Cosmography of Herself: The Autobiography of Rachel Rosenthal," © 1996 Bonnie Marranca; to Denise Meola for "Interview, Rachel Rosenthal," and to *Omni,* © 1992 *Omni;* to Erika Munk for "Brainchild of a Lesser God," and to *The Village Voice,* © 1988 Erika Munk; to Barbara Smith for "Rachel Rosenthal Performs *Charm,*" and to *Artweek,* © 1977 *Artweek;* to Alisa Solomon for "Rosenthal Performs *Futurfax* for Whitney in New York," © 1992 Alisa Solomon, and for "Worm's Eye View," and to *The Village Voice,* © 1987 *The Village Voice;* to Ruth Weisberg for "Autobiographical Journey," and to *Artweek,* © 1980 *Artweek,* and for "Reaching for Revelations," and to *Artweek,* © 1981 *Artweek;* to Ross Wetzsteon for "Stand-up Shaman," and to *The Village Voice,* © 1991 *The Village Voice;* to Melinda Wortz for "Los Angeles," © 1981 Melinda Wortz, reprinted by permission of Ed Wortz. The following writings by Rachel Rosenthal are reprinted by permission of the author: